ExamWise
For
CIW Site Designer

Design Methodology and Technology
CIW Exam 1D0-420

Online testing provided by
BeachFrontQuizzer, Inc.
Friendswood, Texas 77546

Author

Chad M. Bayer

Published by

TotalRecall Publications, Inc.
1103 Middlecreek
Friendswood, TX 77546
281-992-3131

NOTE: THIS IS BOOK IS GUARANTEED:
See details at www.TotalRecallPress.com

TotalRecall Publications, Inc.

This Book is Sponsored by BeachFront Quizzer, Inc..

Printed in United States of America

ISBN: 1-59095-402-5
UPC: 6-43977-43420-3

The sponsoring editor for this book was Bruce Moran and the production supervisor was Corby Tate.

Printed and bound by Data Duplicators of Houston, Texas

Dedication

This book is dedicated to my family, thanks for the support.

Chad M. Bayer

ExamWise™
For
CIW® Site Designer
BY

Chad M. Bayer

About the Author

Chad Bayer has been working in the computer industry for over 6 years and is currently CIW Certifiable. His background is quite varied in regards to CIW and is interested in both the engineering of software and hardware.

Chad is working towards his computer engineering degree at the University of Texas in Dallas.

About the Book

Part of the TotalRecall: IT Question Book CIW certification series, this new Self Help and Interactive Exam Study Aid is now available for candidate's preparing to sit the CIW 1D0-420 Design Methodology and Technology exam. The book covers the information associated with each of the exam topics in detail and includes information found in no other book.

Using the book will help readers determine if they are ready for the CIW 1D0-420- certification exam. This book provides Questions, Answers and Explanations that explain the concepts in a clear and easy-to-understand manner. This book is designed for the Experienced user that desires to build their confidence by refreshing their knowledge of CIW material.

About Online Testing

www.TotalRecallPress.com practice tests include Self Help and Interactive Exam Study Aid with instant feed back for simulated and adaptive testing with detailed explanations.

Register your book purchase at **www.TotalRecallPress.com** or send an email to **bfquiz@swbell.net** for your free 30 day Registration.

Located in the back of this book are the instructions for obtaining your Free 30 day Registration for the online practice test. The Registration is good for access to only the CIW Fundamentals Exam.

THIS BOOK IS GUARANTEED: See details at **www.TotalRecallPress.com**

1D0-420 Exam Preparation Guide

Web Publishing Concepts, Web Design Concepts, Navigation and Presentation Concepts, Third Party Applications, Scripting and Advanced HTML Features, Working with Graphics and Multimedia.

You will find the CIW 1D0-420 Exam guide located at their web site.
http://www.ciwcertified.com/exams/1d0420.asp?comm=home&llm=4

Note:	**Exam subject matter and skills being measured are subject to change at any time without prior notice and at CIW's sole discretion**

Information you will find in their document will include the following.

Certification Credit

The CIW Site Designer Exam is a requirement for the following CIW certifications: CIW Certified Instructor, Master CIW Web Site Manager, and Master CIW Designer.

Exam Audience

Web authors, marketing and communications professionals, PR professionals, Webmasters, graphic designers, desktop designers, technical writers, and library scientists. Candidates should have the following prerequisite completed before taking the exam: CIW Foundations certification.

Prerequisites

Candidates must complete the following prerequisites prior to sitting the CIW Site Designer exam.

1. Candidates are required to complete the CIW Certification Agreement online before the CIW Certificate will be shipped to you.

2. Passing the CIW Foundations exam 1D0-410 is required for those candidates to achieve CIW Professional, Master CIW Designer, and/or Master CIW Web Site Manager certification designation. Students may sit the CIW Site Designer exam prior to the CIW Foundations exam, however it is recommended that students take (and pass) these exams in sequential order.

Exam Information

Students who have taken CIW courses are encouraged to continue their studies and apply their new skills before attempting the 1D0-420 Site Designer examination. Skills taught in the CIW Site Designer courses are best reinforced with real-world experience.

The candidate is responsible for learning the content and achieving a passing score on the CIW Site Designer exam.

Candidates taking the 1D0-420 Site Designer exam will be subject for the following:

1. Each delivery of the exam will include 10 non-scored beta items, appearing randomly.
2. The examination period will be increased from 75 minutes to 90 minutes.

To achieve a passing score on the exam, candidates must:

1. Correctly answer at least 45 of the 60 scored questions to achieve a total score of 75% or greater.

This scoring method applies to the Site Designer examination.

Web Publishing Concepts
Web Design Concepts
Navigation and Presentation Concepts
Third Party Applications
Scripting and Advanced HTML Features
Working with Graphics and Multimedia

Total Questions Scored	**60** Questions
Beta Questions are randomly delivered throughout exam	10 Questions
Total Questions presented on each exam	**70** Questions

Each item offers four solutions or distracters. Exam candidates must select the one best solution for each item.

Skills Measured

Site Designer skills are not product-or system-specific. They are a combination of minimal technical and non-technical skills and knowledge required for those interested in developing specific Internet skills as a Web site designer. The 1D0-420 exam tests the following common core of Internet skills:

- Explain and implement Web design concepts, including page layout, multimedia, font and color selection, graphic images, audience usability, file hierarchy, and navigation.
- Manage Web site development processes.
- Develop a Web strategy with goals and tactics to support it, and implement techniques such as mindmapping and site metaphor concepts.
- Select and implement basic Web technologies, such as HTML tables and frames, metadata, and Cascading Style Sheets.
- Use Web production applications and tools to create and manage pages and sites, create animated GIFs, edit graphic image files, and create multimedia files.
- Describe and implement advanced Web technologies, including scripting languages, Dynamic HTML, Extensible Markup Language (XML), server-side technologies, Java applets, and plug-ins.
- Describe the functions of Web servers, server administration ports, cookies, databases, and database management systems.
- Identify the Internet governing organizations.
- Understand how to research Internet standards and register a domain name.
- Complete development of a functional Web site.
- Compare in-house Web site hosting to hosting with an Internet Service Provider.
- Publish sites to the Web using various tools and techniques.

Current CIW Exams

http://www.ciwcertified.com/exams/general.asp?comm=home&llm=4

CIW ASSOCIATE CERTIFICATE: Requires passing

- CIW Foundations (exam 1D0-410)

CIW PROFESSIONAL CERTIFICATE: Requires

CIW Associate certification (CIW Foundations exam 1D0-410)

and passing any one of the following CIW job-role exams:

- CIW Site Designer (exam 1D0-420)
- CIW E-Commerce Designer (exam 1D0-425)
- CIW Server Administrator (exam 1D0-450)
- CIW Internetworking Professional (exam 1D0-460)
- CIW Security Professional (exam 1D0-470)
- CIW Application Developer (exam 1D0-430)
- CIW Database Specialist (exam 1D0-441)
- CIW Enterprise Specialist (exam 1D0-442)

Table of Contents

Total Recall

Chapter 1:
Web Publishing Concepts

1. When you implement a site design with over 100MB of data in size, what factor will you consider regarding the production server?

A. storage

B. processor

C. bandwidth

D. memory

E. reliability

2. When you implement a site design with very complicated decision support function provided to the users, what factor will you consider regarding the production server?

A. storage

B. processor

C. bandwidth

D. memory

E. reliability

1. When you implement a site design with over 100MB of data in size, what factor will you consider regarding the production server?

A. storage

B. processor

C. bandwidth

D. memory

***E. reliability**

Explanation: Reliability is always the most important concern. A serious web site should be running 24 x 7.

---

2. When you implement a site design with very complicated decision support function provided to the users, what factor will you consider regarding the production server?

A. storage

***B. processor**

C. bandwidth

D. memory

E. reliability

Explanation: For a decision support system, heavy duty number crunching occupies most of the CPU time.

3. When you implement a site design with an ever growing bank of data, what factor will you consider regarding the production server?

A. storage

B. processor

C. bandwidth

D. memory

E. reliability

---

4. When you implement a site design, you set up the production servers to use failover cluster. What kind of proactive measure is this?

A. storage

B. processor

C. bandwidth

D. memory

E. reliability

3. When you implement a site design with an ever growing bank of data, what factor will you consider regarding the production server?

***A. storage**

B. processor

C. bandwidth

D. memory

E. reliability

Explanation: You want to have enough storage space to accommodate the growing storage need of the data bank.

---

4. When you implement a site design, you set up the production servers to use failover cluster. What kind of proactive measure is this?

A. storage

B. processor

C. bandwidth

D. memory

***E. reliability**

Explanation: Reliability is always the most important concern. A serious web site should be running 24 x 7.

5. You need to decide on the implementation detail of your site. You need to ensure that no hacker can steal data from your server. What technology do you need?

A. anti-virus

B. firewall

C. spying

D. net spider

E. No Answer is Correct

---

6. You need to decide on the implementation detail of your public web site. You need to ensure that no hacker can penetrate into your internal network. What technology do you need?

A. anti-virus

B. SSL

C. DMZ

D. net spider

E. No Answer is Correct

5. You need to decide on the implementation detail of your site. You need to ensure that no hacker can steal data from your server. What technology do you need?

A. anti-virus

***B. firewall**

C. spying

D. net spider

E. No Answer is Correct

Explanation: You should put your web server behind the firewall for protection against hackers' attacks.

---

6. You need to decide on the implementation detail of your public web site. You need to ensure that no hacker can penetrate into your internal network. What technology do you need?

A. anti-virus

B. SSL

***C. DMZ**

D. net spider

E. No Answer is Correct

Explanation: A Demilitarized zone provides an extra layer of protection for your internal network.

7. You need to decide on the implementation detail of your public retail web site. You need to ensure that no hacker can steal information from transmitted packet. What technology do you need?

A. anti-virus

B. SSL

C. DMZ

D. Firewall

E. No Answer is Correct

---

8. You need to decide on the implementation detail of your public retail web site. You need to ensure 100% safe credit card transaction processing. What technology do you need?

A. SET

B. SSL

C. DMZ

D. Firewall

E. No Answer is Correct

7. You need to decide on the implementation detail of your public retail web site. You need to ensure that no hacker can steal information from transmitted packet. What technology do you need?

A. anti-virus

***B. SSL**

C. DMZ

D. Firewall

E. No Answer is Correct

Explanation: Secure Socket Layer ensures safe data transmission by using encryption.

---

8. You need to decide on the implementation detail of your public retail web site. You need to ensure 100% safe credit card transaction processing. What technology do you need?

***A. SET**

B. SSL

C. DMZ

D. Firewall

E. No Answer is Correct

Explanation: SET is the industry standard for online credit card transaction security processing.

9. You need to decide on the implementation detail of your public retail web site. You need to show your customers' your site identity before they commit a transaction. What technology do you need?

A. SET

B. SSL

C. DMZ

D. Firewall

E. Certificate

---

10. When you implement your site, you come upon a situation where the power goes off for the whole building. What proactive measure should you take to maintain the 24 x 7 availability of your site?

A. RAID

B. Cluster

C. Removable media

D. Tape backup

E. UPS

9. You need to decide on the implementation detail of your public retail web site. You need to show your customers' your site identity before they commit a transaction. What technology do you need?

   A. SET

   B. SSL

   C. DMZ

   D. Firewall

***E. Certificate**

Explanation: You should apply for a certificate from a CA for your site. One of the most popular CA is Verisign (www.verisign.com).

---

10. When you implement your site, you come upon a situation where the power goes off for the whole building. What proactive measure should you take to maintain the 24 x 7 availability of your site?

   A. RAID

   B. Cluster

   C. Removable media

   D. Tape backup

***E. UPS**

Explanation: RAID and Cluster would not work if the power goes off for the whole building. A good UPS is a must-have.

11. You want to implement an online shopping mall. You have a NT server with SQL Server already. What software will you use to build the mall based on the equipment you have now?

A. Site Server

B. Site Server Commerce Edition

C. FrontPage

D. Visual Interdev

E. No Answer is Correct

---

12. You want to implement an online shopping mall. You need to decide on what OS and platform the site should run on. You have an extremely tight budget. Which of the following will you choose as the server OS?

A. Redhat Linux

B. Solaris

C. NT

D. Win2000

E. WinME

11. You want to implement an online shopping mall. You have a NT server with SQL Server already. What software will you use to build the mall based on the equipment you have now?

A. Site Server

***B. Site Server Commerce Edition**

C. FrontPage

D. Visual Interdev

E. No Answer is Correct

Explanation: Site Server Commerce allows you to build the entire Commerce site with the concept of pipes. It works best with SQL Server as the back end.

---

12. You want to implement an online shopping mall. You need to decide on what OS and platform the site should run on. You have an extremely tight budget. Which of the following will you choose as the server OS?

***A. Redhat Linux**

B. Solaris

C. NT

D. Win2000

E. WinME

Explanation: Linux is a low cost yet powerful and reliable OS suitable as a web server.

13. You are implementing your web site. You have been told by the marketing department that most of the visitors will be using version 2 or below browsers. Which of the following technology should be avoided (Choose all that apply)?

A. Java

B. Shockwave

C. Flash

D. JavaScript

E. VBScript

---

14. You are implementing your web site. You have been told by the marketing department that most of the visitors will want to receive page updates automatically. What technology will you deploy?

A. Push

B. Pull

C. Broadcast

D. Multicast

E. No Answer is Correct

13. You are implementing your web site. You have been told by the marketing department that most of the visitors will be using version 2 or below browsers. Which of the following technology should be avoided (Choose all that apply)?

***A. Java**

***B. Shockwave**

***C. Flash**

***D. JavaScript**

***E. VBScript**

Explanation: Version 2 browsers basically support nothing fancy. You want to build pages with only simple text and simple graphics for them.

---

14. You are implementing your web site. You have been told by the marketing department that most of the visitors will want to receive page updates automatically. What technology will you deploy?

***A. Push**

B. Pull

C. Broadcast

D. Multicast

E. No Answer is Correct

Explanation: Push technology is appropriate when bandwidth is plentiful.

15. You are implementing your web site. You have been told by the marketing department that most of the visitors will want to receive page updates automatically. However, bandwidth is very limited on their side. What technology will you deploy?

A. Push

B. Pull

C. Broadcast

D. Multicast

E. No Answer is Correct

---

16. In HTML, every code revolves around ___________ ?

A. tags

B. symbols

C. text

D. quotes

E. No Answer is Correct

15. You are implementing your web site. You have been told by the marketing department that most of the visitors will want to receive page updates automatically. However, bandwidth is very limited on their side. What technology will you deploy?

A. Push

B. Pull

C. Broadcast

D. Multicast

***E. No Answer is Correct**

Explanation: Push technology is appropriate only when bandwidth is plentiful. When bandwidth is not enough, you should consider allowing visitors to subscribe to a list instead.

---

16. In HTML, every code revolves around ___________ ?

***A. tags**

B. symbols

C. text

D. quotes

E. No Answer is Correct

Explanation: Refer to the web link for detailed explanation.

17. In HTML, Tags can be written in
(Choose all that apply)?

A. uppercase

B. lower case

C. mixed cases

D. nonstandard characters

E. No Answer is Correct

---

18. In HTML, the difference between the opening tag and a closing tag is that:

A. the opening tag has a slash

B. the closing tag has a slash

C. the opening tag has a quote

D. no difference

E. No Answer is Correct

17. In HTML, Tags can be written in
(Choose all that apply)?

***A. uppercase**

***B. lower case**

***C. mixed cases**

D. nonstandard characters

E. No Answer is Correct

Explanation: Refer to the web link for detailed explanation.

---

18. In HTML, the difference between the opening tag and a closing tag is that:

A. the opening tag has a slash

***B. the closing tag has a slash**

C. the opening tag has a quote

D. no difference

E. No Answer is Correct

Explanation: Refer to the web link for detailed explanation.

19. What tags are presented at the beginning and end of every HTML file?

A. <HTML>...</HTML>

B. <HEAD>...</HEAD>

C. <TITLE>...</TITLE>

D. <BODY>...</BODY>

E. No Answer is Correct

20. What tags are used in HTML to enclose the contents of your page?

A. <HTML>...</HTML>

B. <HEAD>...</HEAD>

C. <TITLE>...</TITLE>

D. <BODY>...</BODY>

E. No Answer is Correct

19. What tags are presented at the beginning and end of every HTML file?

***A. <HTML>...</HTML>**

B. <HEAD>...</HEAD>

C. <TITLE>...</TITLE>

D. <BODY>...</BODY>

E. No Answer is Correct

Explanation: Refer to the web link for detailed explanation.

---

20. What tags are used in HTML to enclose the contents of your page?

A. <HTML>...</HTML>

B. <HEAD>...</HEAD>

C. <TITLE>...</TITLE>

***D. <BODY>...</BODY>**

E. No Answer is Correct

Explanation: Refer to the web link for detailed explanation.

21. In HTML, what tags are usually put directly after the first HTML tag?

A. <HTML>...</HTML>

B. <HEAD>...</HEAD>

C. <TITLE>...</TITLE>

D. <BODY>...</BODY>

E. No Answer is Correct

---

22. What tags in HTML are used to connect to other documents on the web?

A. <HTML>...</HTML>

B. <HEAD>...</HEAD>

C. <TITLE>...</TITLE>

D. <BODY>...</BODY>

E. No Answer is Correct

21. In HTML, what tags are usually put directly after the first HTML tag?

A. <HTML>...</HTML>

***B. <HEAD>...</HEAD>**

C. <TITLE>...</TITLE>

D. <BODY>...</BODY>

E. No Answer is Correct

Explanation: Refer to the web link for detailed explanation.

---

22. What tags in HTML are used to connect to other documents on the web?

A. <HTML>...</HTML>

B. <HEAD>...</HEAD>

C. <TITLE>...</TITLE>

D. <BODY>...</BODY>

***E. No Answer is Correct**

Explanation: The correct answer is the anchor tag.

23. What tag in HTML will you use for adding picture into the page?

A. <HTML>...</HTML>

B. <HEAD>...</HEAD>

C. <TITLE>...</TITLE>

D. <IMG>

E. No Answer is Correct

---

24. In HTML, what will you use to include the name of the file you want to link to?

A. <HTML>...</HTML>

B. <HEAD>...</HEAD>

C. <TITLE>...</TITLE>

D. <IMG>

E. No Answer is Correct

23. What tag in HTML will you use for adding picture into the page?

A. <HTML>...</HTML>

B. <HEAD>...</HEAD>

C. <TITLE>...</TITLE>

***D. <IMG>**

E. No Answer is Correct

Explanation: Refer to the web link for detailed explanation.

---

24. In HTML, what will you use to include the name of the file you want to link to?

A. <HTML>...</HTML>

B. <HEAD>...</HEAD>

C. <TITLE>...</TITLE>

D. <IMG>

***E. No Answer is Correct**

Explanation: All the choices here are tags. We actually need the HREF attribute.

25. You have the following HTML code fragment:

<H1>enormous</H1>

<H2>big</H2>

<H3>normal</H3>

What construct is this?

A. headers

B. labels

C. columns

D. rows

E. No Answer is Correct

---

26. Which group is responsible for defining the HTML standard?

A. IEEE

B. IANA

C. W3C

D. OFTF

E. No Answer is Correct

25. You have the following HTML code fragment:

<H1>enormous</H1>

<H2>big</H2>

<H3>normal</H3>

What construct is this?

***A. headers**

B. labels

C. columns

D. rows

E. No Answer is Correct

Explanation: Refer to the web link for detailed explanation.

---

26. Which group is responsible for defining the HTML standard?

A. IEEE

B. IANA

***C. W3C**

D. OFTF

E. No Answer is Correct

Explanation: W3C's home page is at: www.w3c.org.

27. You have the following HTML code fragment:

<ul>

<li>first list item</li>

<li>second list item</li>

<li>third list item</li>

</ul>

What construct is this?

A. unordered list

B. ordered list

C. gray list

D. numbered list

E. No Answer is Correct

---

28. You have the following HTML code fragment:

<ol>

<li>first list item</li>

<li>second list item</li>

<li>third list item</li>

</ol>

What construct is this?

A. unordered list

B. ordered list

C. gray list

D. numbered list

E. No Answer is Correct

27. You have the following HTML code fragment:

```
<ul>
 <li>first list item</li>
 <li>second list item</li>
 <li>third list item</li>
</ul>
```

What construct is this?

***A. unordered list**

B. ordered list

C. gray list

D. numbered list

E. No Answer is Correct

Explanation: Please refer to the web link for example and explanation.

---

28. You have the following HTML code fragment:

```
<ol>
 <li>first list item</li>
 <li>second list item</li>
 <li>third list item</li>
</ol>
```

What construct is this?

A. unordered list

***B. ordered list**

C. gray list

D. numbered list

E. No Answer is Correct

Explanation: Please refer to the web link for example and explanation.

29. You have the following HTML code fragment:

```
<dl>
 <dt>the first term</dt>
 <dd>its definition</dd>
 <dt>the second term</dt>
 <dd>its definition</dd>
</dl>
```

What construct is this?

A. unordered list

B. ordered list

C. gray list

D. numbered list

E. No Answer is Correct

---

30. What is the latest HTML specification as of December 2000?

A. version 5.0

B. version 4.0

C. version 3.0

D. version 2.0

E. No Answer is Correct

29. You have the following HTML code fragment:

```
<dl>
 <dt>the first term</dt>
 <dd>its definition</dd>
 <dt>the second term</dt>
 <dd>its definition</dd>
</dl>
```

What construct is this?

A. unordered list

B. ordered list

C. gray list

D. numbered list

***E. No Answer is Correct**

Explanation: This is a definition list. Please refer to the web link for example and explanation.

---

30. What is the latest HTML specification as of December 2000?

A. version 5.0

***B. version 4.0**

C. version 3.0

D. version 2.0

E. No Answer is Correct

Explanation: W3C's HTML 4.0 is the authorative specification for HTML.

31. What is the definition of metadata?

A. data about data

B. data about system

C. data about state

D. data about object

E. No Answer is Correct

---

32. What is the function of metadata?

A. provides implementation detail on the contents of data

B. provides execution instruction on the contents of data

C. provides search mechanism on the contents of data

D. provides descriptive information on the contents of data

E. No Answer is Correct

31. What is the definition of metadata?

***A. data about data**

B. data about system

C. data about state

D. data about object

E. No Answer is Correct

Explanation: Please refer to the web link for more information.

---

32. What is the function of metadata?

A. provides implementation detail on the contents of data

B. provides execution instruction on the contents of data

C. provides search mechanism on the contents of data

***D. provides descriptive information on the contents of data**

E. No Answer is Correct

Explanation: Please refer to the web link for more information.

33. Where do we find the usage of metadata in HTML page?

A. between the <title></title> tags

B. between the <head></head> tags

C. between the <body></body> tags

D. between the <end></end> tags

E. No Answer is Correct

---

34. Why do we want to include metadata tag in our HTML document?

A. to describe the data records of the web page

B. to describe the tags of the web page

C. to describe the contents of the web page

D. to describe the server platform of the web page

E. No Answer is Correct

33. Where do we find the usage of metadata in HTML page?

A. between the <title></title> tags

***B. between the <head></head> tags**

C. between the <body></body> tags

D. between the <end></end> tags

E. No Answer is Correct

Explanation: Please refer to the web link for more information.

---

34. Why do we want to include metadata tag in our HTML document?

A. to describe the data records of the web page

B. to describe the tags of the web page

***C. to describe the contents of the web page**

D. to describe the server platform of the web page

E. No Answer is Correct

Explanation: Please refer to the web link for more information.

35. Metadata can provide functions similar to an index by deploying what components?

A. server

B. client

C. data engine

D. data fields

E. No Answer is Correct

36. As the site designer, why would you care about the use of metadata?

A. search engines have begun to include the ability to make use of the HTML meta tag

B. search engines have begun to exclude the ability to remove HTML meta tag in Web documents

C. search engines have begun to exclude the ability to filter the HTML meta tag in Web documents

D. search engines have begun to include the ability to generate HTML meta tag in Web documents

E. No Answer is Correct

35. Metadata can provide functions similar to an index by deploying what components?

A. server

B. client

C. data engine

***D. data fields**

E. No Answer is Correct

Explanation: Please refer to the web link for more information.

---

36. As the site designer, why would you care about the use of metadata?

***A. search engines have begun to include the ability to make use of the HTML meta tag**

B. search engines have begun to exclude the ability to remove HTML meta tag in Web documents

C. search engines have begun to exclude the ability to filter the HTML meta tag in Web documents

D. search engines have begun to include the ability to generate HTML meta tag in Web documents

E. No Answer is Correct

Explanation: Please refer to the web link for more information.

37. Which of the following are valid metadata element types (Choose all that apply)?

A. Creator

B. Subjects

C. Keywords

D. Title

E. No Answer is Correct

---

38. You want to include the date associated with the creation or availability of a resource in your metadat

a. What element should you use?

A. Creator

B. Subjects

C. Keywords

D. Title

E. Date

37. Which of the following are valid metadata element types (Choose all that apply)?

***A. Creator**

***B. Subjects**

***C. Keywords**

***D. Title**

E. No Answer is Correct

Explanation: Please refer to the web link for more information.

---

38. You want to include the date associated with the creation or availability of a resource in your metadat

a. What element should you use?

A. Creator

B. Subjects

C. Keywords

D. Title

***E. Date**

Explanation: Please refer to the web link for more information.

39. You want to include the category of your resource in your metadat

a. What element should you use?

A. Resource Type

B. Subjects

C. Keywords

D. Resource

E. Item

---

40. You want to be able to uniquely identify a resource in your metadat

a. What element should you use?

A. Resource Type

B. Subjects

C. Keywords

D. Resource

E. Resource Identifier

39. You want to include the category of your resource in your metadat

a. What element should you use?

***A. Resource Type**

B. Subjects

C. Keywords

D. Resource

E. Item

Explanation: Please refer to the web link for more information.

---

40. You want to be able to uniquely identify a resource in your metadat

a. What element should you use?

A. Resource Type

B. Subjects

C. Keywords

D. Resource

***E. Resource Identifier**

Explanation: Please refer to the web link for more information.

41. What rule expresses the notion that a discrete resource should have a discrete metadata record?

A. 1:1

B. One Resource Rule

C. Discrete Resource Rule

D. 1:2

E. No Answer is Correct

---

42. How do search engines find out about the content of your web site?

A. inspect the metadata

B. inspect the IP

C. inspect the DNS record

D. inspect the IP pointer

E. No Answer is Correct

41. What rule expresses the notion that a discrete resource should have a discrete metadata record?

***A. 1:1**

B. One Resource Rule

C. Discrete Resource Rule

D. 1:2

E. No Answer is Correct

Explanation: Please refer to the web link for more information.

---

42. How do search engines find out about the content of your web site?

***A. inspect the metadata**

B. inspect the IP

C. inspect the DNS record

D. inspect the IP pointer

E. No Answer is Correct

Explanation: This is why it is important to include a site description with the meta tag in your HTML document.

43. Which of the following is true concerning how search engines use the metadata in your web documents?

A. all engines do the same

B. different engines make use of the metadata differently

C. most engines ignore the metadata

D. most engines filter out the metadata

E. No Answer is Correct

---

44. To include metadata in your web document, what tag should you use?

A. <metas>

B. <metadata>

C. <meta data>

D. <meta>

E. No Answer is Correct

43. Which of the following is true concerning how search engines use the metadata in your web documents?

A. all engines do the same

***B. different engines make use of the metadata differently**

C. most engines ignore the metadata

D. most engines filter out the metadata

E. No Answer is Correct

Explanation: This really depends on the implementation of the different search engines.

---

44. To include metadata in your web document, what tag should you use?

A. <metas>

B. <metadata>

C. <meta data>

***D. <meta>**

E. No Answer is Correct

Explanation: You should memorize this for the exam.

45. What are valid arguments in the metadata tag of your HTML codes (Choose all that apply)?

A. name

B. engine

C. content

D. version

E. No Answer is Correct

---

46. You designed your web page so that a hyperlink has a destination that starts with https://. What kind of link is this?

A. SSL

B. SET

C. SAS

D. RAS

E. No Answer is Correct

45. What are valid arguments in the metadata tag of your HTML codes (Choose all that apply)?

***A. name**

B. engine

***C. content**

D. version

E. No Answer is Correct

Explanation: You should memorize this for the exam.

---

46. You designed your web page so that a hyperlink has a destination that starts with https://. What kind of link is this?

***A. SSL**

B. SET

C. SAS

D. RAS

E. No Answer is Correct

Explanation: When you connect to a site using HTTPS, SSL is running for security purpose.

47. You are setting up a server for your web site. Which port does your HTTP server use?

A. 20

B. 22

C. 25

D. 80

E. 81

---

48. People are complaining that they cannot connect to your HTTP server. You check everything, and it seems like there is nothing wrong with the software and hardware. Which of the following may be a cause of the problem?

A. Port 80 is blocked by the firewall

B. Server service is not working

C. HTTP service is set to sleep

D. Windows is currently locked

E. No Answer is Correct

47. You are setting up a server for your web site. Which port does your HTTP server use?

A. 20

B. 22

C. 25

***D. 80**

E. 81

Explanation: HTTP uses port 80.

---

48. People are complaining that they cannot connect to your HTTP server. You check everything, and it seems like there is nothing wrong with the software and hardware. Which of the following may be a cause of the problem?

***A. Port 80 is blocked by the firewall**

B. Server service is not working

C. HTTP service is set to sleep

D. Windows is currently locked

E. No Answer is Correct

Explanation: HTTP server uses port 80. If this port is blocked, the server will not receive any request.

49. You are setting up a server for your web site. Which of the following is a common choice for HTTP server on the Windows platform?

A. PHP

B. PGP

C. INetD

D. HTTPD

E. IIS

---

50. You are running a Linux system with the Apache server. Where will you place the HTML files?

A. /home/httpd/html

B. /home/html

C. /httpd/html

D. /httpd/htm

E. No Answer is Correct

49. You are setting up a server for your web site. Which of the following is a common choice for HTTP server on the Windows platform?

A. PHP

B. PGP

C. INetD

D. HTTPD

***E. IIS**

Explanation: IIS comes with different versions of NT/Win2000 Servers .

---

50. You are running a Linux system with the Apache server. Where will you place the HTML files?

***A. /home/httpd/html**

B. /home/html

C. /httpd/html

D. /httpd/htm

E. No Answer is Correct

Explanation: Please refer to the web link for more information.

51. You are setting up a Linux server for your web site. What files should you place in the /home/httpd/cgi-bin directory of your Apache HTTP server?

A. Executables

B. HTML

C. SHTML

D. Acrobat

E. No Answer is Correct

---

52. You are setting up a server for your web site. This server will be running the HTTP service. HTTP belongs to which layer of the OSI model?

A. Application Layer

B. Presentation Layer

C. Session Layer

D. Transport Layer

E. Network Layer

51. You are setting up a Linux server for your web site. What files should you place in the /home/httpd/cgi-bin directory of your Apache HTTP server?

***A. Executables**

B. HTML

C. SHTML

D. Acrobat

E. No Answer is Correct

Explanation: Please refer to the web link for more information.

---

52. You are setting up a server for your web site. This server will be running the HTTP service. HTTP belongs to which layer of the OSI model?

***A. Application Layer**

B. Presentation Layer

C. Session Layer

D. Transport Layer

E. Network Layer

Explanation: Please refer to the web link for more information.

53. You are setting up a server for your web site. Your peer Mary asks you to deploy SSL. At which layer of the OSI model does SSL function?

A. Application Layer Only

B. Presentation Layer Only

C. Between Session Layer and Application Layer

D. Between Transport Layer and Application Layer

E. No Answer is Correct

---

54. You are setting up a server for your web site. Your server will deploy SSL for security purpose. Which port should you enable for SSL to work?

A. 80

B. 110

C. 440

D. 443

E. 445

53. You are setting up a server for your web site. Your peer Mary asks you to deploy SSL. At which layer of the OSI model does SSL function?

A. Application Layer Only

B. Presentation Layer Only

C. Between Session Layer and Application Layer

***D. Between Transport Layer and Application Layer**

E. No Answer is Correct

Explanation: Please refer to the web link for more information.

---

54. You are setting up a server for your web site. Your server will deploy SSL for security purpose. Which port should you enable for SSL to work?

A. 80

B. 110

C. 440

***D. 443**

E. 445

Explanation: Please refer to the web link for more information.

55. You are setting up a server for your web site. To allow for web page access, which service within your server must be enabled?

A. HTTPS

B. HTTP Host Header

C. HTTP

D. FTP

E. SNMP

---

56. You have only one IP address available. However, you want your HTTP server to host couple web sites. What option do you have?

A. Virtual site

B. Virtual directory

C. Virtual mall

D. SSL

E. Virtual server

55. You are setting up a server for your web site. To allow for web page access, which service within your server must be enabled?

A. HTTPS

B. HTTP Host Header

***C. HTTP**

D. FTP

E. SNMP

Explanation: HTTPS offers security which is entirely optional. Host header is another optional feature. Only HTTP is REQUIRED.

---

56. You have only one IP address available. However, you want your HTTP server to host couple web sites. What option do you have?

A. Virtual site

***B. Virtual directory**

C. Virtual mall

D. SSL

E. Virtual server

Explanation: Virtual directory is equivalent to alias. For example: www.xyz.com/~versionA

57. You are running IIS as the web server platform. You have only one NIC available. However, you want your HTTP server to host couple web sites. You do have multiple IP addresses available for use. What option do you have?

A. Virtual site

B. Virtual directory

C. Virtual mall

D. SSL

E. Virtual server

---

58. You are deploying virtual directories in your HTTP server. You want to allow one click access to these directories. How do you enable this?

A. Links

B. Host header

C. Host encrypted

D. Virtual server

E. No Answer is Correct

57. You are running IIS as the web server platform. You have only one NIC available. However, you want your HTTP server to host couple web sites. You do have multiple IP addresses available for use. What option do you have?

A. Virtual site

B. Virtual directory

C. Virtual mall

D. SSL

***E. Virtual server**

Explanation: With virtual server, you can associate the same NIC with couple IP addresses at the same time.

---

58. You are deploying virtual directories in your HTTP server. You want to allow one click access to these directories. How do you enable this?

***A. Links**

B. Host header

C. Host encrypted

D. Virtual server

E. No Answer is Correct

Explanation: Please refer to the web link or more information.

59. You are deploying virtual directories in your HTTP server. You want to allow access to these directories without the use of anchor tag. How do you enable this?

A. Links

B. Host header

C. Host encrypted

D. Virtual server

E. No Answer is Correct

---

60. You are setting up a server for your web site. What type of permission is required for the CGI applications in your HTTP server?

A. Read

B. Write

C. Change

D. Execute

E. No Answer is Correct

59. You are deploying virtual directories in your HTTP server. You want to allow access to these directories without the use of anchor tag. How do you enable this?

A. Links

B. Host header

C. Host encrypted

D. Virtual server

***E. No Answer is Correct**

Explanation: You will need to inform the users to type the alias in the URL name space. Please refer to the web link or more information.

---

60. You are setting up a server for your web site. What type of permission is required for the CGI applications in your HTTP server?

A. Read

B. Write

C. Change

***D. Execute**

E. No Answer is Correct

Explanation: Please refer to the web link or more information.

61. Which organization develops the HTML standard?

A. W3C

B. IEEE

C. InterNIC

D. ISP

E. No Answer is Correct

---

62. What is the latest standard defined by W3C on HTML?

A. HTML 3

B. DHTML

C. SHTML

D. XHTML

E. No Answer is Correct

61. Which organization develops the HTML standard?

***A. W3C**

B. IEEE

C. InterNIC

D. ISP

E. No Answer is Correct

Explanation: Basically most of the web design related standards are developed by W3C. Please refer to the web link for more information.

---

62. What is the latest standard defined by W3C on HTML?

A. HTML 3

B. DHTML

C. SHTML

***D. XHTML**

E. No Answer is Correct

Explanation: Basically most of the web design related standards are developed by W3C. Please refer to the web link for more information.

63. What is W3C's standard on platform- and language-neutral interface that will allow programs and scripts to dynamically access and update the content, structure and style of documents?

A. DCOM

B. DOM

C. OBJECTLIB

D. DHTML

E. No Answer is Correct

---

64. What is W3C's standard on the universal format for structured documents and data on the Web?

A. DCOM

B. DOM

C. OBJECTLIB

D. DHTML

E. XML

63. What is W3C's standard on platform- and language-neutral interface that will allow programs and scripts to dynamically access and update the content, structure and style of documents?

A. DCOM

B. DOM

C. OBJECTLIB

***D. DHTML**

E. No Answer is Correct

Explanation: DOM stands for Document Object Model. Basically most of the web design related standards are developed by W3C. Please refer to the web link for more information.

---

64. What is W3C's standard on the universal format for structured documents and data on the Web?

A. DCOM

B. DOM

C. OBJECTLIB

D. DHTML

***E. XML**

Explanation: Basically most of the web design related standards are developed by W3C. Please refer to the web link for more information.

65. What is W3C's standard on maintaining fonts, colors and spacing to Web documents?

A. DCOM

B. DOM

C. CSS

D. DHTML

E. XML

---

66. What does the term W3C stands for?

A. a web address

B. an .org web address

C. World Wide Web Consortium

D. World Wide Web Construction

E. No Answer is Correct

65. What is W3C's standard on maintaining fonts, colors and spacing to Web documents?

A. DCOM

B. DOM

***C. CSS**

D. DHTML

E. XML

Explanation: CSS stands for Cascading Style Sheets. Basically most of the web design related standards are developed by W3C. Please refer to the web link for more information.

---

66. What does the term W3C stands for?

A. a web address

B. an .org web address

***C. World Wide Web Consortium**

D. World Wide Web Construction

E. No Answer is Correct

Explanation: Basically most of the web design related standards are developed by W3C. Please refer to the web link for more information.

67. When was the W3C Founded?

A. 1987

B. 1990

C. 1994

D. 1996

E. 1997

---

68. Who is always regarded as the inventor of the web?

A. Tim Berners-Lee

B. John Mark

C. David Komansky

D. Bill Gate

E. Al Gore

67. When was the W3C Founded?

A. 1987

B. 1990

***C. 1994**

D. 1996

E. 1997

Explanation: In October 1994, Tim Berners-Lee founded the World Wide Web Consortium (W3C).

---

68. Who is always regarded as the inventor of the web?

***A. Tim Berners-Lee**

B. John Mark

C. David Komansky

D. Bill Gate

E. Al Gore

Explanation: In October 1994, Tim Berners-Lee founded the World Wide Web Consortium (W3C).

69. Where was W3C founded in 1994?

A. MIT/LCS

B. UC Berkeley

C. Stanford

D. RIT

E. No Answer is Correct

---

70. Which organization was the first European W3C host in history?

A. INRIA

B. CERN

C. W3C

D. IEEE

E. No Answer is Correct

69. Where was W3C founded in 1994?

***A. MIT/LCS**

B. UC Berkeley

C. Stanford

D. RIT

E. No Answer is Correct

Explanation: World Wide Web Consortium (W3C) was found at the Massachusetts Institute of Technology Laboratory for Computer Science [MIT/LCS] in collaboration with CERN.

---

70. Which organization was the first European W3C host in history?

***A. INRIA**

B. CERN

C. W3C

D. IEEE

E. No Answer is Correct

Explanation: It stands for Institute National de Recherché en Informatique et Automatique.

71. W3C was founded by Tim Berners Lee at MIT in collaboration with which organization?

A. INRIA

B. CERN

C. W3C

D. IEEE

E. No Answer is Correct

---

72. What are the domains of W3C web framework (Choose all that apply)?

A. Architecture Domain

B. User Interface Domain

C. Technology and Society Domain

D. Web Accessibility Initiative

E. No Answer is Correct

71. W3C was founded by Tim Berners Lee at MIT in collaboration with which organization?

A. INRIA

***B. CERN**

C. W3C

D. IEEE

E. No Answer is Correct

Explanation: People always describe CERN as where the Web originated.

---

72. What are the domains of W3C web framework (Choose all that apply)?

***A. Architecture Domain**

***B. User Interface Domain**

***C. Technology and Society Domain**

***D. Web Accessibility Initiative**

E. No Answer is Correct

Explanation: Refer to the web link for more information.

73. Among the domains of W3C web framework, which one governs the underlying technologies of the Web?

A. Architecture Domain

B. User Interface Domain

C. Technology and Society Domain

D. Web Accessibility Initiative

E. No Answer is Correct

---

74. Among the domains of W3C web framework, which one governs the works on the formats and languages for presenting information to users?

A. Architecture Domain

B. User Interface Domain

C. Technology and Society Domain

D. Web Accessibility Initiative

E. No Answer is Correct

73. Among the domains of W3C web framework, which one governs the underlying technologies of the Web?

***A. Architecture Domain**

B. User Interface Domain

C. Technology and Society Domain

D. Web Accessibility Initiative

E. No Answer is Correct

Explanation: Refer to the web link for more information.

---

74. Among the domains of W3C web framework, which one governs the works on the formats and languages for presenting information to users?

A. Architecture Domain

***B. User Interface Domain**

C. Technology and Society Domain

D. Web Accessibility Initiative

E. No Answer is Correct

Explanation: Refer to the web link for more information.

75. Among the domains of W3C web framework, which one governs the works on the social, legal, and public policy concerns?

A. Architecture Domain

B. User Interface Domain

C. Technology and Society Domain

D. Web Accessibility Initiative

E. No Answer is Correct

---

76. It is always better for you to design your web site on:

A. workstation

B. server

C. palm

D. dock

E. No Answer is Correct

75. Among the domains of W3C web framework, which one governs the works on the social, legal, and public policy concerns?

A. Architecture Domain

B. User Interface Domain

***C. Technology and Society Domain**

D. Web Accessibility Initiative

E. No Answer is Correct

Explanation: Refer to the web link for more information.

---

76. It is always better for you to design your web site on:

***A. workstation**

B. server

C. palm

D. dock

E. No Answer is Correct

Explanation: The design should be done on the workstation first before uploading to the web server.

77. You have a project team of 10 members. To ensure that members will not accidentally overwrite each others' works, what technology should you deploy?

A. version control

B. save control

C. write permission

D. share permission

E. No Answer is Correct

---

78. What software tool allows you to actually load your creations to the web server?

A. HTTP

B. XCOPY

C. RSH

D. FTP

E. No Answer is Correct

77. You have a project team of 10 members. To ensure that members will not accidentally overwrite each others' works, what technology should you deploy?

***A. version control**

B. save control

C. write permission

D. share permission

E. No Answer is Correct

Explanation: A good example of such software is the MS Visual SourceSafe.

---

78. What software tool allows you to actually load your creations to the web server?

A. HTTP

B. XCOPY

C. RSH

***D. FTP**

E. No Answer is Correct

Explanation: Most of the time we use FTP client to upload the files to the server.

79. What must be carefully set in the web server software so that we can upload our creation successfully?

A. permission

B. speed

C. link

D. bandwidth

E. No Answer is Correct

---

80. What component of FrontPage allows for extended functionality when running on IIS?

A. FP server extension

B. FP server accelerator

C. FP server optimizer

D. FP theme chooser

E. FP style generator

79. What must be carefully set in the web server software so that we can upload our creation successfully?

***A. permission**

B. speed

C. link

D. bandwidth

E. No Answer is Correct

Explanation: Without proper access permission we may not be able to write files on the server's drive.

---

80. What component of FrontPage allows for extended functionality when running on IIS?

***A. FP server extension**

B. FP server accelerator

C. FP server optimizer

D. FP theme chooser

E. FP style generator

Explanation: FP server extension allows additional functionality and control for FrontPage users. However, not every web server in the market supports the use of this extension kit.

81. You have a project team of 10 members developing ASP pages. To ensure that members will not accidentally overwrite each others works, what software should you deploy?

A. Visual Interdev

B. Visual Gen

C. Visual EnCAD

D. Visual SourceSafe

E. No Answer is Correct

---

82. Before you publish your pages to the server, what essential action should you perform?

A. testing

B. training

C. tuning

D. masking

E. No Answer is Correct

81. You have a project team of 10 members developing ASP pages. To ensure that members will not accidentally overwrite each others works, what software should you deploy?

A. Visual Interdev

B. Visual Gen

C. Visual EnCAD

***D. Visual SourceSafe**

E. No Answer is Correct

Explanation: Visual SourceSafe is an example of version control software.

---

82. Before you publish your pages to the server, what essential action should you perform?

***A. testing**

B. training

C. tuning

D. masking

E. No Answer is Correct

83. You may want to consider the increase of __________ for your 4 way web server when the number of visitors keep on increasing.

A. hard drive

B. RAM

C. CDROM

D. CPU

E. No Answer is Correct

---

84. Before you publish your site, you want to conduct a series of testing. What type of server should you consider for the testing purpose?

A. performance server

B. http server

C. ftp server

D. staging server

E. No Answer is Correct

83. You may want to consider the increase of __________ for your 4 way web server when the number of visitors keep on increasing.

A. hard drive

***B. RAM**

C. CDROM

D. CPU

E. No Answer is Correct

Explanation: Since your web server is already a 4-way (4 CPUs system), processing power is not the top concern. RAM is essential to the performance of the system.

---

84. Before you publish your site, you want to conduct a series of testing. What type of server should you consider for the testing purpose?

A. performance server

B. http server

C. ftp server

***D. staging server**

E. No Answer is Correct

Explanation: You may upload your works to the staging server, test them, and then finally transfer them to the production server.

85. To be able to successfully publish your works to the web server, what protocol must be running on the network?

A. IPX

B. NetBEUI

C. DLC

D. AppleTalk

E. No Answer is Correct

---

86. When you upload your works to the web server, in which directory should you place the CGI scripts in general?

A. SBIN

B. CBIN

C. CGI-BIN

D. Binary

E. No Answer is Correct

85. To be able to successfully publish your works to the web server, what protocol must be running on the network?

A. IPX

B. NetBEUI

C. DLC

D. AppleTalk

***E. No Answer is Correct**

Explanation: Anything related to the Web requires only TCP/IP.

---

86. When you upload your works to the web server, in which directory should you place the CGI scripts in general?

A. SBIN

B. CBIN

***C. CGI-BIN**

D. Binary

E. No Answer is Correct

Explanation: Many web servers have a predefined directory structure. A lot of these structures have a directory called CGI-BIN to hold the CGI scripts.

87. You want to be sure that your web site can handle requests even during the peak hours. What kind of test should you conduct?

A. debug

B. speed test

C. CPU test

D. stress test

E. No Answer is Correct

---

88. To publish your works to a third party Unix web server, what software tool will you use?

A. HTTP

B. XCOPY

C. RSH

D. FTP

E. No Answer is Correct

87. You want to be sure that your web site can handle requests even during the peak hours. What kind of test should you conduct?

A. debug

B. speed test

C. CPU test

***D. stress test**

E. No Answer is Correct

Explanation: You are encouraged to run a stress test to make sure that your site will not go down when heavy traffic is flooding in.

---

88. To publish your works to a third party Unix web server, what software tool will you use?

A. HTTP

B. XCOPY

C. RSH

***D. FTP**

E. No Answer is Correct

Explanation: Most of the time we use FTP client to upload the files to the server.

89. Your site has been published to the server with a URL
http://www.abcserver.com/~yourDIR

What kind of structure is this?

A. virtual IP

B. virtual server

C. virtual directory

D. real server

E. No Answer is Correct

---

90. Your site has been published to the server with a URL http://www.yoursite.com

This server also hosts the following sites:

http://www.Asite.com

http://www.Bsite.com

What kind of structure is this?

A. virtual IP

B. virtual server

C. virtual directory

D. real server

E. No Answer is Correct

89. Your site has been published to the server with a URL
http://www.abcserver.com/~yourDIR

What kind of structure is this?

A. virtual IP

B. virtual server

***C. virtual directory**

D. real server

E. No Answer is Correct

Explanation: This is also called an alias. With alias, a single domain name can be used to host different web sites.

---

90. Your site has been published to the server with a URL http://www.yoursite.com

This server also hosts the following sites:

http://www.Asite.com

http://www.Bsite.com

What kind of structure is this?

A. virtual IP

***B. virtual server**

C. virtual directory

D. real server

E. No Answer is Correct

Explanation: With virtual server a single server assumes multiple IP addresses as well as multiple domain names.

91. The proprietary <LAYER> tag from Netscape has been deprecated in favor of what HTML 4.0 tag for creating layers in a web document?

A. <SPAN>

B. <IFRAME>

C. <FRAME>

D. <DIV>

---

92. By taking the file size of an HTML document and dividing it by the speed of a user's connection, you can determine what?

A. The user's bandwidth

B. The server's throughput

C. The time required to download the image

D. The file format best suited for the image

91. The proprietary <LAYER> tag from Netscape has been deprecated in favor of what HTML 4.0 tag for creating layers in a web document?

A. <SPAN>

B. <IFRAME>

C. <FRAME>

***D. <DIV>**

Explanation: The best way to create layers in an HTML document and still be compatible with all browsers is to use the <DIV> tag. The <SPAN> tag is used primarily for inline formatting. The <IFRAME> tag is an Internet Explorer specific tag used to create a frame anywhere in an HTML document. The <FRAME> tag is used in conjunction with the <FRAMESET> tag to divide the window up into separate windows, each with their own HTML document.

---

92. By taking the file size of an HTML document and dividing it by the speed of a user's connection, you can determine what?

A. The user's bandwidth

B. The servers throughput

***C. The time required to download the image**

D. The file format best suited for the image

Explanation: The time required to download an image can be roughly determined by dividing the file size by the users connection speed. However, this is only a rough estimate because there are additional overhead requirements to transfer the file. Therefore, a 10KB file may need 11KB of bandwidth to actually transfer to the user's machine. File size can sometimes be used to determine which file format is best suited for the image, but other factors usually take precedence. The user's bandwidth is equal to the connection speed that they are capable of. The server's throughput is equal to the connection speed that it is capable of.

93. What new technology combines HTML 4.0 and XML technologies

A. HTML X

B. XML 1.H

C. HTML 5.0

D. XHTML 1.0

---

94. What three variants are described in the W3C's HTML 4.0 recommendation?

A. HTML 4.0 Strict

B. HTML 4.0 Basic

C. HTML 4.0 Advanced

D. HTML 4.0 Transitional

E. HTML 4.0 Frameset

93. What new technology combines HTML 4.0 and XML technologies

A. HTML X

B. XML 1.H

C. HTML 5.0

***D. XHTML 1.0**

Explanation: The newest technology on the block is XHTML 1.0. It uses the same tags as HTML 4.0, but requires that HTML documents use the same syntax and structure rules as XML. It accomplishes this by defining 3 separate Document Type Definitions (DTD's) for HTML documents.

---

94. What three variants are described in the W3C's HTML 4.0 recommendation?

***A. HTML 4.0 Strict**

B. HTML 4.0 Basic

C. HTML 4.0 Advanced

***D. HTML 4.0 Transitional**

***E. HTML 4.0 Frameset**

Explanation: The three variants to the HTML 4.0 recommendation outlined by the W3C are Strict, Transitional, and Frameset. The Strict variant is used for documents without tags associated with layout, such as Cascading Style Sheets. The Transitional variant is used pages that were originally written to the HTML 3.2 standard. The Frameset variant is used for documents that use frames to partition the browser window.

95. What steps need to be taken to create a hyperlink that loads the "index.html" document into a frame named "Main?" Choose two.

A. Add the NAME="Main" attribute to the <FRAMESET> tag.

B. Add the NAME="Main" attribute to the <FRAME> tag.

C. Add the TARGET="Main" attribute to the <A> tag.

D. Add the HREF="index.htm#Main" attribute to the <A> tag.

---

96. You want all of the links on an HTML page to point to the "Main" frame in the "frames.html" document. What line of code would you use to accomplish this?

A. <BASE TARGET="main">

B. <BASE HREF="frames.html#main">

C. <BASE SRC="frames.html#main">

D. <BASETARGET HREF="frames.html#main">

95. What steps need to be taken to create a hyperlink that loads the "index.html" document into a frame named "Main?" Choose two.

A. Add the NAME="Main" attribute to the <FRAMESET> tag.

***B. Add the NAME="Main" attribute to the <FRAME> tag.**

***C. Add the TARGET="Main" attribute to the <A> tag.**

D. Add the HREF="index.htm#Main" attribute to the <A> tag.

Explanation: In order to have a document that is referenced by the <A> tag load into the proper frame in the browser window, you must use the NAME attribute in the <FRAME> tag of the frameset document. In this case the code would read <FRAME NAME="Main">. Then, you would use the TARGET attribute in the <A> tag to load the document in the "Main" frame. The code would read <A HREF="index.html" TARGET="Main">

---

96. You want all of the links on an HTML page to point to the "Main" frame in the "frames.html" document. What line of code would you use to accomplish this?

***A. <BASE TARGET="main">**

B. <BASE HREF="frames.html#main">

C. <BASE SRC="frames.html#main">

D. <BASETARGET HREF="frames.html#main">

Explanation: The <BASE> tag with the TARGET attribute is used to define a default target for all links used on a page. The optional HREF attribute can be used for defining the URL of the targeted document in case the page on which the <BASE> tag resides is read out of context.

97. You wish to add a hyperlink to your webpage that will load the "news.html" document into a separate window. The document is located in the "extra" directory of the "www.totalrecall.com" domain. Enter the proper code below.

A. <A HREF="}{WebURL1=http://www.totalrecall.com/extra/news.html" TARGET="_new">

---

98. Many search engines examine web pages for what tag that provides information about the page?

A. <TITLE>Page Title</TITLE>

B. <META NAME="Keywords" CONTENT="keyword1 keyword2 keyword3">

C. <META HTTP-EQUIV="Keywords" CONTENT="keyword1 keyword2 keyword3">

D. <KEYWORDS>keyword1 keyword2 keyword3</KEYWORD>

97. You wish to add a hyperlink to your webpage that will load the "news.html" document into a separate window. The document is located in the "extra" directory of the "www.totalrecall.com" domain. Enter the proper code below.

A. <A HREF="}{WebURL1=http://www.totalrecall.com/extra/news.html" TARGET="_new">

Explanation: The key to this answer is the "_new" value in the TARGET attribute. This value loads the document into a new window. The "_blank" value would load the document into the current window and clear the current frameset.

---

98. Many search engines examine web pages for what tag that provides information about the page?

A. <TITLE>Page Title</TITLE>

***B. <META NAME="Keywords" CONTENT="keyword1 keyword2 keyword3">**

C. <META HTTP-EQUIV="Keywords" CONTENT="keyword1 keyword2 keyword3">

D. <KEYWORDS>keyword1 keyword2 keyword3</KEYWORD>

Explanation: Search engines such as Alta Vista and Infoseek search web page for metadata contained in the <META> tag. The NAME and CONTENT attributes are used with the <META> tag to list the keywords for the page. The HTTP-EQUIV attribute is used to send information to the web server sending the document. Many search engines ignore <META> tags with the HTTP-EQUIV attribute.

99. From the list below, choose the commonly used values for the HTTP-EQUIV attribute of a <META> tag.

A. TITLE

B. REFRESH

C. EXPIRES

D. AUTHOR

E. SET-COOKIE

---

100. Choose the four types of style sheets available in the HTML 4.0 recommendation from the list below.

A. Embedded

B. Cascading

C. Inline

D. Imported

E. Linked

99. From the list below, choose the commonly used values for the HTTP-EQUIV attribute of a <META> tag.

A. TITLE

***B. REFRESH**

***C. EXPIRES**

D. AUTHOR

***E. SET-COOKIE**

Explanation: The HTTP-EQUIV attribute is used to send information to the web server that is sending the requested page. The REFRESH value is used to redirect the user to a different page. The EXPIRES value is used to set a time and date the content on the page is expired. The SET-COOKIE value is used to set cookie information in the user's browser. Even though any value can be used in the HTTP-EQUIV attribute, only these three listed will be useful in all browsers that access the page.

---

100. Choose the four types of style sheets available in the HTML 4.0 recommendation from the list below.

***A. Embedded**

B. Cascading

***C. Inline**

***D. Imported**

***E. Linked**

Explanation: The four types of style sheets are Linked, Imported, Inline, and Embedded. Cascading Style Sheets refers to the use of multiple style sheets and the order in which they are processed. Any of the four types of style sheets can be used to create Cascading Style Sheets.

101. Given the following code, which style information would apply to the <P> tag?

```
<HTML>
<HEAD>
<TITLE>Style Test</TITLE>
<!--
<STYLE>
P {color: blue; font-family: verdana; font-size: 12pt; background: black;}
</STYLE>
-->
</HEAD>
<BODY>
<P STYLE="color: yellow; font-family: times; font-weight: bold;">What
style am I using?</P>
</BODY>
</HTML>
```

A. Blue 12pt Verdana with a black background

B. Yellow 12 pt Verdana with a white background

C. Yellow 12pt Times Bold with a white background

D. Yellow 12pt Times Bold with a black background

101. Given the following code, which style information would apply to the <P> tag?

```
<HTML>
<HEAD>
<TITLE>Style Test</TITLE>
<!--
<STYLE>
P {color: blue; font-family: verdana; font-size: 12pt; background: black;}
</STYLE>
-->
</HEAD>
<BODY>
<P STYLE="color: yellow; font-family: times; font-weight: bold;">What
style am I using?</P>
</BODY>
</HTML>
```

A. Blue 12pt Verdana with a black background

B. Yellow 12 pt Verdana with a white background

C. Yellow 12pt Times Bold with a white background

***D. Yellow 12pt Times Bold with a black background**

Explanation: When using cascading style sheets, the most recent style rule applied will be used to format a defined element. In this case the inline style rules specified in the <P> tag will override the rules used in the embedded style rule at the beginning of the page. However, because the inline style rules of the <P> tag do not specify different values for the FONT-SIZE or BACKGROUND values, these values are inherited from the embedded style rules.

Chapter 2: Web Design Concepts

1. What is the duty of a web designer?

A. Responsible for the appearance of the Web site

B. Responsible for the programming of the Web site

C. Responsible for the server of the Web site

D. Responsible for the caching of the Web site

E. No Answer is Correct

---

2. Valid skill areas required by a Web Designer should include (Choose all that apply)?

A. Publication design principles

B. Graphic design

C. Marketing

D. Web design

E. No Answer is Correct

1. What is the duty of a web designer?

***A. Responsible for the appearance of the Web site**

B. Responsible for the programming of the Web site

C. Responsible for the server of the Web site

D. Responsible for the caching of the Web site

E. No Answer is Correct

Explanation: The designer should have backgrounds on design concepts and theories.

---

2. Valid skill areas required by a Web Designer should include (Choose all that apply)?

***A. Publication design principles**

***B. Graphic design**

***C. Marketing**

***D. Web design**

E. No Answer is Correct

Explanation: All these concepts help the designer to develop an effective web site.

3. From a traditional designer point of view, what is "web design skill"?

A. internet experience

B. AutoCAD experience

C. dreamweaver experience

D. shockwave experience

E. No Answer is Correct

---

4. When you define the site goal, what factors must be considered (Choose all that apply)?

A. the need of business

B. the need of browsers

C. the need of customers

D. the need of effects

E. No Answer is Correct

3. From a traditional designer point of view, what is "web design skill"?

***A. internet experience**

B. AutoCAD experience

C. dreamweaver experience

D. shockwave experience

E. No Answer is Correct

Explanation: Web design requires interactions, while most traditional designs are "static".

---

4. When you define the site goal, what factors must be considered (Choose all that apply)?

***A. the need of business**

B. the need of browsers

***C. the need of customers**

D. the need of effects

E. No Answer is Correct

Explanation: These are the life blood of your site.

5. What is a story board in site design?

A. the first site prototype

B. the second site prototype

C. the draft document

D. the logic flow of site events

E. No Answer is Correct

---

6. When creating your storyboard, what is the focus?

A. beauty

B. style

C. fashion

D. information flow

E. functions

5. What is a story board in site design?

***A. the first site prototype**

B. the second site prototype

C. the draft document

D. the logic flow of site events

E. No Answer is Correct

Explanation: It is the initial design of the site. You will want to test and further develop this prototype into the final product at a later stage.

---

6. When creating your storyboard, what is the focus?

A. beauty

B. style

C. fashion

D. information flow

***E. functions**

Explanation: You want to focus on the functions of the site at this stage.

7. Which of the following are valid examples of site goals (Choose all that apply)?

A. Generate sales lead

B. Increase web server throughput

C. Increase business visibility

D. Attract new customers

E. No Answer is Correct

---

8. In general, you should design your site on a ?

A. Server

B. laptop

C. workstation

D. Javastation

E. No Answer is Correct

s7. Which of the following are valid examples of site goals (Choose all that apply)?

***A. Generate sales lead**

B. Increase web server throughput

***C. Increase business visibility**

***D. Attract new customers**

E. No Answer is Correct

Explanation: Business objectives are always the appropriate site goals.

---

8. In general, you should design your site on a ?

A. Server

B. laptop

***C. workstation**

D. Javastation

E. No Answer is Correct

Explanation: Generally you should design your site using your workstation, and then upload the site to a web server so that everyone can access it.

9. What will be the best location for the site menu of a site for reference purpose?

A. on the front door

B. on the second page

C. on the exit page

D. on any page

E. No Answer is Correct

---

10. When you design your site, what is true regarding the site navigation structure design?

A. Make sure users can locate information fast enough

B. Make sure users can have a good looking side bar

C. Make sure users can have a good looking navigation panel

D. Make sure users can skip the introductory page

E. No Answer is Correct

9. What will be the best location for the site menu of a site for reference purpose?

***A. on the front door**

B. on the second page

C. on the exit page

D. on any page

E. No Answer is Correct

Explanation: Doing this allow visitors to tell at a glance if the information they are seeking is inside your site.

---

10. When you design your site, what is true regarding the site navigation structure design?

***A. Make sure users can locate information fast enough**

B. Make sure users can have a good looking side bar

C. Make sure users can have a good looking navigation panel

D. Make sure users can skip the introductory page

E. No Answer is Correct

Explanation: Fast information location is the key to a good design.

11. What is the most likely design goal of a generic intranet site?

A. outstanding style

B. attention grabbing design

C. efficient information delivery

D. fast fall back

E. No Answer is Correct

---

12. What would be a valid assumption about visitors of external sites?

A. reader prefers english

B. reader does not read english

C. reader like to surf your site thoroughly

D. the reader has little motivation to stay

E. No Answer is Correct

11. What is the most likely design goal of a generic intranet site?

A. outstanding style

B. attention grabbing design

***C. efficient information delivery**

D. fast fall back

E. No Answer is Correct

Explanation: Intranet is mostly for information retrieval purpose.

---

12. What would be a valid assumption about visitors of external sites?

A. reader prefers english

B. reader does not read english

C. reader like to surf your site thoroughly

***D. the reader has little motivation to stay**

E. No Answer is Correct

Explanation: You need to keep them from leaving your site. They do not have much patience to stay.

13. Which of the following are valid goals for external sites that sell fashions?

A. Maximizing contact time

B. Maximizing download performance

C. Drawing reader deeper into the site

D. Keep server up 24 x 7

E. No Answer is Correct

---

14. Mary has a site that sells clothes and fashions. What type of presentation can she use to enrich her site?

A. voice presentation

B. animation

C. multimedia presentation

D. line arts presentation

E. No Answer is Correct

13. Which of the following are valid goals for external sites that sell fashions?

***A. Maximizing contact time**

B. Maximizing download performance

***C. Drawing reader deeper into the site**

D. Keep server up 24 x 7

E. No Answer is Correct

Explanation: For external sites you need to keep readers from leaving your site. They do not have much patience to stay.

---

14. Mary has a site that sells clothes and fashions. What type of presentation can she use to enrich her site?

A. voice presentation

B. animation

***C. multimedia presentation**

D. line arts presentation

E. No Answer is Correct

Explanation: Content can be enriched with multimedia presentation to grab attentions.

15. An elegant but non-functional cover on your web site is likely to be tedious for which type of users?

A. single visit

B. frequent visit

C. non English speaking

D. users with version 3 browsers

E. No Answer is Correct

---

16. Many users have graphics turned off due to slow connections. In this case, what option will make your page more accessible to them?

A. use ALT text

B. use Tag text

C. use Image

D. use voice

E. No Answer is Correct

15. An elegant but non-functional cover on your web site is likely to be tedious for which type of users?

A. single visit

***B. frequent visit**

C. non English speaking

D. users with version 3 browsers

E. No Answer is Correct

Explanation: Attractive cover is good to grab attention of first time visitor only.

---

16. Many users have graphics turned off due to slow connections. In this case, what option will make your page more accessible to them?

***A. use ALT text**

B. use Tag text

C. use Image

D. use voice

E. No Answer is Correct

Explanation: For more information please refer to the web link.

17. Which of the following is a good design principle regarding the use of link text?

A. Make link text descriptive and detail

B. Make link text descriptive but brief

C. Make link text short and italic

D. Make link text in different colors

E. No Answer is Correct

---

18. Which of the following are NOT recommended design principles regarding the use of link text
(Choose all that apply)?

A. Use link text that can stand alone

B. Use link text that cannot stand alone

C. Use long link text

D. Use BOLD link text

E. Use Arial link text

17. Which of the following is a good design principle regarding the use of link text?

A. Make link text descriptive and detail

***B. Make link text descriptive but brief**

C. Make link text short and italic

D. Make link text in different colors

E. No Answer is Correct

Explanation: For more information please refer to the web link.

---

18. Which of the following are NOT recommended design principles regarding the use of link text
(Choose all that apply)?

A. Use link text that can stand alone

***B. Use link text that cannot stand alone**

***C. Use long link text**

***D. Use BOLD link text**

***E. Use Arial link text**

Explanation: For more information please refer to the web link.

19. Which of the following is a recommended design principle for usability regarding the use of Java Applet?

A. provide submenu

B. provide alternatives

C. provide push buttons

D. provide additional windows

E. No Answer is Correct

---

20. When designing web page for blind users, which of the following is a valid measure?

A. Provide alternatives to tables and frames

B. Provide alternatives to windows

C. Provide alternatives to tables only

D. Provide alternatives to frames only

E. No Answer is Correct

19. Which of the following is a recommended design principle for usability regarding the use of Java Applet?

A. provide submenu

***B. provide alternatives**

C. provide push buttons

D. provide additional windows

E. No Answer is Correct

Explanation: Your audiences will need to have alternatives, as applets are usually inaccessible and sometimes unsupported. For more information please refer to the web link.

---

20. When designing web page for blind users, which of the following is a valid measure?

***A. Provide alternatives to tables and frames**

B. Provide alternatives to windows

C. Provide alternatives to tables only

D. Provide alternatives to frames only

E. No Answer is Correct

Explanation: Tables and frames can cause text to form columns, which can be very confusing for blind readers. For more information please refer to the web link.

21. When you plan for the development of your web site, your focus should be on satisfying the needs of which group of people?

A. developers

B. team members

C. supplier

D. audience

E. No Answer is Correct

---

21. When you plan for the development of your web site, your focus should be on satisfying the needs of which group of people?

A. developers

B. team members

C. supplier

***D. audience**

E. No Answer is Correct

Explanation: You should fulfill the need of your audience. They are your customers.

22. When you first plan for the overall directions of your web site, you should identify a group of people. Which group of people is it?

A. developers

B. team members

C. supplier

D. audience

E. No Answer is Correct

---

22. When you first plan for the overall directions of your web site, you should identify a group of people. Which group of people is it?

A. developers

B. team members

C. supplier

***D. audience**

E. No Answer is Correct

Explanation: You should fulfill the need of your audience. They are your customers.

23. You want to deliver music over the web to your audience. 99% of your audiences are residing in area with broadband access. Which of the following are valid options you should go for (choose 2)?

A. use mono sound

B. use stereo sound

C. use low sampling rate

D. use high sampling rate

E. No Answer is Correct

---

24. You want to deliver music over the web to your audience. 99% of your audiences are residing in area with dial up access. Which of the following are valid options you should go for (choose 2)?

A. use mono sound

B. use stereo sound

C. use low sampling rate

D. use high sampling rate

E. No Answer is Correct

23. You want to deliver music over the web to your audience. 99% of your audiences are residing in area with broadband access. Which of the following are valid options you should go for (choose 2)?

A. use mono sound

***B. use stereo sound**

C. use low sampling rate

***D. use high sampling rate**

E. No Answer is Correct

Explanation: Broadband users prefer higher quality, as bandwidth is plentiful for them.

---

24. You want to deliver music over the web to your audience. 99% of your audiences are residing in area with dial up access. Which of the following are valid options you should go for (choose 2)?

***A. use mono sound**

B. use stereo sound

***C. use low sampling rate**

D. use high sampling rate

E. No Answer is Correct

Explanation: Broadband users prefer higher quality, as bandwidth is plentiful for them. Dial up users have slow connection, so quality is too expensive for them.

25. You want to deliver a large amount of library reference information over your intranet to your audience. 99% of your audiences are frequent visitors. Which of the following are valid options you should go for?

A. use a Flash front door

B. use a Shockwave front door

C. use a multimedia introduction for the site

D. use a textual index as the first page

E. No Answer is Correct

---

26. Your creative director wants to provide colorful pictures of weapons in your site. However, 50% of your audiences are kids below the age of 15. Should you approve his request?

A. YES

B. NO

25. You want to deliver a large amount of library reference information over your intranet to your audience. 99% of your audiences are frequent visitors. Which of the following are valid options you should go for?

A. use a Flash front door

B. use a Shockwave front door

C. use a multimedia introduction for the site

***D. use a textual index as the first page**

E. No Answer is Correct

Explanation: Fast searching is the key to internal intranet type operation.

---

26. Your creative director wants to provide colorful pictures of weapons in your site. However, 50% of your audiences are kids below the age of 15. Should you approve his request?

A. YES

***B. NO**

Explanation: Be extremely careful when planning for the site content. Your content must match the needs of your audience.

27. Your web site has visitors from all over the world. Many of them do not speak or read English. Which of the following option should you go for?

A. use Unicode

B. use English

C. develop different versions with different languages

D. use Unicode input locale

E. No Answer is Correct

---

28. One of the potential drawbacks of using CSS when designing page is that:

A. CSS can render pages inaccessible to people with visual or cognitive disabilities.

B. CSS can scramble the HTML code

C. CSS can distract visitor's attention

D. CSS consumes too much RAM

E. No Answer is Correct

27. Your web site has visitors from all over the world. Many of them do not speak or read English. Which of the following option should you go for?

A. use Unicode

B. use English

***C. develop different versions with different languages**

D. use Unicode input locale

E. No Answer is Correct

Explanation: If budget is allowed, you should have different versions of the site in different languages.

---

28. One of the potential drawbacks of using CSS when designing page is that:

***A. CSS can render pages inaccessible to people with visual or cognitive disabilities.**

B. CSS can scramble the HTML code

C. CSS can distract visitor's attention

D. CSS consumes too much RAM

E. No Answer is Correct

Explanation: For more information please refer to the web link.

29. Before designing your page, you noticed that some of your audiences are handicapped. For users who cannot control a mouse smoothly, you should:

A. provide good keyboard navigation with the tab key

B. provide alternative input devices

C. consider the use of voice input

D. consider the use of sound wave control

E. No Answer is Correct

---

30. When the TAB key moves between links and image map areas on your web page, the correct order of movement should be (choose 2)

A. left to right

B. top to bottom

C. right to left

D. bottom to top

E. no order is necessary

29. Before designing your page, you noticed that some of your audiences are handicapped. For users who cannot control a mouse smoothly, you should:

***A. provide good keyboard navigation with the tab key**

B. provide alternative input devices

C. consider the use of voice input

D. consider the use of sound wave control

E. No Answer is Correct

Explanation: For more information please refer to the web link.

---

30. When the TAB key moves between links and image map areas on your web page, the correct order of movement should be (choose 2)

***A. left to right**

***B. top to bottom**

C. right to left

D. bottom to top

E. no order is necessary

Explanation: these are the default order defined in the HTML. For more information please refer to the web link.

31. In which stage of the web development process will you define target audience, purpose, and objectives?

A. Planning

B. Analysis

C. Design

D. Implementation

E. Promotion

32. In which stage of the web development process will you define the policies for information development and use?

A. Planning

B. Analysis

C. Design

D. Implementation

E. Promotion

31. In which stage of the web development process will you define target audience, purpose, and objectives?

***A. Planning**

B. Analysis

C. Design

D. Implementation

E. Promotion

Explanation: Please refer to the web link for more information.

---

32. In which stage of the web development process will you define the policies for information development and use?

***A. Planning**

B. Analysis

C. Design

D. Implementation

E. Promotion

Explanation: Please refer to the web link for more information.

33. In which stage of the web development process will you deploy validation tools to check the technical construction of the web site?

A. Planning

B. Analysis

C. Design

D. Implementation

E. Promotion

---

34. You are verifying the correctness of your domain information. In which stage of the web development process are you currently at?

A. Planning

B. Analysis

C. Design

D. Implementation

E. Promotion

33. In which stage of the web development process will you deploy validation tools to check the technical construction of the web site?

A. Planning

***B. Analysis**

C. Design

D. Implementation

E. Promotion

Explanation: Please refer to the web link for more information.

---

34. You are verifying the correctness of your domain information. In which stage of the web development process are you currently at?

A. Planning

***B. Analysis**

C. Design

D. Implementation

E. Promotion

Explanation: Please refer to the web link for more information.

35. At which stage of the web development process should you attempt to connect pages along the routes of use?

A. Planning

B. Analysis

C. Design

D. Implementation

E. Promotion

36. You are creating an extendable directory and file structure for your web site. This is an activity in which stage of the web development process?

A. Planning

B. Analysis

C. Design

D. Implementation

E. Promotion

35. At which stage of the web development process should you attempt to connect pages along the routes of use?

A. Planning

B. Analysis

***C. Design**

D. Implementation

E. Promotion

Explanation: Please refer to the web link for more information.

---

36. You are creating an extendable directory and file structure for your web site. This is an activity in which stage of the web development process?

A. Planning

B. Analysis

C. Design

***D. Implementation**

E. Promotion

Explanation: Please refer to the web link for more information.

37. You are developing a web site for your company's trading business. Your clients will be using different browsers. You want to make sure that they can all view the pages correctly. At which stage would you do this?

A. Planning

B. Analysis

C. Design

D. Implementation

E. Promotion

---

38. You are advised to actively and innovatively connect with users to meet their needs. At which stage of the web development process should you do this?

A. Planning

B. Analysis

C. Design

D. Implementation

E. Promotion

37. You are developing a web site for your company's trading business. Your clients will be using different browsers. You want to make sure that they can all view the pages correctly. At which stage would you do this?

A. Planning

B. Analysis

C. Design

***D. Implementation**

E. Promotion

Explanation: Please refer to the web link for more information.

---

38. You are advised to actively and innovatively connect with users to meet their needs. At which stage of the web development process should you do this?

A. Planning

B. Analysis

C. Design

D. Implementation

***E. Promotion**

Explanation: Please refer to the web link for more information.

39. Your Supremesite.COM project is about to launch. At which stage of the web development process would you need to follow the online community norms and practices for a successful site launch?

A. Planning

B. Analysis

C. Design

D. Implementation

E. Promotion

---

40. In your web development process, you will be working with a lot of documents. Which of the following is a store of knowledge about the target audience for the web?

A. Planning statement

B. Analysis document

C. Design statement

D. Implementation List

E. Audience Information

39. Your Supremesite.COM project is about to launch. At which stage of the web development process would you need to follow the online community norms and practices for a successful site launch?

A. Planning

B. Analysis

C. Design

D. Implementation

***E. Promotion**

Explanation: Please refer to the web link for more information.

---

40. In your web development process, you will be working with a lot of documents. Which of the following is a store of knowledge about the target audience for the web?

A. Planning statement

B. Analysis document

C. Design statement

D. Implementation List

***E. Audience Information**

Explanation: Please refer to the web link for more information.

41. In your web development process, you will be working with a lot of documents. Which of the following is a store of knowledge about the actual audience who uses the information?

A. Planning statement

B. Analysis document

C. Design statement

D. Audience Implementation List

E. Audience Information

---

42. In your web development process, you will be working with a lot of documents. Which of the following is a collection of knowledge and information about the subject domain your web site will cover?

A. Planning statement

B. Analysis document

C. Subject Design statement

D. Implementation List

E. No Answer is Correct

41. In your web development process, you will be working with a lot of documents. Which of the following is a store of knowledge about the actual audience who uses the information?

A. Planning statement

B. Analysis document

C. Design statement

D. Audience Implementation List

***E. Audience Information**

Explanation: Please refer to the web link for more information.

---

42. In your web development process, you will be working with a lot of documents. Which of the following is a collection of knowledge and information about the subject domain your web site will cover?

A. Planning statement

B. Analysis document

C. Subject Design statement

D. Implementation List

***E. No Answer is Correct**

Explanation: Domain information document is what you need. Please refer to the web link for more information.

43. What document will you use for the detailed description of the constraints and elements that will go into your web site?

A. Constraint Planning statement

B. Analysis document

C. Design statement

D. Implementation List

E. Web specification

---

44. In your web development process, what document will be used to define the specific goals your web site should accomplish?

A. Planning statement

B. Goals document

C. Design aims statement

D. Implementation List

E. Objectives List

43. What document will you use for the detailed description of the constraints and elements that will go into your web site?

A. Constraint Planning statement

B. Analysis document

C. Design statement

D. Implementation List

***E. Web specification**

Explanation: Please refer to the web link for more information.

---

44. In your web development process, what document will be used to define the specific goals your web site should accomplish?

A. Planning statement

B. Goals document

C. Design aims statement

D. Implementation List

***E. Objectives List**

Explanation: Please refer to the web link for more information.

45. In your web development process, you defined a purpose statement. What is this statement for?

A. As an articulation of the reason for your web's existence

B. As a list of site logical design goals

C. As a list of site physical design goals

D. As a list of site design priorities

E. No Answer is Correct

---

46. In the web design process, you may need to use the techniques of mindmapping. What correctly describe this mindmapping process?

A. Use images, and sounds to bring mere words to life

B. Use vectors to combine objects

C. Use HTML to transform objects

D. Use XML to simulate objects

E. No Answer is Correct

45. In your web development process, you defined a purpose statement. What is this statement for?

***A. As an articulation of the reason for your web's existence**

B. As a list of site logical design goals

C. As a list of site physical design goals

D. As a list of site design priorities

E. No Answer is Correct

Explanation: Please refer to the web link for more information.

---

46. In the web design process, you may need to use the techniques of mindmapping. What correctly describe this mindmapping process?

***A. Use images, and sounds to bring mere words to life**

B. Use vectors to combine objects

C. Use HTML to transform objects

D. Use XML to simulate objects

E. No Answer is Correct

Explanation: Refer to the web link for more information.

47. In the web design process, you may need to use the techniques of mindmapping. What correctly describe the application of the mindmapping process?

A. organizing thoughts

B. organizing codes

C. organizing links

D. organizing graphics

E. No Answer is Correct

---

48. In the web design process, you may need to use the techniques of mindmapping. What is the major difference between mindmapping and the traditional thinking methods?

A. think sequentially

B. do not think sequentially

C. think logically

D. do not think logically

E. No Answer is Correct

47. In the web design process, you may need to use the techniques of mindmapping. What correctly describe the application of the mindmapping process?

***A. organizing thoughts**

B. organizing codes

C. organizing links

D. organizing graphics

E. No Answer is Correct

Explanation: Refer to the web link for more information.

---

48. In the web design process, you may need to use the techniques of mindmapping. What is the major difference between mindmapping and the traditional thinking methods?

A. think sequentially

***B. do not think sequentially**

C. think logically

D. do not think logically

E. No Answer is Correct

Explanation: Refer to the web link for more information.

49. In the web design process, you may need to use the techniques of mindmapping. You want to construct a mind map. Which of the following elements can you include in the mind map
(Choose all that apply)?

A. words

B. lines

C. logic

D. colors

E. images

---

50. In the web design process, you may need to use the techniques of mindmapping. In a mind map, what do we use to represent a subject?

A. central image

B. main branches

C. main themes

D. nodal structure

E. No Answer is Correct

49. In the web design process, you may need to use the techniques of mindmapping. You want to construct a mind map. Which of the following elements can you include in the mind map
(Choose all that apply)?

***A. words**

***B. lines**

***C. logic**

***D. colors**

***E. images**

Explanation: Refer to the web link for more information.

---

50. In the web design process, you may need to use the techniques of mindmapping. In a mind map, what do we use to represent a subject?

***A. central image**

B. main branches

C. main themes

D. nodal structure

E. No Answer is Correct

Explanation: Refer to the web link for more information.

51. In the web design process, you may need to use the techniques of mindmapping. In your mind map, what will radiate from the central image as main branches?

A. central image

B. main branches

C. main themes

D. nodal structure

E. No Answer is Correct

---

52. In the web design process, you may need to use the techniques of mindmapping. In your mind map, what will be linked to the main themes?

A. central image

B. main branches

C. main themes

D. nodal structure

E. No Answer is Correct

51. In the web design process, you may need to use the techniques of mindmapping. In your mind map, what will radiate from the central image as main branches?

A. central image

B. main branches

***C. main themes**

D. nodal structure

E. No Answer is Correct

Explanation: Refer to the web link for more information.

---

52. In the web design process, you may need to use the techniques of mindmapping. In your mind map, what will be linked to the main themes?

A. central image

B. main branches

C. main themes

D. nodal structure

***E. No Answer is Correct**

Explanation: In your mind map, minor themes are linked to the main themes. Refer to the web link for more information.

53. In the web design process, you may need to use the techniques of mindmapping. In your mind map, all the branches are connected to form a ?

A. central image

B. main branches

C. main themes

D. nodal structure

E. No Answer is Correct

---

54. What is one of the most common applications of mindmapping in your web design process?

A. to plan for a new project

B. to plan for the staff list

C. to plan for the permission setting

D. to plan for the software tools used

E. No Answer is Correct

53. In the web design process, you may need to use the techniques of mindmapping. In your mind map, all the branches are connected to form a ?

A. central image

B. main branches

C. main themes

***D. nodal structure**

E. No Answer is Correct

Explanation: Refer to the web link for more information.

---

54. What is one of the most common applications of mindmapping in your web design process?

***A. to plan for a new project**

B. to plan for the staff list

C. to plan for the permission setting

D. to plan for the software tools used

E. No Answer is Correct

Explanation: Refer to the web link for more information.

55. What is one of the most common applications of mindmapping in your web design process in regards to meeting deadlines?

A. to plan for a resource list

B. to plan for the staff list

C. to plan for the permission setting

D. to plan for the software tools used

E. to plan for a schedule

---

56. What is one of the most common applications of mindmapping in your web design process when your team members have defined more than 5 objectives?

A. prioritize multiple objectives

B. eliminate redundant objectives

C. study different objectives

D. explain different objectives

E. No Answer is Correct

55. What is one of the most common applications of mindmapping in your web design process in regards to meeting deadlines?

A. to plan for a resource list

B. to plan for the staff list

C. to plan for the permission setting

D. to plan for the software tools used

***E. to plan for a schedule**

Explanation: Refer to the web link for more information.

---

56. What is one of the most common applications of mindmapping in your web design process when your team members have defined more than 5 objectives?

***A. prioritize multiple objectives**

B. eliminate redundant objectives

C. study different objectives

D. explain different objectives

E. No Answer is Correct

Explanation: Refer to the web link for more information.

57. You are working on the specifications of your web application. You have the following draft available:

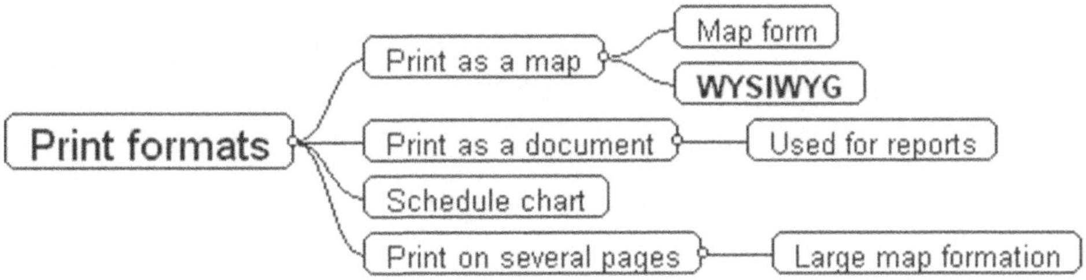

What technique are you using to plan for the above?

A. mind sharing

B. mind capturing

C. project scheduling

D. mind mapping

E. No Answer is Correct

---

58. One of the uses of mindmapping techniques is to effective plan for and run your web design team meeting.

A. True

B. False

57. You are working on the specifications of your web application. You have the following draft available:

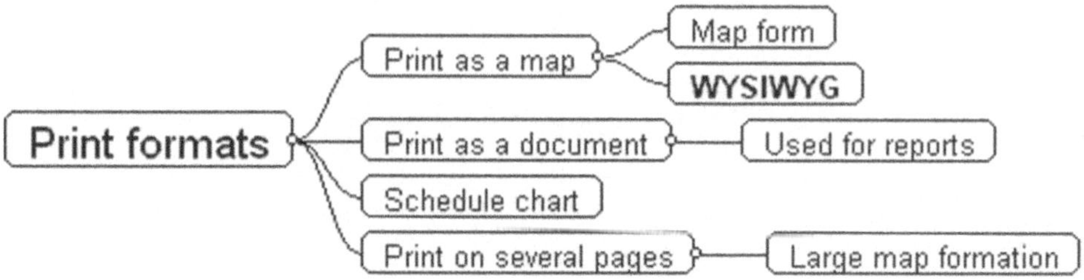

What technique are you using to plan for the above?

A. mind sharing

B. mind capturing

C. project scheduling

***D. mind mapping**

E. No Answer is Correct

Explanation: Refer to the web link for more information.

---

58. One of the uses of mindmapping techniques is to effective plan for and run your web design team meeting.

***A. True**

B. False

Explanation: Mindmapping improves the effectiveness of any meeting by organizing the minutes. Refer to the web link for more information.

59. Your web design team peer John has drawn the following draft on the board:

John told you that this technique will improve your understanding of the relationship between facts. Is it true?

A. True

B. False

---

60. You have a very complicated system waiting to be transformed into a web platform. There are a lot of features, functions and objectives involved. You have also been asked to enrich this system with new functions. You call for a meeting among your web design team. You want to list all the factors and elements in a form that can improve your team members' memory, concentration, innovation and creativity. What format will you use?

A. graphic

B. text

C. index map

D. mind map

E. No Answer is Correct

59. Your web design team peer John has drawn the following draft on the board:

John told you that this technique will improve your understanding of the relationship between facts. Is it true?

***A. True**

B. False

Explanation: Mindmapping improves the effectiveness of the thinking process. Refer to the web link for more information.

---

60. You have a very complicated system waiting to be transformed into a web platform. There are a lot of features, functions and objectives involved. You have also been asked to enrich this system with new functions. You call for a meeting among your web design team. You want to list all the factors and elements in a form that can improve your team members' memory, concentration, innovation and creativity. What format will you use?

A. graphic

B. text

C. index map

***D. mind map**

E. No Answer is Correct

Explanation: Mindmapping improves the effectiveness of the thinking process. Refer to the web link for more information.

61. In general, what is the meaning of the term "Metaphor"?

A. describe the unfamiliar in terms of the familiar.

B. describe the familiar in terms of the unfamiliar.

C. describe the unfamiliar in terms of the unfamiliar.

D. describe the familiar in terms of the familiar.

E. No Answer is Correct

---

62. When we build our internet presence for retail, how do we make use of the concept of metaphor?

A. building the storefront to resemble the look and feel of a real physical store

B. building the storefront to resemble a virtual store

C. building the storefront to resemble an order tracking system

D. building the storefront with electronic shop attendants

E. No Answer is Correct

61. In general, what is the meaning of the term "Metaphor"?

***A. describe the unfamiliar in terms of the familiar.**

B. describe the familiar in terms of the unfamiliar.

C. describe the unfamiliar in terms of the unfamiliar.

D. describe the familiar in terms of the familiar.

E. No Answer is Correct

Explanation: In web terms, we try to build our site to make it looks like something in our real life, so that we won't alienate the visitors.

---

62. When we build our internet presence for retail, how do we make use of the concept of metaphor?

***A. building the storefront to resemble the look and feel of a real physical store**

B. building the storefront to resemble a virtual store

C. building the storefront to resemble an order tracking system

D. building the storefront with electronic shop attendants

E. No Answer is Correct

Explanation: In web terms, we try to build our site to make it looks like something in our real life, so that we won't alienate the visitors.

63. When we design our storefront for customers from different states within the US, which area do we have to pay special attention to?

A. sales tax

B. income tax

C. demographic

D. gender

E. No Answer is Correct

---

64. For your store front options, why would you choose to develop a content site and handle transactions off-line
(Choose all that apply)?

A. Simple Web sites can be developed easily

B. Simple Web sites can be developed quickly

C. Simple Web sites can be developed at low cost

D. Simple Web sites can be driven by database

E. No Answer is Correct

63. When we design our storefront for customers from different states within the US, which area do we have to pay special attention to?

***A. sales tax**

B. income tax

C. demographic

D. gender

E. No Answer is Correct

Explanation: You are encouraged to work with your attorney to develop a tax policy for your online store.

---

64. For your store front options, why would you choose to develop a content site and handle transactions off-line
(Choose all that apply)?

***A. Simple Web sites can be developed easily**

***B. Simple Web sites can be developed quickly**

***C. Simple Web sites can be developed at low cost**

D. Simple Web sites can be driven by database

E. No Answer is Correct

Explanation: For detailed information please refer to the web link.

65. What are the options available for setting up your online store front?

A. Buy a ready-made solution

B. Rent space in a network-based e-commerce solution

C. Build the system from scratch

D. No Answer is Correct

E. All Answers are Correct

---

66. To have an instant store front for your company, which of the following options will you choose?

A. Buy a ready-made solution

B. Rent space in a network-based e-commerce solution

C. Build the system from scratch

D. No Answer is Correct

E. All Answers are Correct

65. What are the options available for setting up your online store front?

A. Buy a ready-made solution

B. Rent space in a network-based e-commerce solution

C. Build the system from scratch

D. No Answer is Correct

***E. All Answers are Correct**

Explanation: For detailed information please refer to the web link.

---

66. To have an instant store front for your company, which of the following options will you choose?

A. Buy a ready-made solution

***B. Rent space in a network-based e-commerce solution**

C. Build the system from scratch

D. No Answer is Correct

E. All Answers are Correct

Explanation: For detailed information please refer to the web link.

67. To have store front for your company that supports unique and complex functions, which of the following options will you choose?

A. Buy a ready-made solution

B. Rent space in a network-based e-commerce solution

C. Build the system from scratch

D. A and B

E. A, B and C

---

68. What is true regarding a multihomed e-commerce platform?

A. Multiple single storefronts reside on one server

B. Multiple combined storefronts reside on one server

C. Multiple single storefronts reside on multiple servers

D. Single storefront reside on one server

E. Single storefront reside on multiple servers

67. To have store front for your company that supports unique and complex functions, which of the following options will you choose?

A. Buy a ready-made solution

B. Rent space in a network-based e-commerce solution

***C. Build the system from scratch**

D. A and B

E. A, B and C

Explanation: For detailed information please refer to the web link.

---

68. What is true regarding a multihomed e-commerce platform?

***A. Multiple single storefronts reside on one server**

B. Multiple combined storefronts reside on one server

C. Multiple single storefronts reside on multiple servers

D. Single storefront reside on one server

E. Single storefront reside on multiple servers

Explanation: For detailed information please refer to the web link.

69. Which of the following is true concerning an online mall (Choose all that apply)?

A. multiple storefronts in a mall environment

B. the same URL and database

C. shared registration, shopping cart, checkout

D. virtual IP

E. No Answer is Correct

---

70. Which of the following are valid back end tasks of your storefront (Choose all that apply)?

A. payment processing

B. tax calculation

C. order routing

D. selling

E. promotion

69. Which of the following is true concerning an online mall (Choose all that apply)?

***A. multiple storefronts in a mall environment**

***B. the same URL and database**

***C. shared registration, shopping cart, checkout**

D. virtual IP

E. No Answer is Correct

Explanation: For detailed information please refer to the web link.

---

70. Which of the following are valid back end tasks of your storefront (Choose all that apply)?

***A. payment processing**

***B. tax calculation**

***C. order routing**

D. selling

E. promotion

Explanation: Refer to the web link for more information.

71. Transaction server has which of the following roles in an electronic storefront (Choose all that apply)?

A. handles the necessary authorization requests

B. records transaction

C. settlement of transaction information with the merchant

D. deliver email notification

E. No Answer is Correct

---

72. What are the functions of SET in your storefront operation (Choose all that apply)?

A. provides message integrity

B. authentication of financial data

C. encryption of sensitive information.

D. compression of large volume of data

E. No Answer is Correct

71. Transaction server has which of the following roles in an electronic storefront (Choose all that apply)?

***A. handles the necessary authorization requests**

***B. records transaction**

***C. settlement of transaction information with the merchant**

D. deliver email notification

E. No Answer is Correct

Explanation: Refer to the web link for more information.

---

72. What are the functions of SET in your storefront operation (Choose all that apply)?

***A. provides message integrity**

***B. authentication of financial data**

***C. encryption of sensitive information.**

D. compression of large volume of data

E. No Answer is Correct

Explanation: Refer to the web link for more information.

73. What is the role of a commerce-service provider in your storefront operation?

A. offline fulfillment

B. online transaction

C. online tech support

D. order tracing

E. No Answer is Correct

74. To be able to learn about the shopping and surfing patterns of your customers, what should you deploy with your storefront?

A. database

B. log

C. metaphor

D. trending

E. No Answer is Correct

73. What is the role of a commerce-service provider in your storefront operation?

A. offline fulfillment

***B. online transaction**

C. online tech support

D. order tracing

E. No Answer is Correct

Explanation: Refer to the web link for more information.

---

74. To be able to learn about the shopping and surfing patterns of your customers, what should you deploy with your storefront?

A. database

***B. log**

C. metaphor

D. trending

E. No Answer is Correct

Explanation: Refer to the web link for more information.

75. How do you track your customers in your store front to determine which banner ads are effective?

A. assign each banner ad a specific unique code and use that code in the referring URL

B. assign each banner ad a common code and use that code in the referring URL

C. assign each banner ad a specific code and a pattern

D. assign each banner ad a specific code and use that code in your store product database

E. No Answer is Correct

75. How do you track your customers in your store front to determine which banner ads are effective?

***A. assign each banner ad a specific unique code and use that code in the referring URL**

B. assign each banner ad a common code and use that code in the referring URL

C. assign each banner ad a specific code and a pattern

D. assign each banner ad a specific code and use that code in your store product database

E. No Answer is Correct

Explanation: Refer to the web link for more information.

Chapter 3:
Navigation and Presentation Concepts

1. When you design your web page layout, at which resolution should you optimize it for?

   A. 640 x 480

   B. 800 x 600

   C. 1024 x 768

   D. 320 x 200

   E. No Answer is Correct

---

2. How do you disable the space between cells in your table layout?

   A. CELLSPACING="0"

   B. CELLSPACING=off

   C. CELLPADDING="0"

   D. CELLPADDING=off

   E. No Answer is Correct

1. When you design your web page layout, at which resolution should you optimize it for?

***A. 640 x 480**

B. 800 x 600

C. 1024 x 768

D. 320 x 200

E. No Answer is Correct

Explanation: While most users can use higher resolutions, standard VGA screens are still commonly used everywhere.

---

2. How do you disable the space between cells in your table layout?

***A. CELLSPACING="0"**

B. CELLSPACING=off

C. CELLPADDING="0"

D. CELLPADDING=off

E. No Answer is Correct

Explanation: You must manually set the cell spacing to 0.

3. How do you disable the padding between cells in your table layout?

A. CELLSPACING="0"

B. CELLSPACING=off

C. CELLPADDING="0"

D. CELLPADDING=off

E. No Answer is Correct

---

4. How would you create header text for your web page layout, such as the following?

A. use table

B. use frame

C. use line break

D. use text box

E. No Answer is Correct

3. How do you disable the padding between cells in your table layout?

A. CELLSPACING="0"

B. CELLSPACING=off

***C. CELLPADDING="0"**

D. CELLPADDING=off

E. No Answer is Correct

Explanation: You must manually set the cell padding value to 0.

---

4. How would you create header text for your web page layout, such as the following?

***A. use table**

B. use frame

C. use line break

D. use text box

E. No Answer is Correct

Explanation: A single row table will do the job.

5. When designing your page layout, how do you push the header a bit to the right ?

A. use &nsp;

B. use &nbs;

C. use &nbp;

D. use

E. No Answer is Correct

---

6. What is the appropriate work width for a page designed for standard VGA screen?

A. 640 pixels

B. 630 pixels

C. 600 pixels

D. 480 pixels

E. No Answer is Correct

5. When designing your page layout, how do you push the header a bit to the right ?

A. use &nsp;

B. use &nbs;

C. use &nbp;

***D. use **

E. No Answer is Correct

Explanation: You may find this character in many web page codes frequently.

---

6. What is the appropriate work width for a page designed for standard VGA screen?

A. 640 pixels

B. 630 pixels

***C. 600 pixels**

D. 480 pixels

E. No Answer is Correct

Explanation: The screen is 640 pixels wide. However, you need to reserve some room for window borders and scroll bars.

7. To be able to create dropshadows effects in your page layout, you are encouraged to use ________ ?

A. CSS

B. ASP

C. JavaScript

D. Table

E. Frames

---

8. In general, most browsers use which font face for proportional fonts ?

A. Times

B. Carrier

C. Arial

D. Geneva

E. No Answer is Correct

7. To be able to create dropshadows effects in your page layout, you are encouraged to use ________ ?

***A. CSS**

B. ASP

C. JavaScript

D. Table

E. Frames

Explanation: CSS allows extremely fancy styles in your layout.

---

8. In general, most browsers use which font face for proportional fonts ?

***A. Times**

B. Carrier

C. Arial

D. Geneva

E. No Answer is Correct

Explanation: Times is the most common default.

9. In your page layout, you want to specify a section of the text to use ARIAL as the font face. How do you do this?

A. <FONT="Arial">...</FONT>

B. <FONT FACE="Arial">...</FONT>

C. <FONT TYPE="Arial">...</FONT>

D. <FONT Arial>...</FONT>

E. No Answer is Correct

---

10. You want to use alternative fonts for your web page. However, some of your clients may not have the corresponding fonts available in their system. How would you handle this?

A. specify several fonts in the FACE attribute

B. specify several fonts in the BODY attribute

C. develop different pages for different clients

D. use Unicode

E. No Answer is Correct

9. In your page layout, you want to specify a section of the text to use ARIAL as the font face. How do you do this?

A. <FONT="Arial">...</FONT>

***B. <FONT FACE="Arial">...</FONT>**

C. <FONT TYPE="Arial">...</FONT>

D. <FONT Arial>...</FONT>

E. No Answer is Correct

Explanation: Remember this syntax for the exam.

---

10. You want to use alternative fonts for your web page. However, some of your clients may not have the corresponding fonts available in their system. How would you handle this?

***A. specify several fonts in the FACE attribute**

B. specify several fonts in the BODY attribute

C. develop different pages for different clients

D. use Unicode

E. No Answer is Correct

Explanation: Example code fragment: <FONT FACE="Arial,Helvetica,Sansserif">... </FONT>

11. What will be a good way to layout your web page?

A. use all graphics

B. use frames

C. use tables

D. use scripts

E. No Answer is Correct

---

12. In tables, you can define multiple columns and rows, as well as to have them (Choose all that apply)?

A. merge

B. split

C. dropshadow

D. rollover

E. No Answer is Correct

11. What will be a good way to layout your web page?

A. use all graphics

B. use frames

***C. use tables**

D. use scripts

E. No Answer is Correct

Explanation: Without CSS, table is the preferred way to layout a page.

---

12. In tables, you can define multiple columns and rows, as well as to have them (Choose all that apply)?

***A. merge**

***B. split**

C. dropshadow

D. rollover

E. No Answer is Correct

Explanation: If you are using a GUI page authoring tool, you can split or merge cells within a table.

13. To make it clear to a visitor that he is still at your site while browsing around, what key factor should you enforce?

A. freeform

B. integrity

C. consistency

D. flexibility

E. No Answer is Correct

---

14. Which of the following is true concerning good page layout design (Choose all that apply)?

A. The most important information should be visible right away

B. If the page is longer than one screen, make it clear to your visitor

C. Visitors are more likely to click a link before they will scroll

D. Text should be around 10 to 12 words wide across page

E. No Answer is Correct

13. To make it clear to a visitor that he is still at your site while browsing around, what key factor should you enforce?

A. freeform

B. integrity

***C. consistency**

D. flexibility

E. No Answer is Correct

Explanation: You should always choose a consistent approach to your site.

---

14. Which of the following is true concerning good page layout design (Choose all that apply)?

***A. The most important information should be visible right away**

***B. If the page is longer than one screen, make it clear to your visitor**

***C. Visitors are more likely to click a link before they will scroll**

***D. Text should be around 10 to 12 words wide across page**

E. No Answer is Correct

Explanation: Refer to the web link for good design principles.

15. In order to avoid screen scrolling, you prefer to use links. Which of the following is true concerning the use of links in your page design?

A. You should use as many links as possible.

B. Too many links on a page may be confusing

C. Too many links on a page will show unity

D. Too many links on a page will crash the browser easily

E. No Answer is Correct

---

16. Why is it important to have good navigation architecture for your site?

A. this makes pages easier to be found

B. this makes pages look better

C. this ensures a good looking navigation bar

D. this ensures a good looking site panel

E. No Answer is Correct

15. In order to avoid screen scrolling, you prefer to use links. Which of the following is true concerning the use of links in your page design?

A. You should use as many links as possible.

***B. Too many links on a page may be confusing**

C. Too many links on a page will show unity

D. Too many links on a page will crash the browser easily

E. No Answer is Correct

Explanation: Refer to the web link for good design principles.

---

16. Why is it important to have a good navigation architecture for your site?

***A. this makes pages easier to be found**

B. this makes pages look better

C. this ensures a good looking navigation bar

D. this ensures a good looking site panel

E. No Answer is Correct

Explanation: This allows visitors to locate the desired pages easily.

17. What is a front door page?

A. the exit point of the site

B. the entry point of a page

C. the entry point of the site

D. the entry point of the browser

E. No Answer is Correct

---

18. What is the use of Utility navigation?

A. facilitate navigation

B. facilitate graphic display

C. facilitate downloading

D. facilitate screen refresh

E. No Answer is Correct

17. What is a front door page?

A. the exit point of the site

B. the entry point of a page

***C. the entry point of the site**

D. the entry point of the browser

E. No Answer is Correct

Explanation: It is the entry page.

---

18. What is the use of Utility navigation?

***A. facilitate navigation**

B. facilitate graphic display

C. facilitate downloading

D. facilitate screen refresh

E. No Answer is Correct

Explanation: An example of this is the site index page.

19. Which of the following are the major site map types (Choose all that apply)?

A. Table-based site map

B. Indexed site map

C. Image map

D. Automatically generated site map

E. No Answer is Correct

---

20. What are Topical navigation links in site navigation (Choose all that apply)?

A. links that connect topic of one page to another page

B. cross reference

C. links that connect topic of one page to the exit page

D. links that connect topic of one page to the front door

E. No Answer is Correct

19. Which of the following are the major site map types (Choose all that apply)?

***A. Table-based site map**

***B. Indexed site map**

***C. Image map**

***D. Automatically generated site map**

E. No Answer is Correct

Explanation: All these are valid site map types.

---

20. What are Topical navigation links in site navigation (Choose all that apply)?

***A. links that connect topic of one page to another page**

***B. cross reference**

C. links that connect topic of one page to the exit page

D. links that connect topic of one page to the front door

E. No Answer is Correct

Explanation: Cross reference is an example of this link type.

21. What are the characteristics of a Linear Layout for a site (Choose all that apply)?

A. Unidirectional

B. Bidirectional

C. Good for procedure instructions

D. Good for multipath instructions

E. No Answer is Correct

---

22. Which of the following is true concerning the use of BACK and FORWARD buttons (Choose all that apply)?

A. Radical shifts in context cannot confuse Web users

B. Radical shifts in context can assist Web users in navigation

C. Radical shifts in context can be productive

D. Radical shifts in context can easily confuse Web users

E. No Answer is Correct

21. What are the characteristics of a Linear Layout for a site (Choose all that apply)?

***A. Unidirectional**

B. Bidirectional

***C. Good for procedure instructions**

D. Good for multipath instructions

E. No Answer is Correct

Explanation: This type of navigation works like a book.

---

22. Which of the following is true concerning the use of BACK and FORWARD buttons (Choose all that apply)?

A. Radical shifts in context cannot confuse Web users

B. Radical shifts in context can assist Web users in navigation

C. Radical shifts in context can be productive

***D. Radical shifts in context can easily confuse Web users**

E. No Answer is Correct

Explanation: Users need organized cues and interface elements to follow.

23. What is the difference between the "Next Page" and "Previous Page" buttons in a document VS the "Back" and "Forward" buttons in the Web viewers?

A. fixed links to other associated documents provided by the author of the page

B. fixed links to other associated documents provided by the author of the browser

C. fixed links to other associated documents provided by the operating systems

D. fixed links to other associated documents provided by the network platforms

E. No Answer is Correct

---

24. What type of navigation structure is similar to a tree?

A. Unidirectional

B. Linear

C. Hierarchical

D. Bidirectional

E. No Answer is Correct

23. What is the difference between the "Next Page" and "Previous Page" buttons in a document VS the "Back" and "Forward" buttons in the Web viewers?

***A. fixed links to other associated documents provided by the author of the page**

B. fixed links to other associated documents provided by the author of the browser

C. fixed links to other associated documents provided by the operating systems

D. fixed links to other associated documents provided by the network platforms

E. No Answer is Correct

Explanation: The author needs to manually create the "Next Page" and the "Previous Page" buttons.

---

24. What type of navigation structure is similar to a tree?

A. Unidirectional

B. Linear

***C. Hierarchical**

D. Bidirectional

E. No Answer is Correct

Explanation: This is a relatively flexible structure.

25. What should a site map provide in order to be really productive?

A. Overview

B. Orientation

C. Free Form navigation

D. Followed Path

E. No Answer is Correct

---

26. An Indexed site map is best to be displayed as?

A. a table of content

B. an index page

C. a cross reference page

D. a virtual table

E. No Answer is Correct

25. What should a site map provide in order to be really productive?

***A. Overview**

***B. Orientation**

***C. Free Form navigation**

D. Followed Path

E. No Answer is Correct

Explanation: A site map helps visitors to locate the desired pages.

---

26. An Indexed site map is best to be displayed as?

***A. a table of content**

B. an index page

C. a cross reference page

D. a virtual table

E. No Answer is Correct

Explanation: A TOC matches the function of an indexed site map.

27. Why would you want to use a text only site map for navigation (Choose all that apply)?

A. supported by every browser

B. looks better

C. faster to download

D. more colorful

E. No Answer is Correct

---

28. How do we call the navigation structure that combines Linear and Hierarchical navigation?

A. Combined Layout

B. Integrated Layout

C. Mixed Layout

D. Procedural Layout

E. No Answer is Correct

27. Why would you want to use a text only site map for navigation (Choose all that apply)?

***A. supported by every browser**

B. looks better

***C. faster to download**

D. more colorful

E. No Answer is Correct

Explanation: For older browser or slow connection this is a good choice.

---

28. How do we call the navigation structure that combines Linear and Hierarchical navigation?

***A. Combined Layout**

B. Integrated Layout

C. Mixed Layout

D. Procedural Layout

E. No Answer is Correct

Explanation: This is the most flexible architecture for navigation.

29. What type of navigation structure is this?

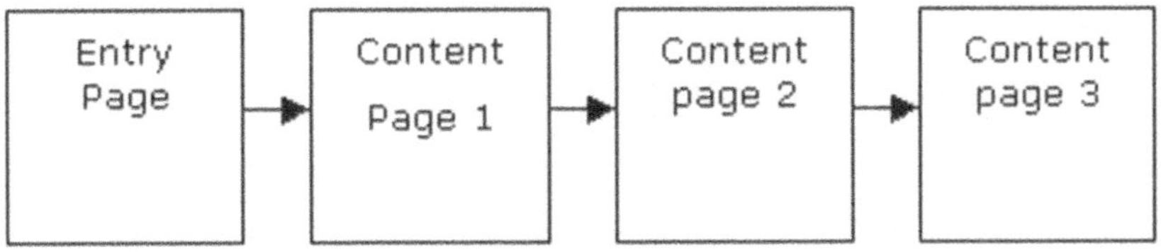

A. Multidirectional

B. Linear

C. Hierarchical

D. Bidirectional

E. No Answer is Correct

29. What type of navigation structure is this?

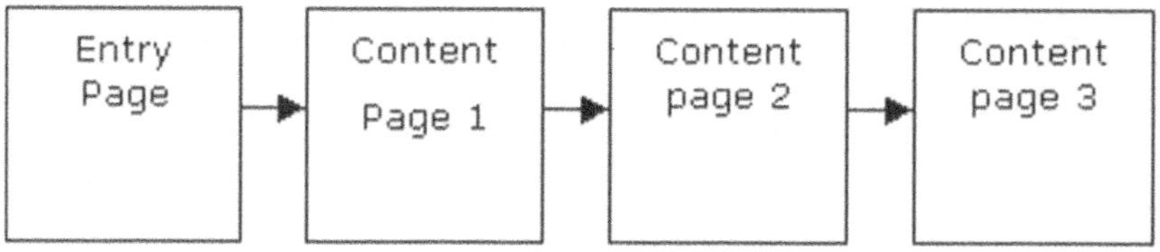

A. Multidirectional

***B. Linear**

C. Hierarchical

D. Bidirectional

E. No Answer is Correct

Explanation: This is unidirectional navigation.

30. What type of navigation structure is this?

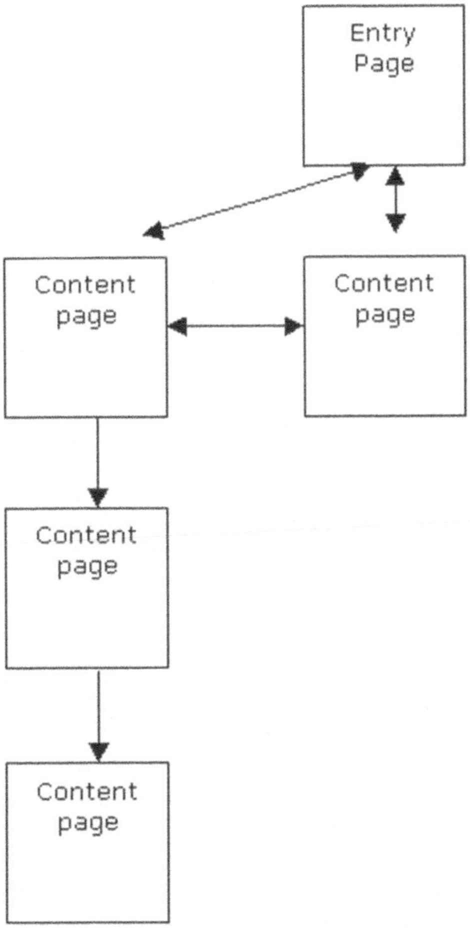

A. Multidirectional

B. Linear

C. Hierarchical

D. Bidirectional

E. Combined

30. What type of navigation structure is this?

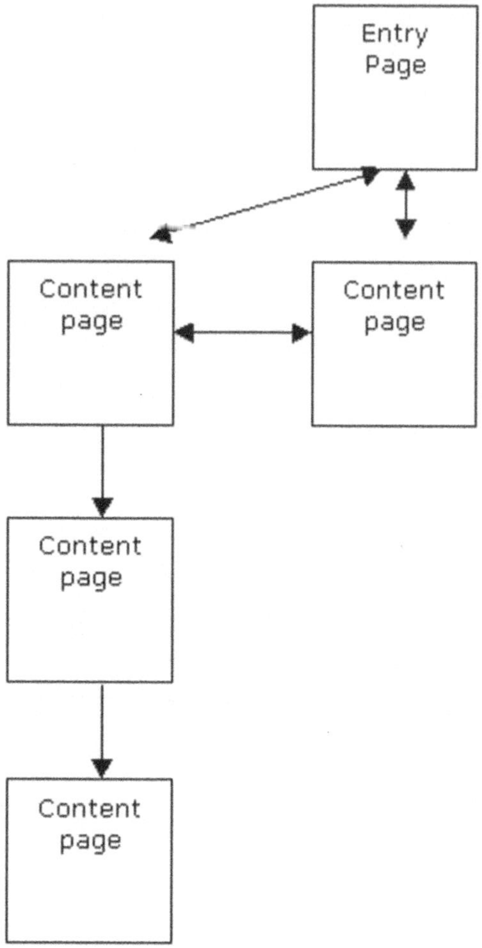

A. Multidirectional

B. Linear

C. Hierarchical

D. Bidirectional

***E. Combined**

Explanation: This includes linear and hierarchical navigation.

31. What tags would you use to construct a table in your web page?

A. <TD> and </TD> tags

B. <TR> and </TR> tags

C. <TD> tag only

D. <TAD> and </TAD> tags

E. No Answer is Correct

---

32. In your table, you can have your cells arranged in a way similar to having ________________ .

A. rows and columns

B. windows and toolbars

C. frames and windows

D. frames

E. toolbar

31. What tags would you use to construct a table in your web page?

***A. <TD> and </TD> tags**

***B. <TR> and </TR> tags**

C. <TD> tag only

D. <TAD> and </TAD> tags

E. No Answer is Correct

Explanation: Table is enclosed in <TD> and </TD> tags.

---

32. In your table, you can have your cells arranged in a way similar to having ________________ .

***A. rows and columns**

B. windows and toolbars

C. frames and windows

D. frames

E. toolbar

Explanation: You can define table rows and columns within a table.

33. How do you use table to create wrap-around effects for image?

A. take a composite image and split it into pieces first, then re-combine it in the cells of table later

B. take a composite image and split it into pieces and distribute them in the cells of table with space between them

C. draw the image with the table tool

D. use table shape image

E. No Answer is Correct

---

34. You want to approximate wrapping text around a graphic. How would you do this?

A. use window

B. use frame

C. use scrollbar

D. use table

E. use XML

33. How do you use table to create wrap-around effects for image?

***A. take a composite image and split it into pieces first, then re-combine it in the cells of table later**

B. take a composite image and split it into pieces and distribute them in the cells of table with space between them

C. draw the image with the table tool

D. use table shape image

E. No Answer is Correct

Explanation: There are graphic packages in the market that can help you achieve this.

---

34. You want to approximate wrapping text around a graphic. How would you do this?

A. use window

B. use frame

C. use scrollbar

***D. use table**

E. use XML

Explanation: You may split the image into couple parts and then combine them together with the text in a table

35. How are table row tags defined?

A. Table rows are defined by the <TR></TR> tags

B. Table rows are defined by <TR> tag only

C. Table rows are defined by <Row></Row> tags

D. Table rows are defined by <Rows></Rows> tags

E. No Answer is Correct

---

36. How are table headings defined?

A. the <TH></TH> tags

B. the <TH> tag only

C. the <Row></Row> tags

D. the <Rows></Rows> tags

E. No Answer is Correct

35. How are table row tags defined?

***A. Table rows are defined by the <TR></TR> tags**

B. Table rows are defined by <TR> tag only

C. Table rows are defined by <Row></Row> tags

D. Table rows are defined by <Rows></Rows> tags

E. No Answer is Correct

Explanation: Table rows are defined by the <TR></TR> tags.

---

36. How are table headings defined?

***A. the <TH></TH> tags**

B. the <TH> tag only

C. the <Row></Row> tags

D. the <Rows></Rows> tags

E. No Answer is Correct

Explanation: Table headings are defined by the <TH></TH> tags.

37. What are valid vertical alignment parameters of a table cell
(Choose all that apply)?

A. center

B. middle

C. bottom

D. baseline

E. No Answer is Correct

---

38. What are valid parameters to justify all the text in a row or cell to the left, right or center of the cell
(Choose all that apply)?

A. left

B. center

C. right

D. top

E. bottom

37. What are valid vertical alignment parameters of a table cell
(Choose all that apply)?

A. center

***B. middle**

***C. bottom**

***D. baseline**

E. No Answer is Correct

Explanation: These are parameters for VALIGN.

38. What are valid parameters to justify all the text in a row or cell to the left, right or center of the cell
(Choose all that apply)?

***A. left**

***B. center**

***C. right**

D. top

E. bottom

Explanation: These are parameters for ALIGN

39. How do you specify that lines within a cell should not be broken to fit the cell width?

A. use NOWRAPS

B. use NOWRAP

C. use NOWRAPPING

D. use WRAP=no

E. No Answer is Correct

---

40. You want to specify how many columns a cell should span. How would you do this?

A. use COLSPAN

B. use ROWSPAN

C. use COL=span

D. use span=1

E. use spanning=true

39. How do you specify that lines within a cell should not be broken to fit the cell width?

A. use NOWRAPS

***B. use NOWRAP**

C. use NOWRAPPING

D. use WRAP=no

E. No Answer is Correct

Explanation: You may use NOWRAP together with the <TD> or <TH> tag.

---

40. You want to specify how many columns a cell should span. How would you do this?

***A. use COLSPAN**

B. use ROWSPAN

C. use COL=span

D. use span=1

E. use spanning=true

Explanation: This allows you to combine cells.

41. To specify the text alignment for table columns, you will use (choose 2):

A. <COL>

B. <COLGROUP>

C. <ROW>

D. <ROWGROUP>

E. No Answer is Correct

---

42. You want to have graphics in tables. What browsers are required (Choose all that apply)?

A. IE 3

B. IE 4

C. Netscape 3

D. Netscape 4

E. Netscape 2

41. To specify the text alignment for table columns, you will use (choose 2):

***A. <COL>**

***B. <COLGROUP>**

C. <ROW>

D. <ROWGROUP>

E. No Answer is Correct

Explanation: Note that these are not supported by Netscape or IE2 and older.

---

42. You want to have graphics in tables. What browsers are required (Choose all that apply)?

***A. IE 3**

***B. IE 4**

C. Netscape 3

***D. Netscape 4**

E. Netscape 2

Explanation: Currently, graphics in tables are supported by MS Internet Explorer 3 and Netscape Navigator 4 upwards.

43. What are the difference between table graphic rendering in Netscape vs. IE browsers (Choose all that apply)?

A. Netscape repeats background graphic in each cell body

B. IE tiles graphic behind the whole table

C. Netscape renders graphic in 16bit color mode only

D. IE renders graphic in 256 color mode only

E. No Answer is Correct

---

44. How do you create an empty cell within a table?

A. place a non-breaking space special character in the cell

B. place a break character in the cell

C. place a transparent bar in the cell

D. use the <BR> tag

E. No Answer is Correct

43. What are the difference between table graphic rendering in Netscape vs. IE browsers (Choose all that apply)?

***A. Netscape repeats background graphic in each cell body**

***B. IE tiles graphic behind the whole table**

C. Netscape renders graphic in 16bit color mode only

D. IE renders graphic in 256 color mode only

E. No Answer is Correct

Explanation: You have to keep multi browser compatibility in mind when using graphics in browser.

---

44. How do you create an empty cell within a table?

***A. place a non-breaking space special character in the cell**

B. place a break character in the cell

C. place a transparent bar in the cell

D. use the <BR> tag

E. No Answer is Correct

Explanation: For example: <TD> </TD>

45. How do you center your table on your web page?

A. include VALIGN="center" in the <TABLE> tag

B. include ALIGN="center" in the <TABLE> tag

C. include VALIGN="center" in the <TD> tag

D. include ALIGN="center" in the <TH> tag

E. No Answer is Correct

---

46. What is the primary purpose of using frame?

A. to display multiple HTML documents on a single page

B. to display single HTML documents on multiple pages

C. to display single HTML documents on single page

D. to display single HTML documents on multiple windows

E. to display multiple HTML documents on single toolbar

45. How do you center your table on your web page?

A. include VALIGN="center" in the <TABLE> tag

***B. include ALIGN="center" in the <TABLE> tag**

C. include VALIGN="center" in the <TD> tag

D. include ALIGN="center" in the <TH> tag

E. No Answer is Correct

Explanation: This alignment is for the entire table, not for a particular cell.

---

46. What is the primary purpose of using frame?

***A. to display multiple HTML documents on a single page**

B. to display single HTML documents on multiple pages

C. to display single HTML documents on single page

D. to display single HTML documents on multiple windows

E. to display multiple HTML documents on single toolbar

Explanation: With the frame page you can display multiple HTML documents on a single page.

47. Under what kind of situation will you consider the use of frame page?

A. for site with contents that change infrequently

B. for site with contents that change frequently

C. for site with contents that do not change

D. for site with contents that change once a month

E. for site with contents that change once a week

---

48. You want to achieve the following: by clicking a link in one part of the screen can change the contents of the other part of the screen.

What can you use to achieve this?

A. Frame

B. Table

C. Anchor

D. HTML

E. XML

47. Under what kind of situation will you consider the use of frame page?

A. for site with contents that change infrequently

***B. for site with contents that change frequently**

C. for site with contents that do not change

D. for site with contents that change once a month

E. for site with contents that change once a week

Explanation: For example, in situation where you have one file specially for navigation, if you need to add or remove pages, you will only have to modify that one file.

---

48. You want to achieve the following: by clicking a link in one part of the screen can change the contents of the other part of the screen.

What can you use to achieve this?

***A. Frame**

B. Table

C. Anchor

D. HTML

E. XML

Explanation: With frames you can dynamically change the content.

49. Which of the following is true regarding the frame definition page?

A. <BODY> tag is replaced by the <FRAME> tag.

B. <BODY> tag is replaced by the <FRAMES> tag.

C. <BODY> tag is replaced by the <FRAMESET> tag.

D. <BODY> tag is replaced by the <FRSET> tag.

E. <BODY> tag is replaced by the <FRAMESETS> tag.

---

50. <FRAMESET> container contains the ____________ elements to describe the frames that make up the page.

A. <FRAME>

B. <FRAMES>

C. <BODY>

D. <ELEMENT>

E. <LIST>

49. Which of the following is true regarding the frame definition page?

A. <BODY> tag is replaced by the <FRAME> tag.

B. <BODY> tag is replaced by the <FRAMES> tag.

***C. <BODY> tag is replaced by the <FRAMESET> tag.**

D. <BODY> tag is replaced by the <FRSET> tag.

E. <BODY> tag is replaced by the <FRAMESETS> tag.

Explanation: Frame page does not contain body HTML tags. It contains only the parameters for the frames and the URLs of the HTML.

---

50. <FRAMESET> container contains the ____________ elements to describe the frames that make up the page.

***A. <FRAME>**

B. <FRAMES>

C. <BODY>

D. <ELEMENT>

E. <LIST>

Explanation: <FRAME> is the element within <FRAMESET>.

51. You like to provide content for non-frame browsers. What element should you use?

A. <NOFRAMES>

B. <NOFRAME>

C. <FRAMES>

D. <HTML>

E. No Answer is Correct

---

52. You just set the FRAMESPACING, FRAMEBORDER and BORDER attributes to 0. Why would you do this?

A. to create a link between the frames in Netscape and Microsoft browsers

B. to create a border between the frames in Netscape and Microsoft browsers

C. to create a separator line between the frames in Netscape and Microsoft browsers

D. to create a dotted divider between the frames in Netscape and Microsoft browsers

E. to create a seamless join between the frames in Netscape and Microsoft browsers

51. You like to provide content for non-frame browsers. What element should you use?

***A. <NOFRAMES>**

B. <NOFRAME>

C. <FRAMES>

D. <HTML>

E. No Answer is Correct

Explanation: You should put content inside the <NOFRAMES> </NOFRAMES> tags.

---

52. You just set the FRAMESPACING, FRAMEBORDER and BORDER attributes to 0. Why would you do this?

A. to create a link between the frames in Netscape and Microsoft browsers

B. to create a border between the frames in Netscape and Microsoft browsers

C. to create a separator line between the frames in Netscape and Microsoft browsers

D. to create a dotted divider between the frames in Netscape and Microsoft browsers

***E. to create a seamless join between the frames in Netscape and Microsoft browsers**

Explanation: The example code fragment of this implementation is as follow:
FRAMEBORDER=0 BORDER=0 FRAMESPACING=0

53. To turn off the border around frames in the frameset, what code would you use?

A. FRAMEBORDER="yes"

B. FRAMEBORDER=0

C. FRAME = noborder

D. FRAME = BORDERLESS

E. FRAMEBORDER= 1

---

54. You like to set the color of the frame borders in your frameset. What code would you use?

A. BORDERCOLOR="#hexcolor|colorname"

B. BORDCOLOR="#hexcolor|colorname"

C. BORDERC="#hexcolor|colorname"

D. BORDER=("#hexcolor|colorname")

E. BORDERCOLOR= (background ="#hexcolor|colorname")

53. To turn off the border around frames in the frameset, what code would you use?

A. FRAMEBORDER="yes"

***B. FRAMEBORDER=0**

C. FRAME = noborder

D. FRAME = BORDERLESS

E. FRAMEBORDER= 1

Explanation: Some browsers also accept FRAMEBORDER="no"

---

54. You like to set the color of the frame borders in your frameset. What code would you use?

***A. BORDERCOLOR="#hexcolor|colorname"**

B. BORDCOLOR="#hexcolor|colorname"

C. BORDERC="#hexcolor|colorname"

D. BORDER=("#hexcolor|colorname")

E. BORDERCOLOR= (background ="#hexcolor|colorname")

Explanation: You can specify color in hex format or as a name, depending on the browser version you support.

55. In your code for the frame you have SCROLLING="auto" . What is it for?

A. tell the browser to decide whether the frame needs scrollbars and display them where necessary

B. tell the browser to decide whether the page needs scrollable toolbars and display them where necessary

C. tell the browser to decide whether the window needs scrolling handles and display them where necessary

D. tell the browser to decide whether the browser needs scrolling window and display them where necessary

E. No Answer is Correct

---

56. You want to prevent the user from resizing the frame. What can you do?

A. RESIZE = No

B. NORESIZE

C. RESIZE = 0

D. Do nothing. This is the default.

E. No Answer is Correct

55. In your code for the frame you have SCROLLING="auto" . What is it for?

***A. tell the browser to decide whether the frame needs scrollbars and display them where necessary**

B. tell the browser to decide whether the page needs scrollable toolbars and display them where necessary

C. tell the browser to decide whether the window needs scrolling handles and display them where necessary

D. tell the browser to decide whether the browser needs scrolling window and display them where necessary

E. No Answer is Correct

Explanation: The browser will automatically determine whether a scrollbar is needed for a frame.

---

56. You want to prevent the user from resizing the frame. What can you do?

A. RESIZE = No

***B. NORESIZE**

C. RESIZE = 0

D. Do nothing. This is the default.

E. No Answer is Correct

Explanation: By default, a user can resize the frames by dragging the frame edges to new positions.

57. Edwin told you that you can place a frameset and its associated frames within another frameset. Is this true?

A. Yes

B. No

C. Yes, only for Netscape browser

D. Yes, only for IE browser

E. Yes, only for Java enabled browser

---

58. What is the MARGINWIDTH parameter for?

A. sets the left and right frame margins

B. sets the top and bottom frame margins

C. sets the color of the frame border

D. sets the clear space around the frame

E. No Answer is Correct

57. Edwin told you that you can place a frameset and its associated frames within another frameset. Is this true?

***A. Yes**

B. No

C. Yes, only for Netscape browser

D. Yes, only for IE browser

E. Yes, only for Java enabled browser

Explanation: Nested frame is possible with any browser that supports frame.

---

58. What is the MARGINWIDTH parameter for?

***A. sets the left and right frame margins**

B. sets the top and bottom frame margins

C. sets the color of the frame border

D. sets the clear space around the frame

E. No Answer is Correct

Explanation: Measurement is in pixels.

59. What is the MARGINHEIGHT parameter for?

A. sets the left and right frame margins in pixels

B. sets the top and bottom frame margins in pixels

C. sets the color of the frame border

D. sets the clear space around the frame

E. No Answer is Correct

---

60. What is the FRAMESPACING parameter for?

A. sets the left and right frame margins in pixels

B. sets the top and bottom frame margins in pixels

C. sets the color of the frame border

D. sets the clear space around the frame

E. No Answer is Correct

59. What is the MARGINHEIGHT parameter for?

A. sets the left and right frame margins in pixels

***B. sets the top and bottom frame margins in pixels**

C. sets the color of the frame border

D. sets the clear space around the frame

E. No Answer is Correct

Explanation: Measurement is in pixels.

---

60. What is the FRAMESPACING parameter for?

A. sets the left and right frame margins in pixels

B. sets the top and bottom frame margins in pixels

C. sets the color of the frame border

***D. sets the clear space around the frame**

E. No Answer is Correct

Explanation: Measurement is in pixels.

61. Which technology allows Windows platform to host different types of database to act as the backend of your web platform?

A. OLE

B. ODBC

C. WINS

D. ASP

E. ACE

---

62. You are designing a totally data driven web site. Which of the following technology is the most appropriate to develop the pages, assuming that your web platform runs on Windows NT?

A. OLE

B. ODBC

C. WINS

D. ASP

E. ACE

61. Which technology allows Windows platform to host different types of database to act as the backend of your web platform?

A. OLE

***B. ODBC**

C. WINS

D. ASP

E. ACE

Explanation: In the control panel you will find the ODBC Manager. By defining data sources you system can provide the web server with backend data service.

---

62. You are designing a totally data driven web site. Which of the following technology is the most appropriate to develop the pages, assuming that your web platform runs on Windows NT?

A. OLE

B. ODBC

C. WINS

***D. ASP**

E. ACE

Explanation: Active Server Page is designed as a web page design language with database driven activities in mind.

63. You are designing a totally data driven web site. Which of the following technology is the most appropriate to develop the pages, assuming that your web platform runs on Linux?

A. OLE

B. ODBC

C. WINS

D. ASP

E. PHP

---

64. Which technology allows Linux platform to host the backend database for your web platform?

A. OLE

B. ODBC

C. MySQL

D. ASP

E. SQL Server 7

63. You are designing a totally data driven web site. Which of the following technology is the most appropriate to develop the pages, assuming that your web platform runs on Linux?

A. OLE

B. ODBC

C. WINS

D. ASP

***E. PHP**

Explanation: PHP together with MySQL is the most popular choice of developing database driven web site in the Linux world.

---

64. Which technology allows Linux platform to host the backend database for your web platform?

A. OLE

B. ODBC

***C. MySQL**

D. ASP

E. SQL Server 7

Explanation: PHP together with MySQL is the most popular choice of developing database driven web site in the Linux world.

65. Which type of database system will best suit the need of your web site if small but frequent updates will be the majority of activities?

A. OLTP

B. Datawarehouse

C. Object DBMS

D. Index DBMS

E. Relay DBMS

---

66. You are using MySQL as the database backend of your web site. What type of database model does your site support?

A. Relational

B. Flat

C. Hierarchical

D. Cylindrical

E. No Answer is Correct

65. Which type of database system will best suit the need of your web site if small but frequent updates will be the majority of activities?

***A. OLTP**

B. Datawarehouse

C. Object DBMS

D. Index DBMS

E. Relay DBMS

Explanation: Online Transaction Processing system is targeted for system with small but frequent updates.

---

66. You are using MySQL as the database backend of your web site. What type of database model does your site support?

***A. Relational**

B. Flat

C. Hierarchical

D. Cylindrical

E. No Answer is Correct

Explanation: Most of the database backend we use today are still in flavor of the relational model.

67. You have a server with Windows NT version 4 SP6 installed. This server has 256M RAM, and is running IIS as the web server. You want to install a database server on the same machine. Which of the following will be your most likely choice?

A. Access

B. SQL Server

C. MySQL

D. Oracle

E. No Answer is Correct

---

68. What type of operation in a RDBMS allows you to select specific sets of records from the database and present them to users?

A. select query with no clause

B. select query with where clause

C. select query with when clause

D. select query with for clause

E. No Answer is Correct

67. You have a server with Windows NT version 4 SP6 installed. This server has 256M RAM, and is running IIS as the web server. You want to install a database server on the same machine. Which of the following will be your most likely choice?

A. Access

***B. SQL Server**

C. MySQL

D. Oracle

E. No Answer is Correct

Explanation: When running on NT platform, IIS works best with SQL Server.

---

68. What type of operation in a RDBMS allows you to select specific sets of records from the database and present them to users?

A. select query with no clause

***B. select query with where clause**

C. select query with when clause

D. select query with for clause

E. No Answer is Correct

Explanation: Example: SELECT Product_name, Product_ID FROM Product_table WHERE Product_ID = 45678

69. To speed up data retrieval in your RDBMS, what operation will you conduct?

A. build index

B. build primary key

C. build foreign key

D. build unique ID

E. No Answer is Correct

---

70. To avoid duplicate keys, what can you do in your RDBMS?

A. build index

B. build primary key

C. build foreign key

D. build unique ID

E. No Answer is Correct

69. To speed up data retrieval in your RDBMS, what operation will you conduct?

***A. build index**

B. build primary key

C. build foreign key

D. build unique ID

E. No Answer is Correct

Explanation: Index facilitates searching at the expense of storage size.

---

70. To avoid duplicate keys, what can you do in your RDBMS?

A. build index

***B. build primary key**

C. build foreign key

D. build unique ID

E. No Answer is Correct

Explanation: Index facilitates searching at the expense of storage size.

71. To allow referential integrity, which of the following will you need to configure in your RDBMS?

A. build index

B. build primary key

C. build foreign key

D. build unique ID

E. No Answer is Correct

---

72. You often hear about the terms clustered and nonclustered. What are these terms related to?

A. build index

B. build primary key

C. build foreign key

D. build unique ID

E. No Answer is Correct

71. To allow referential integrity, which of the following will you need to configure in your RDBMS?

A. build index

B. build primary key

***C. build foreign key**

D. build unique ID

E. No Answer is Correct

Explanation: Refer to the web link for more information.

---

72. You often hear about the terms clustered and nonclustered. What are these terms related to?

***A. build index**

B. build primary key

C. build foreign key

D. build unique ID

E. No Answer is Correct

Explanation: Index facilitates searching at the expense of storage size. To learn more on CLUSTERED VS NONCLUSTERED Index, please refer to the web link.

73. In RDBMS, what is the meaning of Domain Integrity?

A. Data values in each column must be valid.

B. Data values in each column must be unique.

C. Data values in each column must be of the same domain.

D. Data values in each column must not be out of memory scope.

E. No Answer is Correct

---

74. In RDBMS, what is the meaning of Entity Integrity?

A. Data values in each row must be valid.

B. Data values in each row must be unique in the entity.

C. Data values in each row must be of the same domain.

D. Data values in each row must not be out of memory scope.

E. No Answer is Correct

73. In RDBMS, what is the meaning of Domain Integrity?

***A. Data values in each column must be valid.**

B. Data values in each column must be unique.

C. Data values in each column must be of the same domain.

D. Data values in each column must not be out of memory scope.

E. No Answer is Correct

Explanation: Refer to the web link for more information.

---

74. In RDBMS, what is the meaning of Entity Integrity?

A. Data values in each row must be valid.

***B. Data values in each row must be unique in the entity.**

C. Data values in each row must be of the same domain.

D. Data values in each row must not be out of memory scope.

E. No Answer is Correct

Explanation: Refer to the web link for more information.

75. Which of the following normalization level indicates that no table has columns that define similar attributes, and that no column holds multiple values in a single row?

A. 1NF

B. 2NF

C. 3NF

D. 4NF

E. 5NF

---

76. What tag replaces the <BODY> tag in a frameset html document

A. <FRAME>

B. <TABLE>

C. <FRAMEBODY>

D. <FRAMESET>

75. Which of the following normalization level indicates that no table has columns that define similar attributes, and that no column holds multiple values in a single row?

***A. 1NF**

B. 2NF

C. 3NF

D. 4NF

E. 5NF

Explanation: Refer to the web link for more information.

---

76. What tag replaces the <BODY> tag in a frameset html document

A. <FRAME>

B. <TABLE>

C. <FRAMEBODY>

***D. <FRAMESET>**

Explanation: When creating an HTML page that uses frames, the <BODY> tag is replaced with the <FRAMESET> tag. The <FRAMESET> tag is a container tag that tells the browser that this page uses frames. You then use <FRAME> tags to define the parameters of the individual frames used in the document. There is no such thing as a <FRAMEBODY> tag. To use a <TABLE> tag, you must use the <BODY> tag in a standard HTML document.

77. What two True Type fonts are used by most browsers?

A. Verdana

B. Arial

C. Helvetica

D. Courier

E. Times New Roman

---

78. What do web designers commonly use to define a set of standards for formatting style elements on a web site?

A. Style Guides

B. Embedded Style Sheets

C. Inline Style Sheets

D. Cascading Style Sheets

77. What two True Type fonts are used by most browsers?

A. Verdana

***B. Arial**

C. Helvetica

D. Courier

*E. Times New Roman

---

77. What do web designers commonly use to define a set of standards for formatting style elements on a web site?

***A. Style Guides**

B. Embedded Style Sheets

C. Inline Style Sheets

D. Cascading Style Sheets

Explanation: Web designers use Style Guides that are then translated into style sheets for use in the web site. These guides give example of how web developers are to format page elements in particular situations.

79. What tag should be used in favor of the deprecated <B> tag for bolding text in HTML 4.0?

A. <EM>

B. <BOLD>

C. <FONT WEIGHT="bold">

D. <STRONG>

79. What tag should be used in favor of the deprecated <B> tag for bolding text in HTML 4.0?

A. <EM>

B. <BOLD>

C. <FONT WEIGHT="bold">

***D. <STRONG>**

Explanation: The W3C's HTML 4.0 recommendation favors the use of the <STRONG> tag instead of the <B> when bolding a section of type. The reason for this change is that users of aural browser's will hear an infliction of the computer generated voice for words that are surrounded by <STRONG> tags.

Chapter 4:
Third Party Applications

1. How do you create a table in FrontPage Editor?

A. Table - Insert Table

B. Insert - Table

C. Table - Insert Object - Table

D. Edit - Insert Table

E. No Answer is Correct

---

2. What command allows for the merging of table cells in FrontPage?

A. Table - Merge

B. Table - Merge Cells

C. Table - Merge Object - Cells

D. Table - Merge - Cells

E. No Answer is Correct

1. How do you create a table in FrontPage Editor?

***A. Table - Insert Table**

B. Insert - Table

C. Table - Insert Object - Table

D. Edit - Insert Table

E. No Answer is Correct

Explanation: For detailed information please refer to the web link.

---

2. What command allows for the merging of table cells in FrontPage?

A. Table - Merge

***B. Table - Merge Cells**

C. Table - Merge Object - Cells

D. Table - Merge - Cells

E. No Answer is Correct

Explanation: For detailed information please refer to the web link.

3. What command allows for the merging of table columns in FrontPage?

A. Table - Merge Columns

B. Table - Merge Cells

C. Table - Merge Object - Cells

D. Table - Merge - Columns

E. No Answer is Correct

---

4. What command allows for the merging of table rows in FrontPage?

A. Table - Merge Rows

B. Table - Merge Cells

C. Table - Merge Object - Cells

D. Table - Merge - Rows

E. No Answer is Correct

3. What command allows for the merging of table columns in FrontPage?

A. Table - Merge Columns

***B. Table - Merge Cells**

C. Table - Merge Object - Cells

D. Table - Merge - Columns

E. No Answer is Correct

Explanation: For detailed information please refer to the web link.

---

4. What command allows for the merging of table rows in FrontPage?

A. Table - Merge Rows

***B. Table - Merge Cells**

C. Table - Merge Object - Cells

D. Table - Merge - Rows

E. No Answer is Correct

Explanation: For detailed information please refer to the web link.

5. In FrontPage, how can you change the Properties of a Table (Choose all that apply)?

A. Right click inside the table

B. Right click outside the table

C. Choose Table Properties

D. Choose Cell Properties

E. No Answer is Correct

---

6. What element of FrontPage can you deploy for better control of the overall site style?

A. theme

B. list

C. frame

D. table

E. No Answer is Correct

5. In FrontPage, how can you change the Properties of a Table (Choose all that apply)?

***A. Right click inside the table**

B. Right click outside the table

***C. Choose Table Properties**

D. Choose Cell Properties

E. No Answer is Correct

Explanation: For detailed information please refer to the web link.

---

6. What element of FrontPage can you deploy for better control of the overall site style?

***A. theme**

B. list

C. frame

D. table

E. No Answer is Correct

Explanation: For detailed information please refer to the web link.

7. In FrontPage, how would you change the background color of a page?

A. File - View - Page Properties

B. File - Background Properties

C. Edit - Page Properties

D. File - Page Properties

E. No Answer is Correct

---

8. In FrontPage, how would you change the color of the links?

A. File - View - Page Properties

B. File - Background Properties

C. Edit - Page Properties

D. File - Page Properties

E. No Answer is Correct

7. In FrontPage, how would you change the background color of a page?

A. File - View - Page Properties

B. File - Background Properties

C. Edit - Page Properties

***D. File - Page Properties**

E. No Answer is Correct

Explanation: For detailed information please refer to the web link.

---

8. In FrontPage, how would you change the color of the links?

A. File - View - Page Properties

B. File - Background Properties

C. Edit - Page Properties

***D. File - Page Properties**

E. No Answer is Correct

Explanation: For detailed information please refer to the web link.

9. You have the following screen:

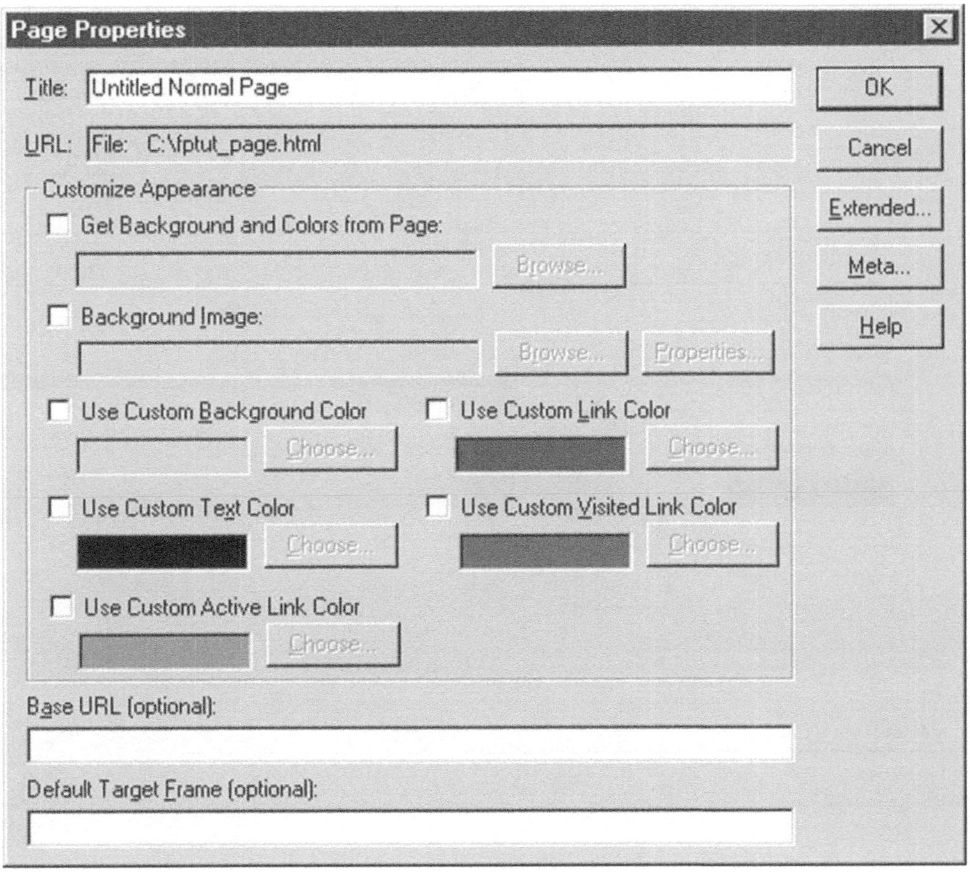

Which option is for retrieving the background image and color from an existing web page in somewhere else?

A. Get Background and Colors from Page

B. Use Custom Link Color

C. Use Custom Text Color

D. Use Custom Visited Link Color

E. Use Custom Active Link Color

9. You have the following screen:

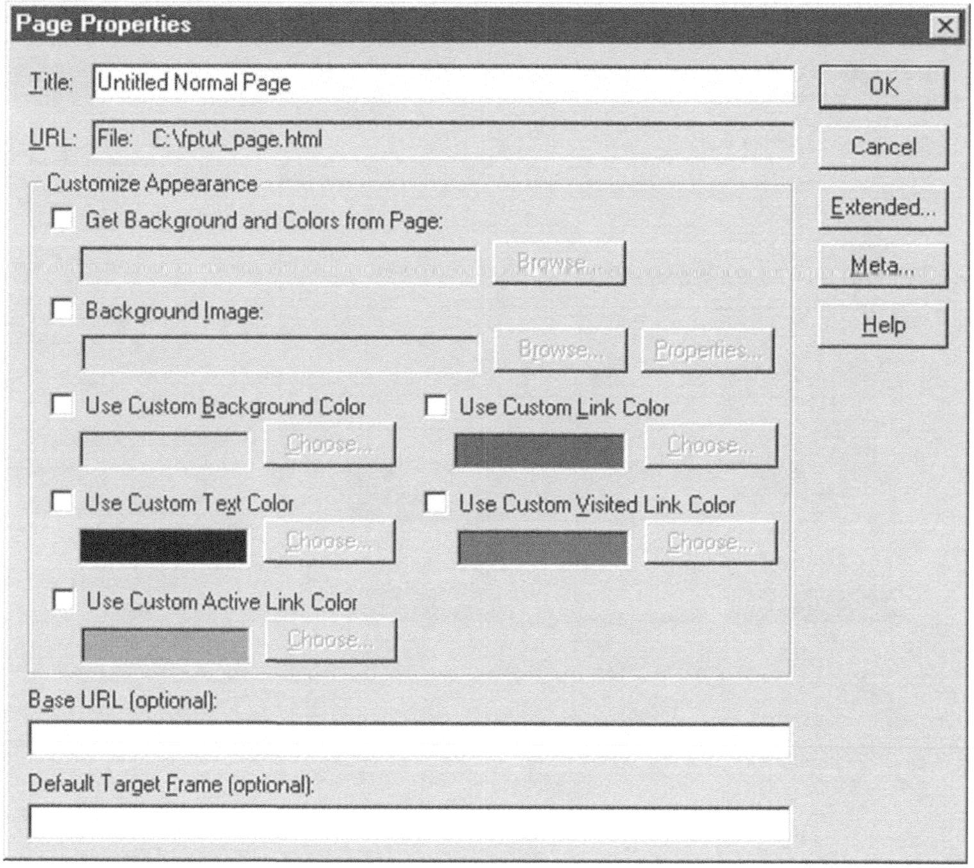

Which option is for retrieving the background image and color from an existing web page in somewhere else?

***A. Get Background and Colors from Page**

B. Use Custom Link Color

C. Use Custom Text Color

D. Use Custom Visited Link Color

E. Use Custom Active Link Color

Explanation: For detailed information please refer to the web link.

10. You have the following screen:

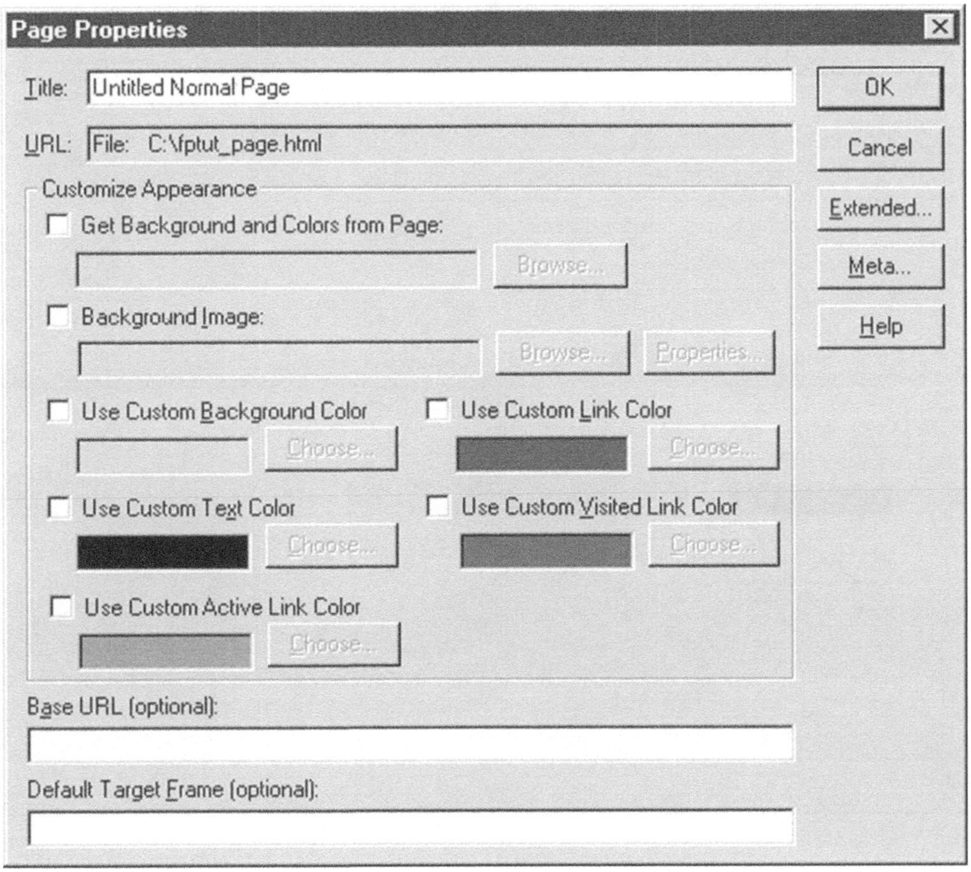

Which option is for specifying the default text color on your page?

A. Get Background and Colors from Page

B. Use Custom Link Color

C. Use Custom Text Color

D. Use Custom Visited Link Color

E. Use Custom Active Link Color

10. You have the following screen:

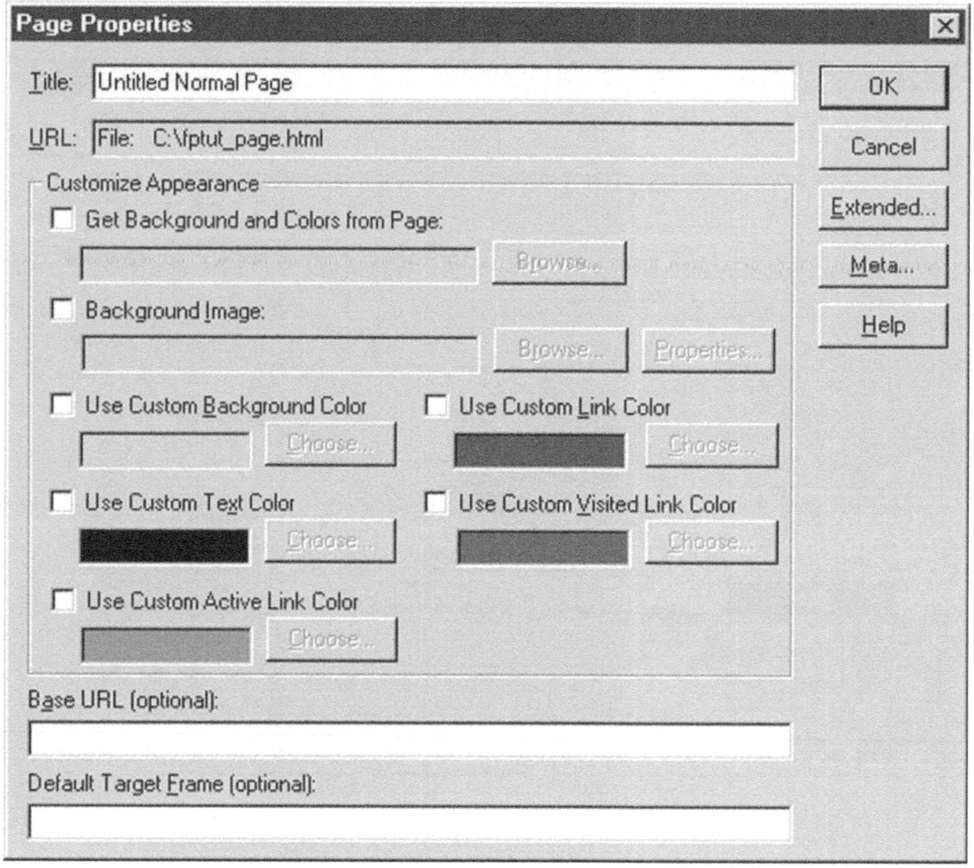

Which option is for specifying the default text color on your page?

A. Get Background and Colors from Page

B. Use Custom Link Color

***C. Use Custom Text Color**

D. Use Custom Visited Link Color

E. Use Custom Active Link Color

Explanation: For detailed information please refer to the web link.

11. You have the following screen:

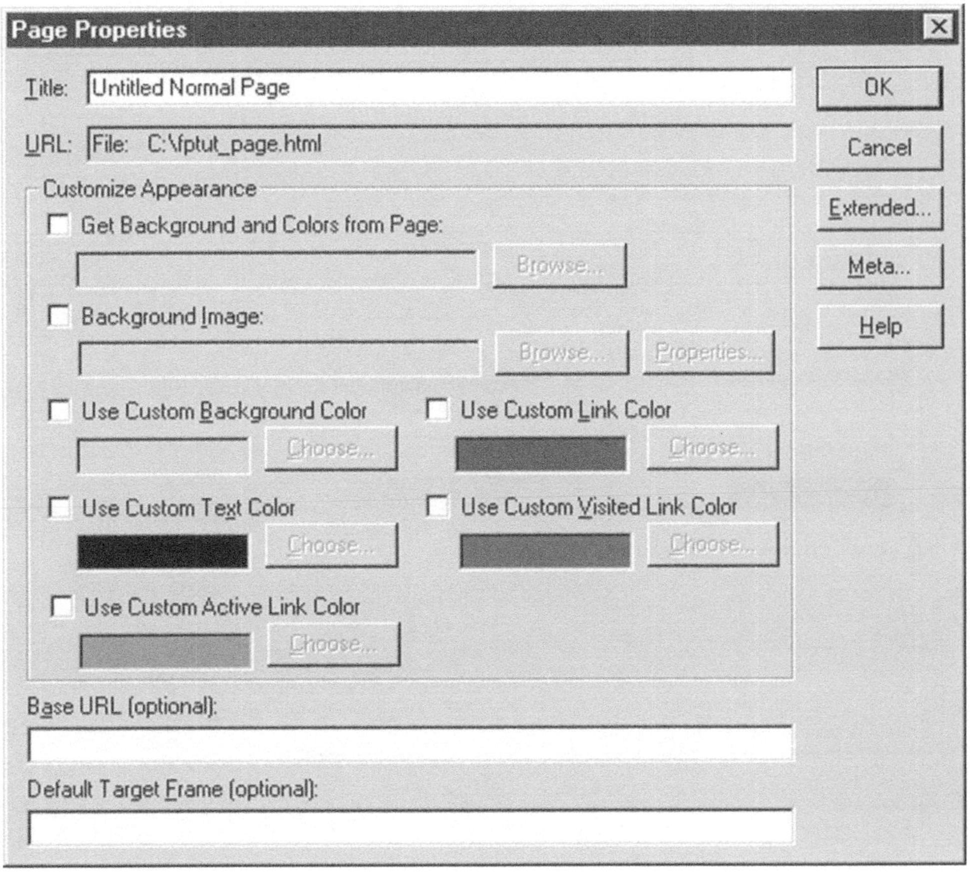

Which option is for setting the color of a link when the user clicks on the link itself?

A. Get Background and Colors from Page

B. Use Custom Link Color

C. Use Custom Text Color

D. Use Custom Visited Link Color

E. Use Custom Active Link Color

11. You have the following screen:

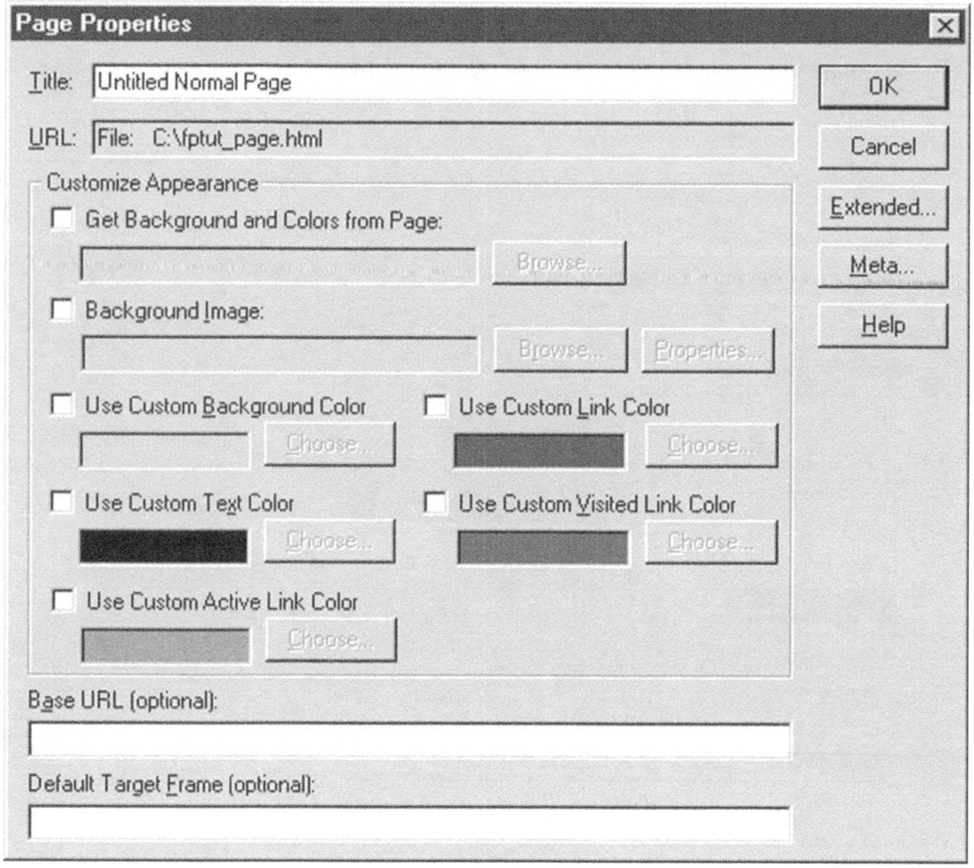

Which option is for setting the color of a link when the user clicks on the link itself?

A. Get Background and Colors from Page

B. Use Custom Link Color

C. Use Custom Text Color

D. Use Custom Visited Link Color

***E. Use Custom Active Link Color**

Explanation: For detailed information please refer to the web link.

12. You have the following screen:

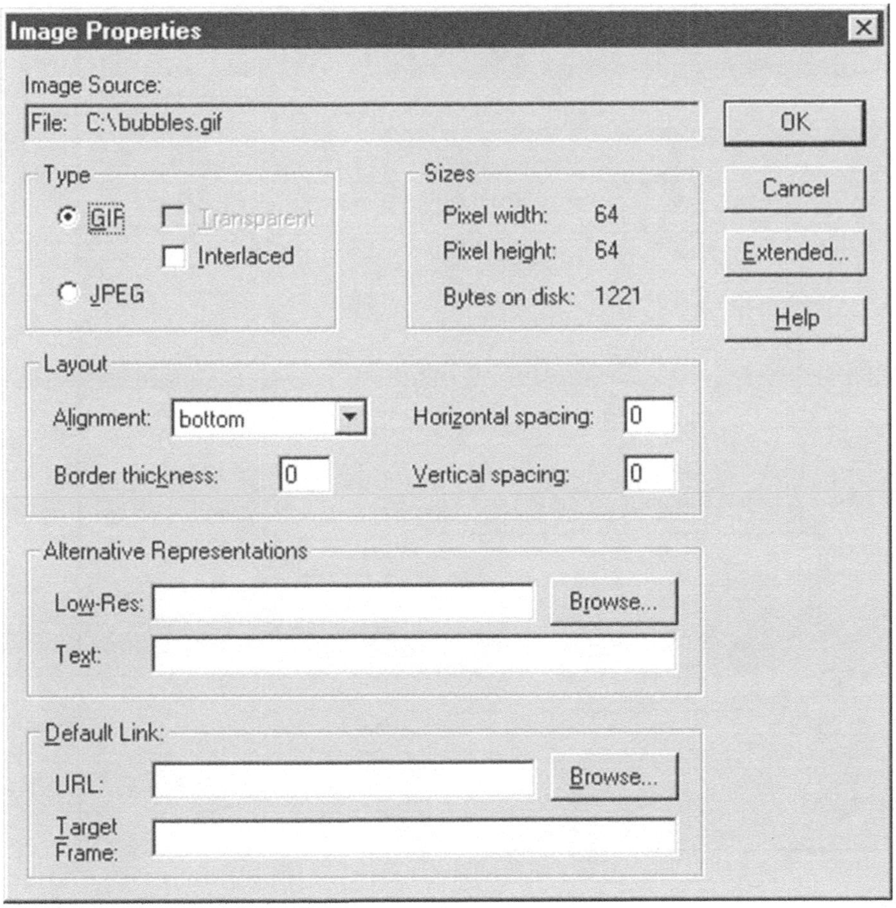

You want to set the spacing in pixels between the picture and adjacent text on the same line. What option do you need to set?

A. Horizontal Spacing

B. Vertical Spacing

C. Border Thickness

D. Low-Res

E. Text

12. You have the following screen:

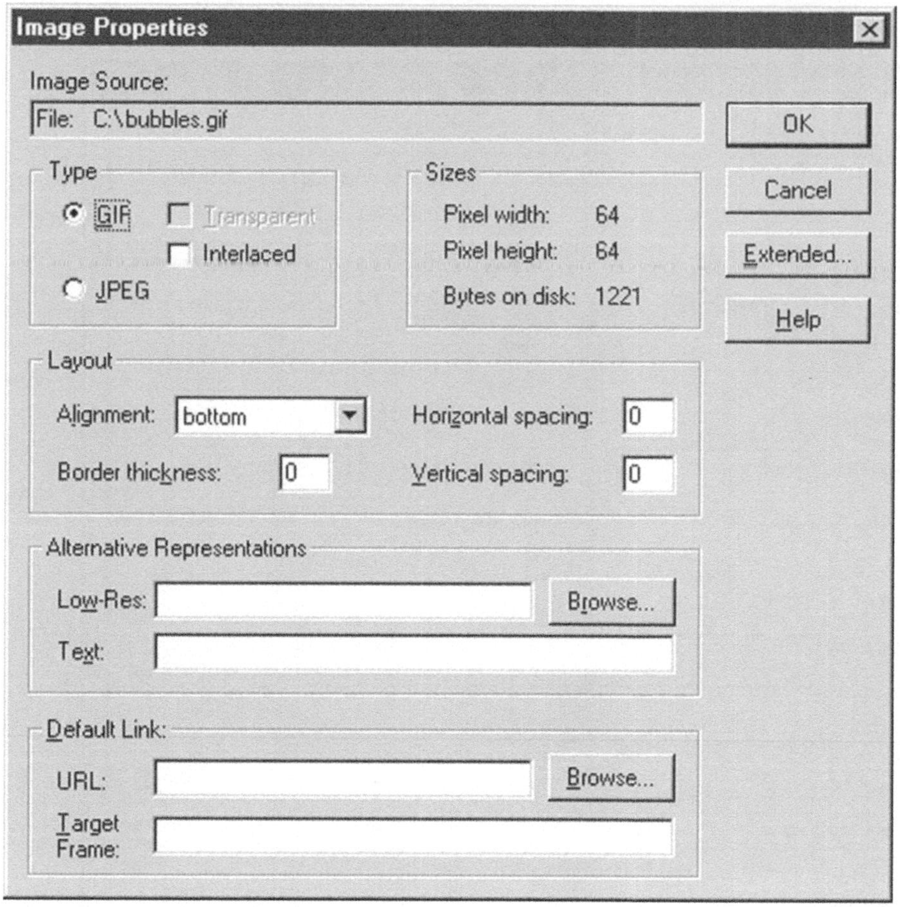

You want to set the spacing in pixels between the picture and adjacent text on the same line. What option do you need to set?

***A. Horizontal Spacing**

B. Vertical Spacing

C. Border Thickness

D. Low-Res

E. Text

Explanation: Vertical VS Horizontal spacing can be confusing. For detailed information please refer to the web link.

13. You have the following screen:

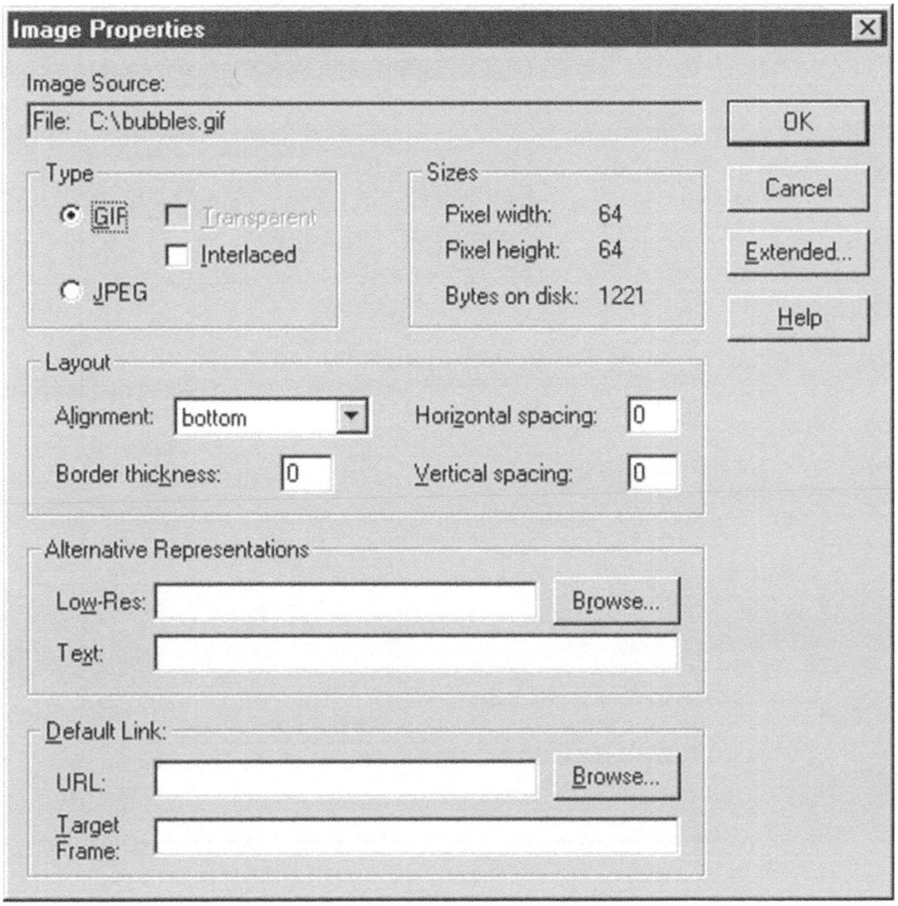

You want to set the spacing in pixels between the picture and adjacent text that is on lines above or below the picture. What option do you need to set?

A. Horizontal Spacing

B. Vertical Spacing

C. Border Thickness

D. Low-Res

E. Text

13. You have the following screen:

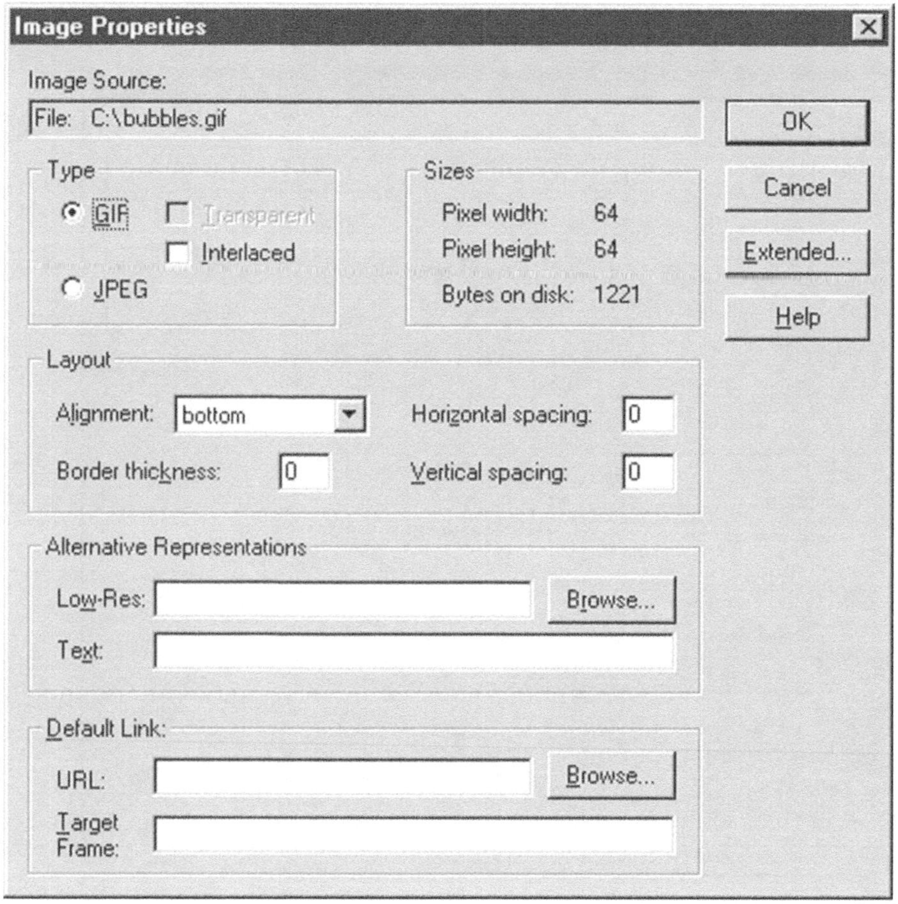

You want to set the spacing in pixels between the picture and adjacent text that is on lines above or below the picture. What option do you need to set?

A. Horizontal Spacing

***B. Vertical Spacing**

C. Border Thickness

D. Low-Res

E. Text

Explanation: Vertical VS Horizontal spacing can be confusing. For detailed information please refer to the web link.

14. You have the following screen:

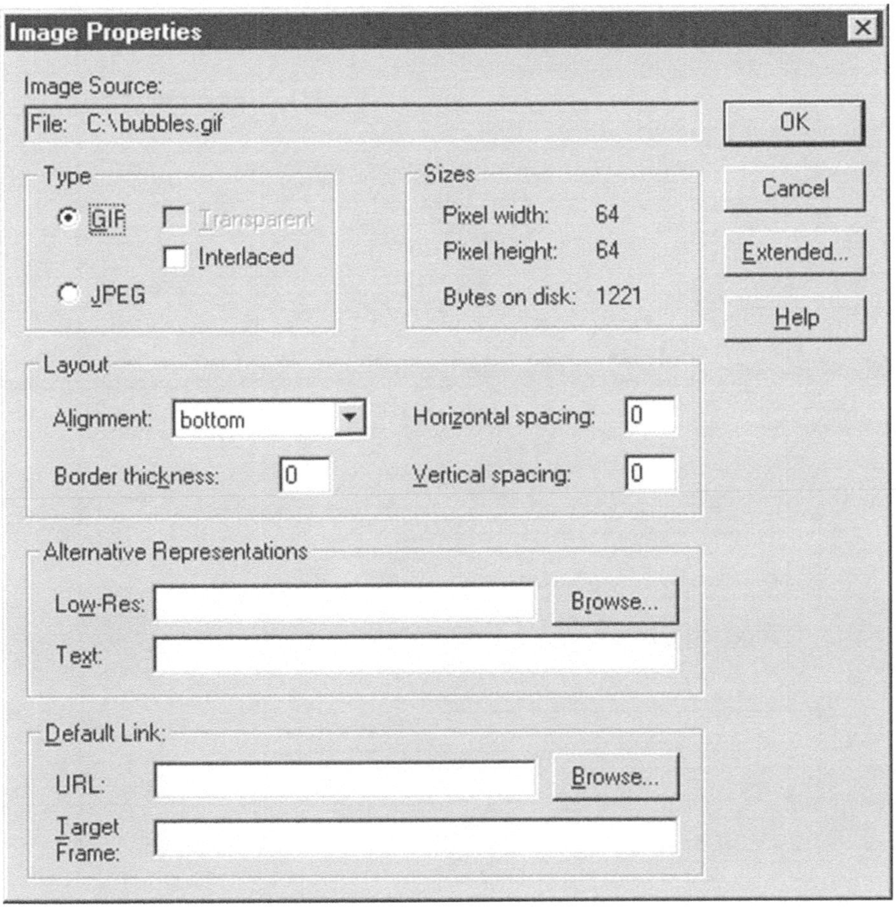

You want to specify a URL to send the user to when they click on your picture. What option do you need to set?

A. Horizontal Spacing

B. Vertical Spacing

C. Border Thickness

D. Text

E. No Answer is Correct

14. You have the following screen:

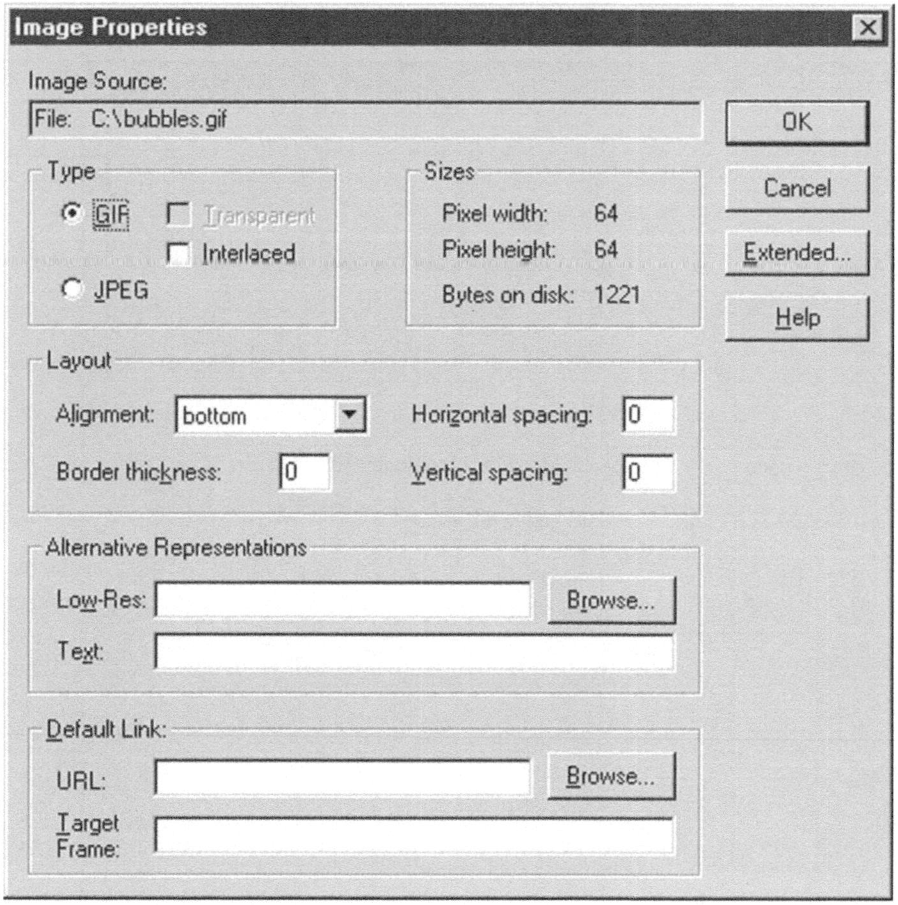

You want to specify a URL to send the user to when they click on your picture. What option do you need to set?

A. Horizontal Spacing

B. Vertical Spacing

C. Border Thickness

D. Text

***E. No Answer is Correct**

Explanation: You actually need to set the URL option. For detailed information please refer to the web link.

15. What image file formats are supported in FrontPage (Choose all that apply)?

A. JPG

B. GIF

C. BMP

D. PNP

E. No Answer is Correct

---

16. You are developing a FrontPage 2000 application. You want to edit an element on one page, and the changes go site wide as soon as you save. What feature should you use?

A. Include Page Component

B. Include Component

C. Insert Page Component

D. Insert Component

E. No Answer is Correct

15. What image file formats are supported in FrontPage (Choose all that apply)?

***A. JPG**

***B. GIF**

C. BMP

D. PNP

E. No Answer is Correct

Explanation: For detailed information please refer to the web link.

---

16. You are developing a FrontPage 2000 application. You want to edit an element on one page, and the changes go site wide as soon as you save. What feature should you use?

***A. Include Page Component**

B. Include Component

C. Insert Page Component

D. Insert Component

E. No Answer is Correct

Explanation: Please refer to the web link for detailed explanation.

17. Which menu path allows for the access of Include Page component in FrontPage?

A. Insert/Include Page

B. Insert/FrontPage Component/Include Page

C. Insert/FrontPage Component

D. Insert/FrontPage Include Page

E. No Answer is Correct

---

18. When working with a FrontPage Web, how do you enable the bottom border of your site to be shared?

A. In FrontPage Editor, choose Tools/Shared Borders.

B. In FrontPage Explorer, choose Shared Borders.

C. In FrontPage Explorer, choose Tools/Shared Borders.

D. In FrontPage Explorer, choose Edit/Shared Borders.

E. No Answer is Correct

17. Which menu path allows for the access of Include Page component in FrontPage?

A. Insert/Include Page

***B. Insert/FrontPage Component/Include Page**

C. Insert/FrontPage Component

D. Insert/FrontPage Include Page

E. No Answer is Correct

Explanation: Please refer to the web link for detailed explanation.

---

18. When working with a FrontPage Web, how do you enable the bottom border of your site to be shared?

A. In FrontPage Editor, choose Tools/Shared Borders.

B. In FrontPage Explorer, choose Shared Borders.

***C. In FrontPage Explorer, choose Tools/Shared Borders.**

D. In FrontPage Explorer, choose Edit/Shared Borders.

E. No Answer is Correct

Explanation: Please refer to the web link for detailed explanation.

19. You have some common textual information that you want to display on more than one page of your site. How would you do this?

A. create a variable

B. create a pointer

C. create a passing parameter

D. create a list

E. No Answer is Correct

---

20. How do you create a variable for use in your FrontPage web?

A. select File/Web Settings in FrontPage Explorer, go to the Parameters tab and click on the Add button

B. select Tools/Web Settings in FrontPage Explorer, go to the Parameters tab and click on the Add button

C. select Edit/Web Settings in FrontPage Explorer, go to the Parameters tab and click on the Add button

D. select Tools/Web Settings in FrontPage Explorer, go to the Parameters tab and click on the Variables button

E. No Answer is Correct

19. You have some common textual information that you want to display on more than one page of your site. How would you do this?

***A. create a variable**

B. create a pointer

C. create a passing parameter

D. create a list

E. No Answer is Correct

Explanation: Please refer to the web link for detailed explanation.

---

20. How do you create a variable for use in your FrontPage web?

A. select File/Web Settings in FrontPage Explorer, go to the Parameters tab and click on the Add button

***B. select Tools/Web Settings in FrontPage Explorer, go to the Parameters tab and click on the Add button**

C. select Edit/Web Settings in FrontPage Explorer, go to the Parameters tab and click on the Add button

D. select Tools/Web Settings in FrontPage Explorer, go to the Parameters tab and click on the Variables button

E. No Answer is Correct

Explanation: Please refer to the web link for detailed explanation.

21. Which borders of your web page can you enable for sharing in FrontPage (Choose all that apply)?

A. Top

B. Bottom

C. Left

D. Right

E. No Answer is Correct

---

22. Which of the following information can be configured to become "submittable" in FrontPage
(Choose all that apply)?

A. Time the form was submitted

B. Date the form was submitted

C. Type of browser

D. Remote computer name

E. User ID of the client

21. Which borders of your web page can you enable for sharing in FrontPage
(Choose all that apply)?

***A. Top**

***B. Bottom**

***C. Left**

***D. Right**

E. No Answer is Correct

Explanation: You may enable or disable sharing of individual border. Please refer to the web link for detailed explanation.

---

22. Which of the following information can be configured to become "submittable" in FrontPage
(Choose all that apply)?

***A. Time the form was submitted**

***B. Date the form was submitted**

***C. Type of browser**

***D. Remote computer name**

***E. User ID of the client**

Explanation: Please refer to the web link for detailed explanation.

23. How do you configure FrontPage to allow users to submit particular information through your page?

A. Choose "Form Properties" - "Options" - "Saved Fields"

B. Choose "Form Properties" - "Saved Fields"

C. Choose "Form Properties" - "Options"

D. Choose "Options" - "Saved Fields"

E. No Answer is Correct

---

24. You receive your submitted input from your web site. The result looks scrambled. To change the way the output looks, you should:

A. Choose "Form Properties" - "Options"

B. Choose "Form Properties" - "Options" - "E-mail Results"

C. Choose "Form Properties" - "Options" - "Results"

D. Choose "Form Properties" - "E-mail Results"

E. No Answer is Correct

23. How do you configure FrontPage to allow users to submit particular information through your page?

***A. Choose "Form Properties" - "Options" - "Saved Fields"**

B. Choose "Form Properties" - "Saved Fields"

C. Choose "Form Properties" - "Options"

D. Choose "Options" - "Saved Fields"

E. No Answer is Correct

Explanation: Please refer to the web link for detailed explanation.

---

24. You receive your submitted input from your web site. The result looks scrambled. To change the way the output looks, you should:

A. Choose "Form Properties" - "Options"

***B. Choose "Form Properties" - "Options" - "E-mail Results"**

C. Choose "Form Properties" - "Options" - "Results"

D. Choose "Form Properties" - "E-mail Results"

E. No Answer is Correct

Explanation: You may enable or disable E-mail results or File results. Please refer to the web link for detailed explanation.

25. What is a subweb in FrontPage?

A. a folder in the C drive that FrontPage treats as a distinct web

B. a folder in the external disk subsystem that FrontPage treats as a distinct web

C. a folder in the root that FrontPage treats as a backup web

D. a folder in the root that FrontPage treats as a distinct web

E. No Answer is Correct

---

26. Which of the following is NOT true concerning a subweb (Choose all that apply)?

A. Creating a subweb does not overwrite the main web

B. Creating a subweb will overwrite the main web

C. Creating a subweb will overwrite another subweb

D. Creating a subweb will overwrite the root of the OS

E. Creating a subweb will overwrite the main web data folder

25. What is a subweb in FrontPage?

A. a folder in the C drive that FrontPage treats as a distinct web

B. a folder in the external disk subsystem that FrontPage treats as a distinct web

C. a folder in the root that FrontPage treats as a backup web

***D. a folder in the root that FrontPage treats as a distinct web**

E. No Answer is Correct

Explanation: Please refer to the web link for detailed explanation.

---

26. Which of the following is NOT true concerning a subweb (Choose all that apply)?

A. Creating a subweb does not overwrite the main web

***B. Creating a subweb will overwrite the main web**

***C. Creating a subweb will overwrite another subweb**

***D. Creating a subweb will overwrite the root of the OS**

***E. Creating a subweb will overwrite the main web data folder**

Explanation: Creating a subweb should not overwrite anything. Please refer to the web link for detailed explanation.

27. How do you create a subweb in FrontPage 2000 Explorer?

A. create a folder, right click on it and mark it as a subweb

B. create a folder, double click on it and check the subweb checkbox

C. create a folder, right click on it and then convert to web

D. create a folder, and then convert to web by running the subweb script

E. No Answer is Correct

---

28. How do you apply permissions to a subweb in FrontPage 2000?

A. In FP Explorer you go to Tools/Security/Permissions and check "use unique permissions for this web."

B. In FP Editor you go to Tools/Security/Permissions and check "use unique permissions for this web."

C. In FP Explorer you go to Tools/Permissions and check "use unique permissions for this web."

D. In FP Editor you go to Tools/Permissions/Security and check "use unique permissions."

E. No Answer is Correct

27. How do you create a subweb in FrontPage 2000 Explorer?

A. create a folder, right click on it and mark it as a subweb

B. create a folder, double click on it and check the subweb checkbox

***C. create a folder, right click on it and then convert to web**

D. create a folder, and then convert to web by running the subweb script

E. No Answer is Correct

Explanation: Please refer to the web link for detailed explanation.

---

28. How do you apply permissions to a subweb in FrontPage 2000?

***A. In FP Explorer you go to Tools/Security/Permissions and check "use unique permissions for this web."**

B. In FP Editor you go to Tools/Security/Permissions and check "use unique permissions for this web."

C. In FP Explorer you go to Tools/Permissions and check "use unique permissions for this web."

D. In FP Editor you go to Tools/Permissions/Security and check "use unique permissions."

E. No Answer is Correct

Explanation: Please refer to the web link for detailed explanation.

29. What option allows for the restriction of browse access to a subweb in your FrontPage 2000 web?

A. "only registered administrator have browse access."

B. "only administrator have browse access."

C. "only unregistered users have browse access."

D. "only registered users have browse access."

E. No Answer is Correct

---

30. In FrontPage, what options are available for orphaned files (Choose all that apply)?

A. purged

B. stored

C. added to site

D. removed

E. No Answer is Correct

29. What option allows for the restriction of browse access to a subweb in your FrontPage 2000 web?

A. "only registered administrator have browse access."

B. "only administrator have browse access."

C. "only unregistered users have browse access."

***D. "only registered users have browse access."**

E. No Answer is Correct

Explanation: Please refer to the web link for detailed explanation.

---

30. In FrontPage, what options are available for orphaned files (Choose all that apply)?

***A. purged**

***B. stored**

***C. added to site**

D. removed

E. No Answer is Correct

Explanation: Please refer to the web link for detailed explanation.

31. You want to add a hit counter into your FrontPage web. How do you insert the counter?

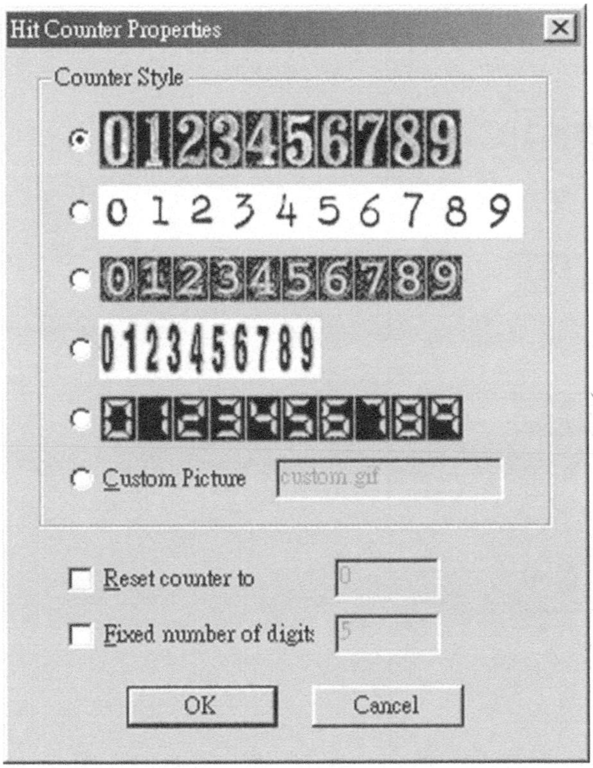

A. Insert - Component - Hit Counter

B. Insert - Hit Counter

C. Insert Component - Hit Counter

D. Insert - Component - Counter

E. No Answer is Correct

31. You want to add a hit counter into your FrontPage web. How do you insert the counter?

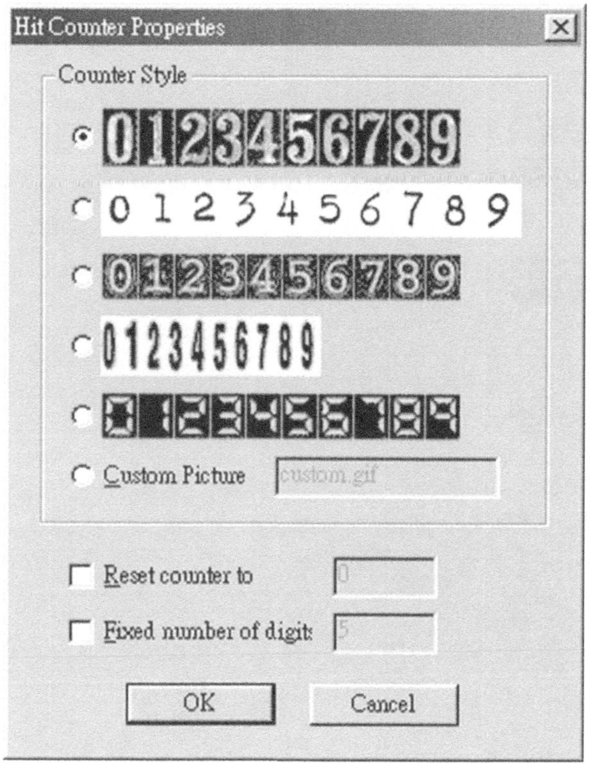

***A. Insert - Component - Hit Counter**

B. Insert - Hit Counter

C. Insert Component - Hit Counter

D. Insert - Component - Counter

E. No Answer is Correct

Explanation: You are encouraged to gain hands on experience with FrontPage 2000 before taking the exam. A trial version can be obtained from http://www.microsoft.com/frontpage/

32. You want to create a button in your FrontPage web that will change its color when the mouse cursor moves on top of it. What native FrontPage function can you use to create this button?

A. Java

B. JavaScript

C. Hover button

D. Animated GIF

E. No Answer is Correct

---

33. You want to tell the size of every file used in your FrontPage web. In which view can you do this?

A. Page

B. Folders

C. Reports

D. Navigation

E. Hyperlinks

32. You want to create a button in your FrontPage web that will change its color when the mouse cursor moves on top of it. What native FrontPage function can you use to create this button?

A. Java

B. JavaScript

***C. Hover button**

D. Animated GIF

E. No Answer is Correct

Explanation: You are encouraged to gain hands on experience with FrontPage 2000 before taking the exam. A trial version can be obtained from http://www.microsoft.com/frontpage/

---

33. You want to tell the size of every file used in your FrontPage web. In which view can you do this?

A. Page

***B. Folders**

C. Reports

D. Navigation

E. Hyperlinks

Explanation: The size of files are presented in KB unit. You are encouraged to gain hands on experience with FrontPage 2000 before taking the exam. A trial version can be obtained from http://www.microsoft.com/frontpage/

34. You want to create a button in your FrontPage web that will change its color when the mouse cursor moves on top of it. How do you access this native FrontPage function for creating the button?

A. Insert - Animation

B. File - Import - Component

C. Options - Enable Hover

D. Insert - Component

E. No Answer is Correct

---

35. In FrontPage, how do you create a horizontal moving line of "Hello How are you?" text with the least amount of coding?

Hello How are You?

A. Use a marquee

B. Use Java

C. Use JavaScript

D. Use DHTML

E. No Answer is Correct

34. You want to create a button in your FrontPage web that will change its color when the mouse cursor moves on top of it. How do you access this native FrontPage function for creating the button?

A. Insert - Animation

B. File - Import - Component

C. Options - Enable Hover

***D. Insert - Component**

E. No Answer is Correct

Explanation: You are encouraged to gain hands on experience with FrontPage 2000 before taking the exam. A trial version can be obtained from http://www.microsoft.com/frontpage/

---

35. In FrontPage, how do you create a horizontal moving line of "Hello How are you?" text with the least amount of coding?

Hello How are You?

***A. Use a marquee**

B. Use Java

C. Use JavaScript

D. Use DHTML

E. No Answer is Correct

Explanation: You are encouraged to gain hands on experience with FrontPage 2000 before taking the exam. A trial version can be obtained from http://www.microsoft.com/frontpage/

36. You want to able to deploy themes in FrontPage. How do you call up the Theme dialog window?

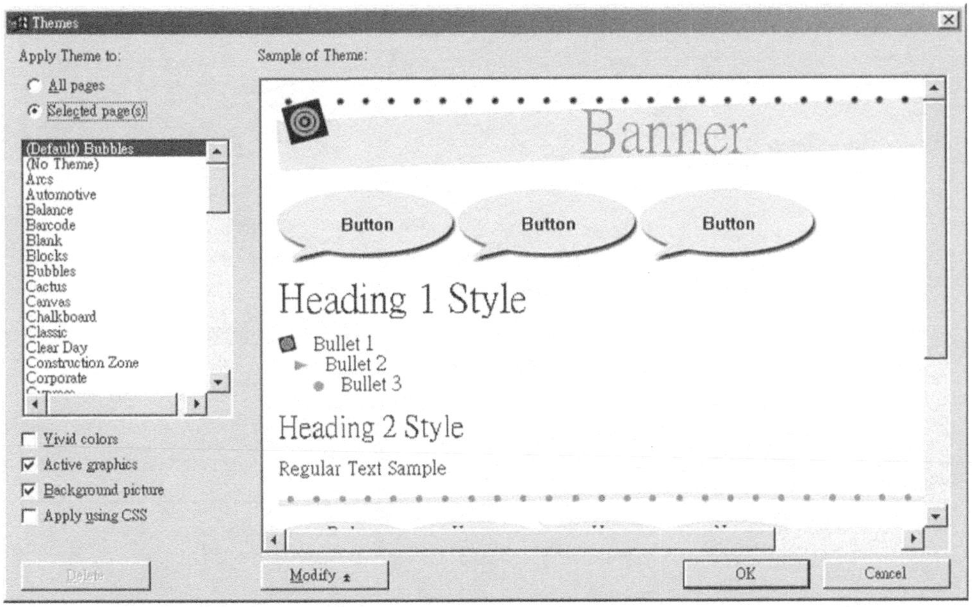

A. Right click on the document and choose Theme

B. Press Alt F

C. Press Ctrl + T

D. Right click on the window title bar and choose Theme

E. No Answer is Correct

36. You want to able to deploy themes in FrontPage. How do you call up the Theme dialog window?

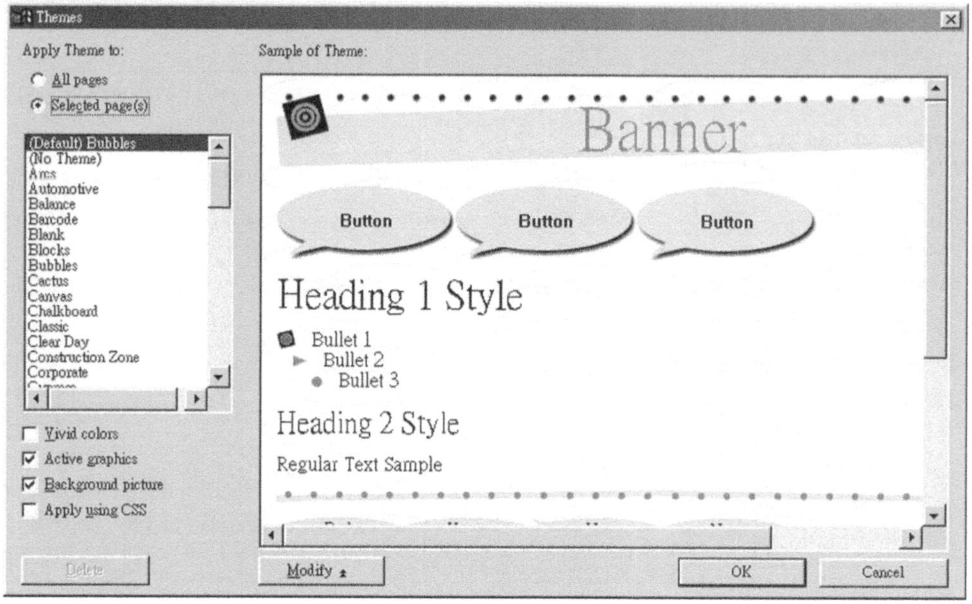

***A. Right click on the document and choose Theme**

B. Press Alt F

C. Press Ctrl + T

D. Right click on the window title bar and choose Theme

E. No Answer is Correct

Explanation: You are encouraged to gain hands on experience with FrontPage 2000 before taking the exam. A trial version can be obtained from http://www.microsoft.com/frontpage/

37. To check for problematic links in your FrontPage web, which view will you choose?

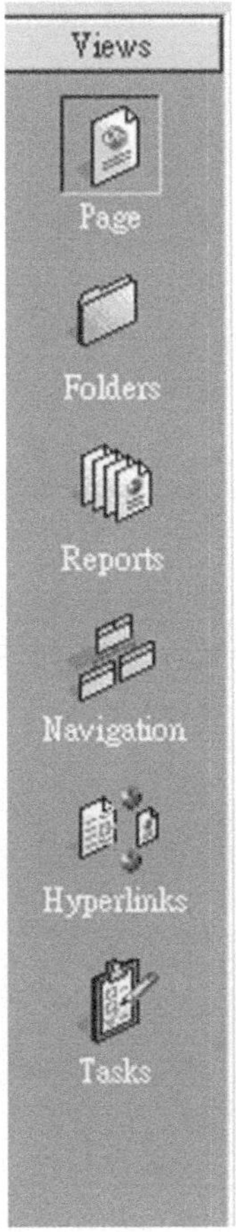

A. Page

B. Folders

C. Reports

D. Navigation

E. Hyperlinks

37. To check for problematic links in your FrontPage web, which view will you choose?

A. Page

B. Folders

C. Reports

D. Navigation

***E. Hyperlinks**

Explanation: You are encouraged to gain hands on experience with FrontPage 2000 before taking the exam. A trial version can be obtained from http://www.microsoft.com/frontpage/

38. You want to have a bird eye view of the current layout of your FrontPage web structure. Which view will you choose?

A. Page

B. Folders

C. Reports

D. Navigation

E. Hyperlinks

38. You want to have a bird eye view of the current layout of your FrontPage web structure. Which view will you choose?

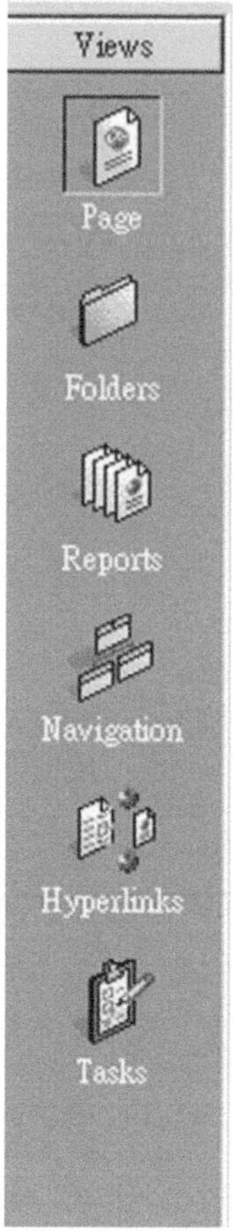

A. Page

B. Folders

C. Reports

***D. Navigation**

E. Hyperlinks

Explanation: You are encouraged to gain hands on experience with FrontPage 2000 before taking the exam. A trial version can be obtained from http://www.microsoft.com/frontpage/

39. You want to be sure that New Page 1 is included in the navigation bar structure of your FrontPage web. How do you do this?

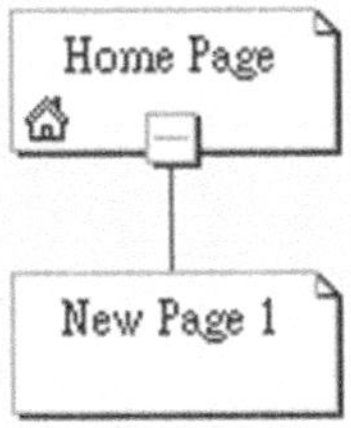

A. In the Navigation view, right click on New Page 1 and choose "Included in Navigation Bars"

B. In the Page view, right click on New Page 1 and choose "Included in Navigation Bars"

C. In the Hyperlink view, right click on New Page 1 and choose "Included in Navigation Bars"

D. Both B and C

E. No Answer is Correct

39. You want to be sure that New Page 1 is included in the navigation bar structure of your FrontPage web. How do you do this?

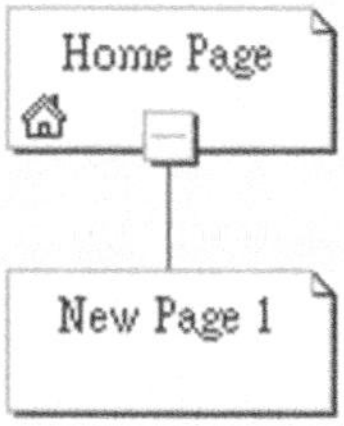

***A. In the Navigation view, right click on New Page 1 and choose "Included in Navigation Bars"**

B. In the Page view, right click on New Page 1 and choose "Included in Navigation Bars"

C. In the Hyperlink view, right click on New Page 1 and choose "Included in Navigation Bars"

D. Both B and C

E. No Answer is Correct

Explanation: You are encouraged to gain hands on experience with FrontPage 2000 before taking the exam. A trial version can be obtained from http://www.microsoft.com/frontpage/

40. In FrontPage, how do you create a new page which has Home Page as its parent and has New Page 1 as the same level neighboring page?

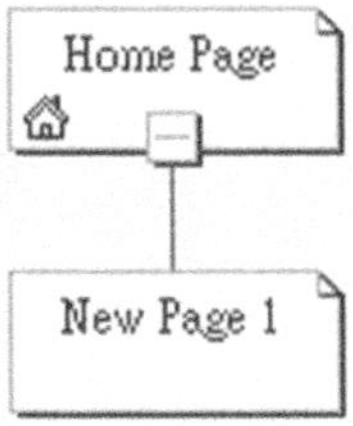

A. In the Navigation view, right click on New Page 1 and choose "New page"

B. In the Navigation view, right click on Home Page and choose "New page"

C. In the Folder view, right click on New Page 1 and choose "New page"

D. In the Folder view, right click on Home Page and choose "New page"

E. No Answer is Correct

40. In FrontPage, how do you create a new page which has Home Page as its parent and has New Page 1 as the same level neighboring page?

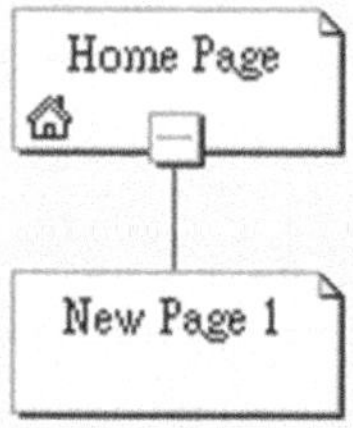

A. In the Navigation view, right click on New Page 1 and choose "New page"

***B. In the Navigation view, right click on Home Page and choose "New page"**

C. In the Folder view, right click on New Page 1 and choose "New page"

D. In the Folder view, right click on Home Page and choose "New page"

E. No Answer is Correct

Explanation: You are encouraged to gain hands on experience with FrontPage 2000 before taking the exam. A trial version can be obtained from http://www.microsoft.com/frontpage/

41. You want to create a new FrontPage web on a server with an IP address of 61.18.131.179 that has the server extension kit installed. Which command will you use?

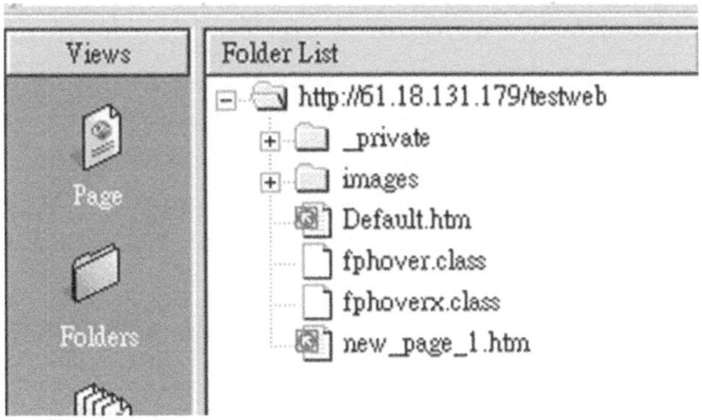

A. File - New - Page

B. File - New - Site

C. File - New - Web

D. File - New - FrontPage Web

E. No Answer is Correct

41. You want to create a new FrontPage web on a server with an IP address of 61.18.131.179 that has the server extension kit installed. Which command will you use?

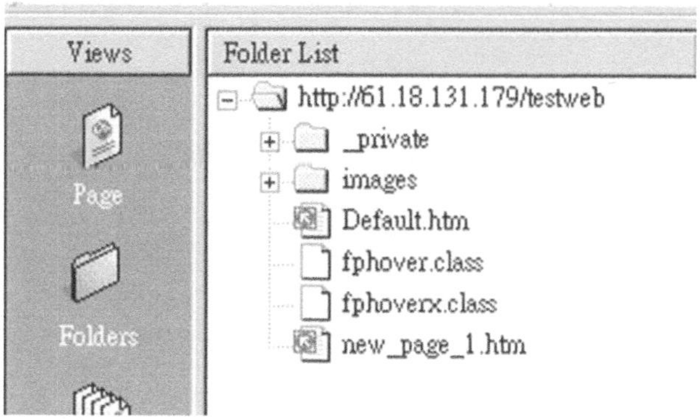

A. File - New - Page

B. File - New - Site

***C. File - New - Web**

D. File - New - FrontPage Web

E. No Answer is Correct

Explanation: You are encouraged to gain hands on experience with FrontPage 2000 before taking the exam. A trial version can be obtained from http://www.microsoft.com/frontpage/

42. You want to create a new FrontPage web on a server with an IP address of 61.18.131.179 that has the server extension kit installed. You want this web to be the ROOT web. Which command will you use?

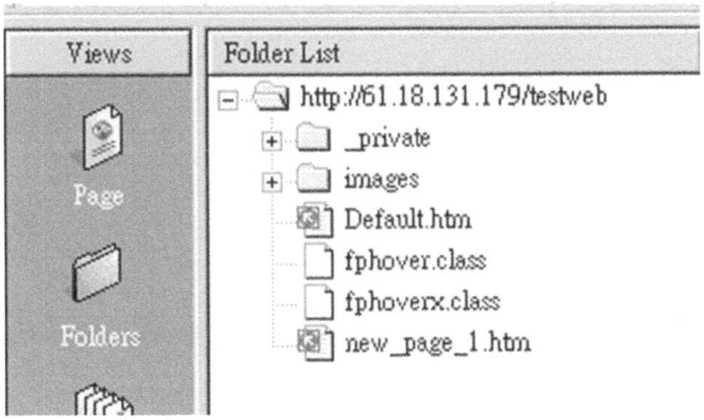

A. File - New - Page

B. File - New - Root Web

C. File - New - Web

D. File - New - FrontPage Web

E. This is not possible.

42. You want to create a new FrontPage web on a server with an IP address of 61.18.131.179 that has the server extension kit installed. You want this web to be the ROOT web. Which command will you use?

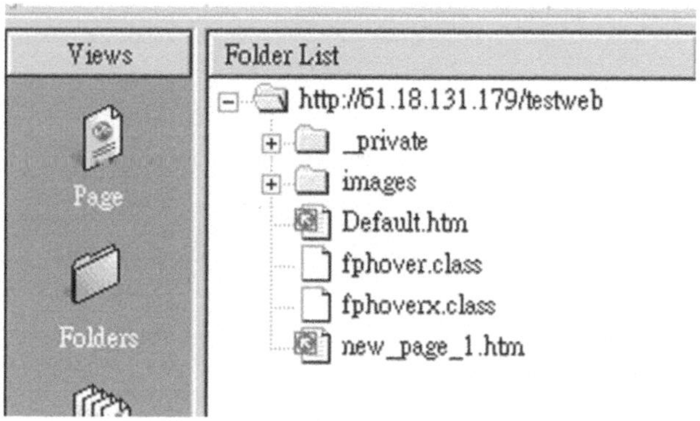

A. File - New - Page

B. File - New - Root Web

C. File - New - Web

D. File - New - FrontPage Web

***E. This is not possible.**

Explanation: A FrontPage web can only be a subweb, not a ROOT web. You are encouraged to gain hands on experience with FrontPage 2000 before taking the exam. A trial version can be obtained from http://www.microsoft.com/frontpage/

43. You suspect that some of the hyperlinks in your FrontPage web are damaged. How do you check for and repair the damaged links?

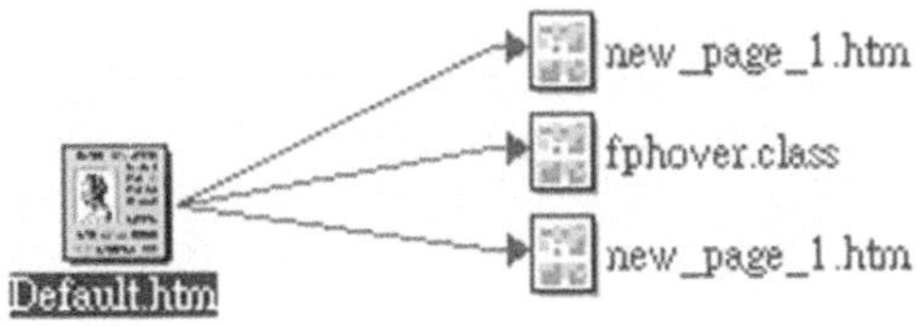

A. Hit F10

B. Hit F11

C. Press Ctrl + G

D. Tools - Recalculate Hyperlinks

E. File - Recalculate Hyperlinks

43. You suspect that some of the hyperlinks in your FrontPage web are damaged. How do you check for and repair the damaged links?

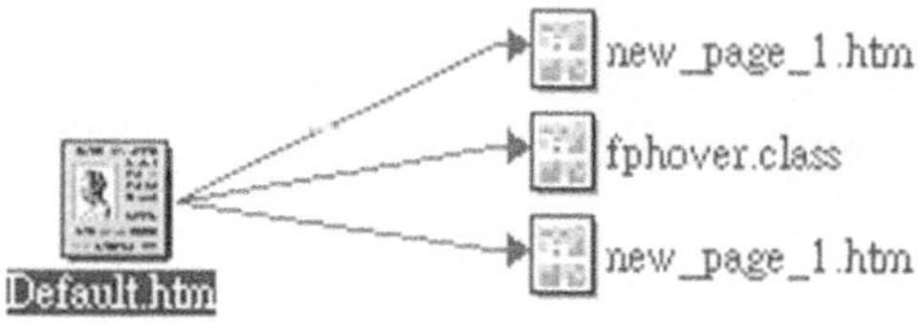

A. Hit F10

B. Hit F11

C. Press Ctrl + G

***D. Tools - Recalculate Hyperlinks**

E. File - Recalculate Hyperlinks

Explanation: You are encouraged to gain hands on experience with FrontPage 2000 before taking the exam. A trial version can be obtained from http://www.microsoft.com/frontpage/

44. In FrontPage, how do you create the fphover.class file as shown in the exhibit?

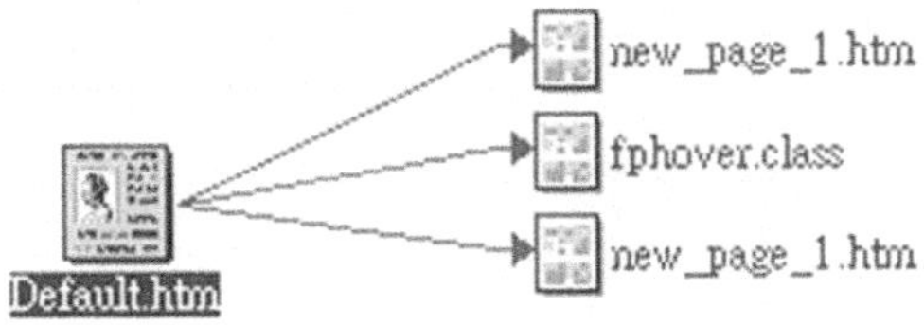

A. File - New - Page

B. File - New - Class

C. Insert - Hover Class

D. Insert - Component - Hover Button

E. No Answer is Correct

44. In FrontPage, how do you create the fphover.class file as shown in the exhibit?

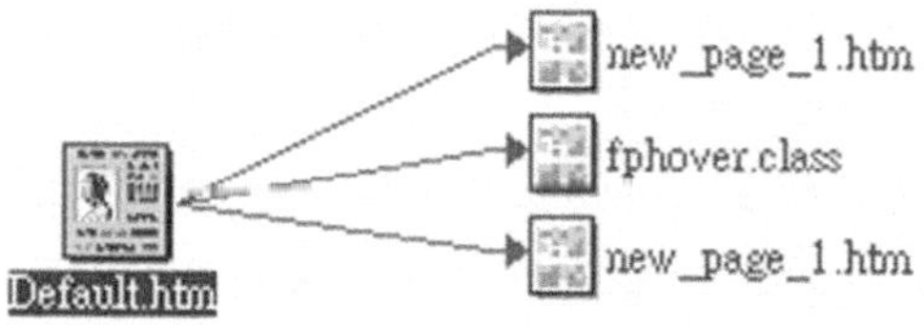

A. File - New - Page

B. File - New - Class

C. Insert - Hover Class

***D. Insert - Component - Hover Button**

E. No Answer is Correct

Explanation: You are encouraged to gain hands on experience with FrontPage 2000 before taking the exam. A trial version can be obtained from http://www.microsoft.com/frontpage/

45. You want to display the site summary window as shown in the exhibit.

Site Summary

Name	Count	Size	Description
All files	4	15KB	All files in the current Web
Pictures	0	0KB	Picture files in the current Web (GIF, JPG, BMP, etc.)
Unlinked files	1	1KB	Files in the current Web that cannot be reached by starting from your home page
Linked files	3	14KB	Files in the current Web that can be reached by starting from your home page
Slow pages	0	0KB	Pages in the current Web exceeding an estimated download time of 30 seconds at 28.8
Older files	0	0KB	Files in the current Web that have not been modified in over 72 days
Recently added files	4	15KB	Files in the current Web that have been created in the last 30 days
Hyperlinks	8		All hyperlinks in the current Web
Unverified hyperli...	0		Hyperlinks pointing to unconfirmed target files
Broken hyperlinks	0		Hyperlinks pointing to unavailable target files
External hyperlinks	0		Hyperlinks pointing to files outside of the current Web
Internal hyperlinks	8		Hyperlinks pointing to other files within the current Web
Component errors	0		Files in the current Web with components reporting an error
Uncompleted tasks	0		Tasks in the current Web that are not yet marked completed
Unused themes	0		Themes in the current Web that are not applied to any file

How do you access this window?

A. Go to File - Site Summary

B. Go to View - Site Summary

C. Go to Window - Site Summary

D. Select the Folder view

E. Select the Report view

45. You want to display the site summary window as shown in the exhibit.

Site Summary

Name	Count	Size	Description
All files	4	15KB	All files in the current Web
Pictures	0	0KB	Picture files in the current Web (GIF, JPG, BMP, etc.)
Unlinked files	1	1KB	Files in the current Web that cannot be reached by starting from your home page
Linked files	3	14KB	Files in the current Web that can be reached by starting from your home page
Slow pages	0	0KB	Pages in the current Web exceeding an estimated download time of 30 seconds at 28.8
Older files	0	0KB	Files in the current Web that have not been modified in over 72 days
Recently added files	4	15KB	Files in the current Web that have been created in the last 30 days
Hyperlinks	8		All hyperlinks in the current Web
Unverified hyperli...	0		Hyperlinks pointing to unconfirmed target files
Broken hyperlinks	0		Hyperlinks pointing to unavailable target files
External hyperlinks	0		Hyperlinks pointing to files outside of the current Web
Internal hyperlinks	8		Hyperlinks pointing to other files within the current Web
Component errors	0		Files in the current Web with components reporting an error
Uncompleted tasks	0		Tasks in the current Web that are not yet marked completed
Unused themes	0		Themes in the current Web that are not applied to any file

How do you access this window?

A. Go to File - Site Summary

B. Go to View - Site Summary

C. Go to Window - Site Summary

D. Select the Folder view

***E. Select the Report view**

Explanation: You are encouraged to gain hands on experience with FrontPage 2000 before taking the exam. A trial version can be obtained from http://www.microsoft.com/frontpage/

46. Which FrontPage view allows for the sharing of workload and responsibilities between the development team members?

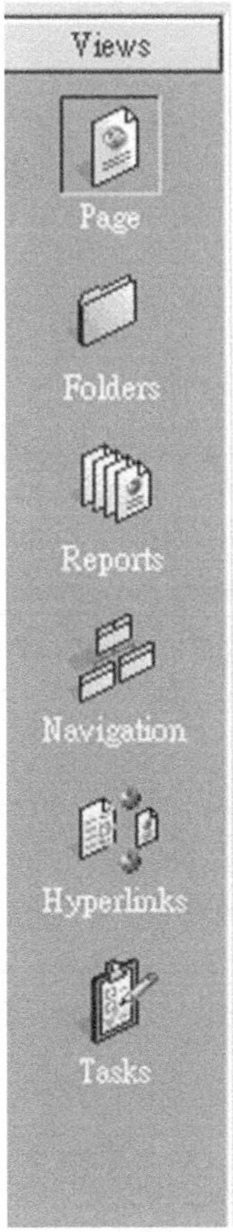

A. Page

B. Folders

C. Reports

D. Tasks

E. Hyperlinks

46. Which FrontPage view allows for the sharing of workload and responsibilities between the development team members?

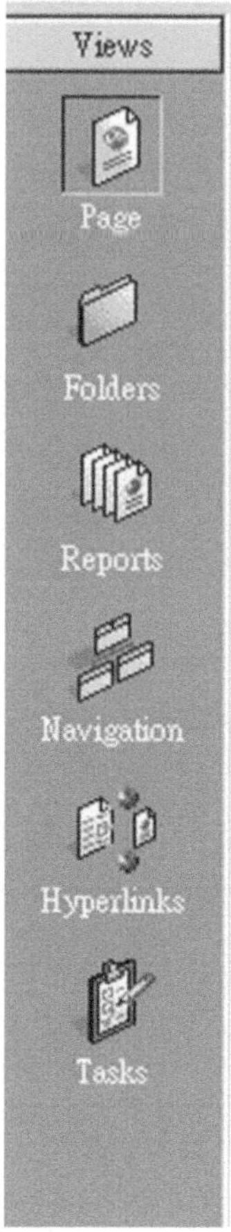

A. Page

B. Folders

C. Reports

***D. Tasks**

E. Hyperlinks

Explanation: You can actually assign tasks of different priorities to different team members. You are encouraged to gain hands on experience with FrontPage 2000 before taking the exam. A trial version can be obtained from http://www.microsoft.com/frontpage/

47. You are using Dreamweaver to develop your web site.

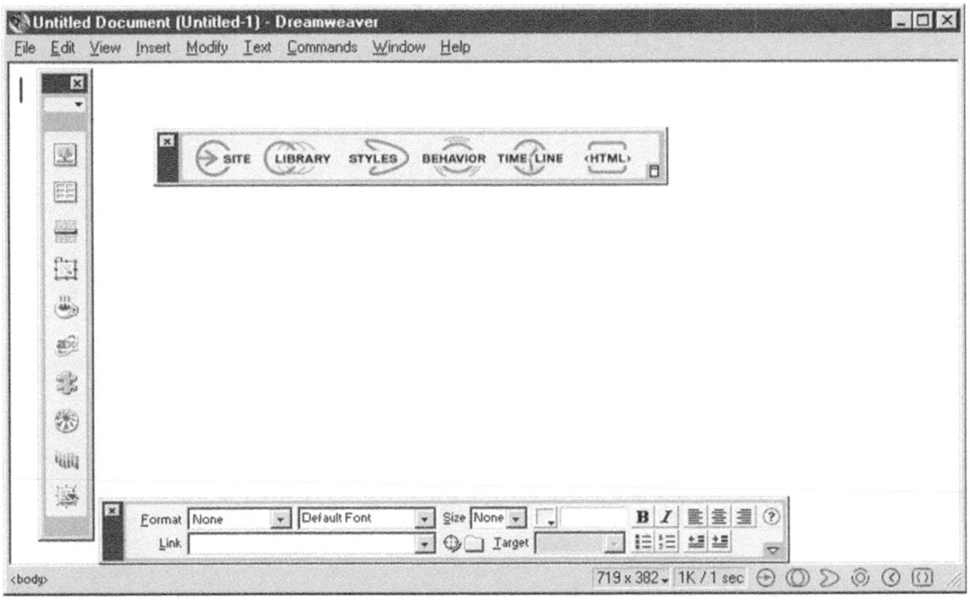

To check the property of an object, which window in the Dreamweaver environment will you use?

A. Document window

B. Property Palette

C. Property Inspector

D. Property Launcher

E. No Answer is Correct

47. You are using Dreamweaver to develop your web site.

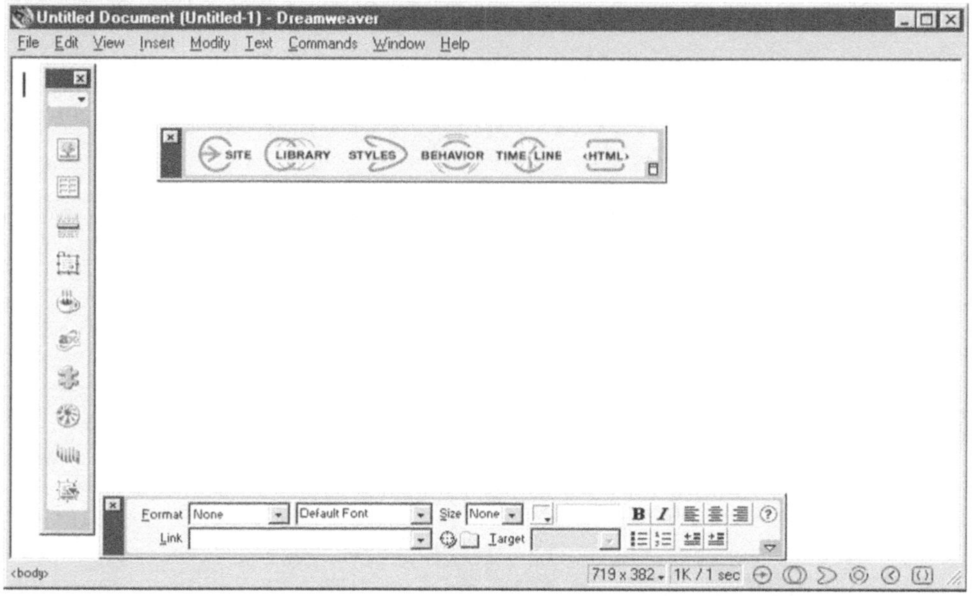

To check the property of an object, which window in the Dreamweaver environment will you use?

A. Document window

B. Property Palette

***C. Property Inspector**

D. Property Launcher

E. No Answer is Correct

Explanation: Choice B and D do not exist. You are encouraged to actually gain hands on experience using Dreamweaver before taking the test. A copy of the Dreamweaver trial version can be downloaded at http://www.macromedia.com/software/dreamweaver/

48. You are using Dreamweaver to develop your web site.

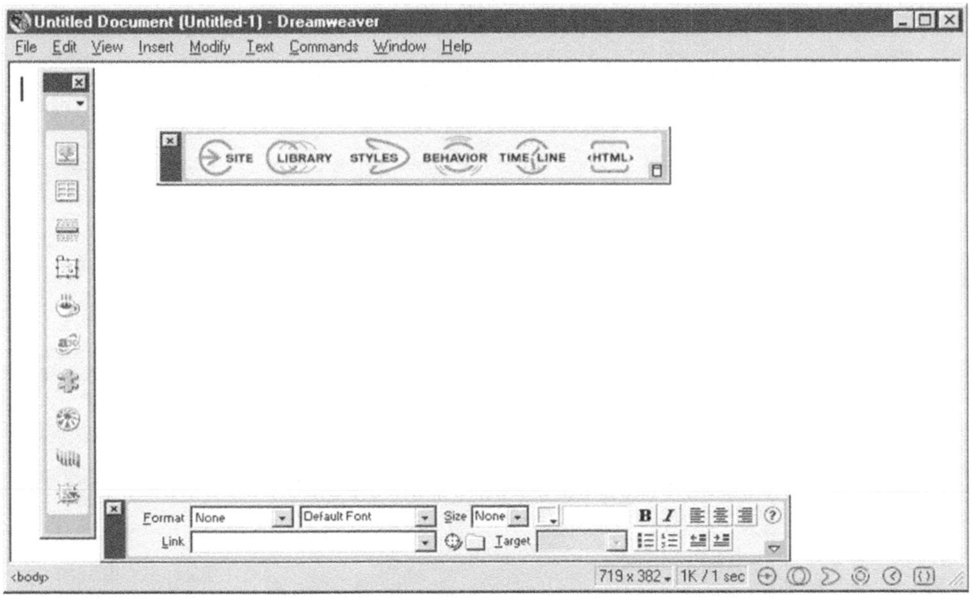

To insert an object onto the document, which window in the Dreamweaver environment will you use?

A. Document window

B. Object Palette

C. Property Inspector

D. App Launcher

E. No Answer is Correct

48. You are using Dreamweaver to develop your web site.

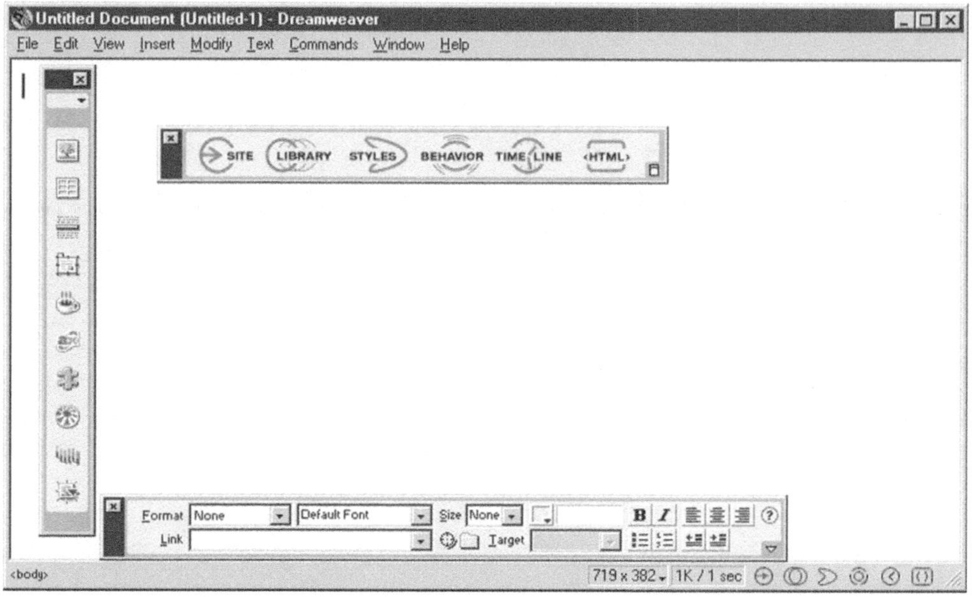

To insert an object onto the document, which window in the Dreamweaver environment will you use?

A. Document window

***B. Object Palette**

C. Property Inspector

D. App Launcher

E. No Answer is Correct

Explanation: You are encouraged to actually gain hands on experience using Dreamweaver before taking the test. A copy of the Dreamweaver trial version can be downloaded at http://www.macromedia.com/software/dreamweaver/

49. You are using Dreamweaver to develop your web site.

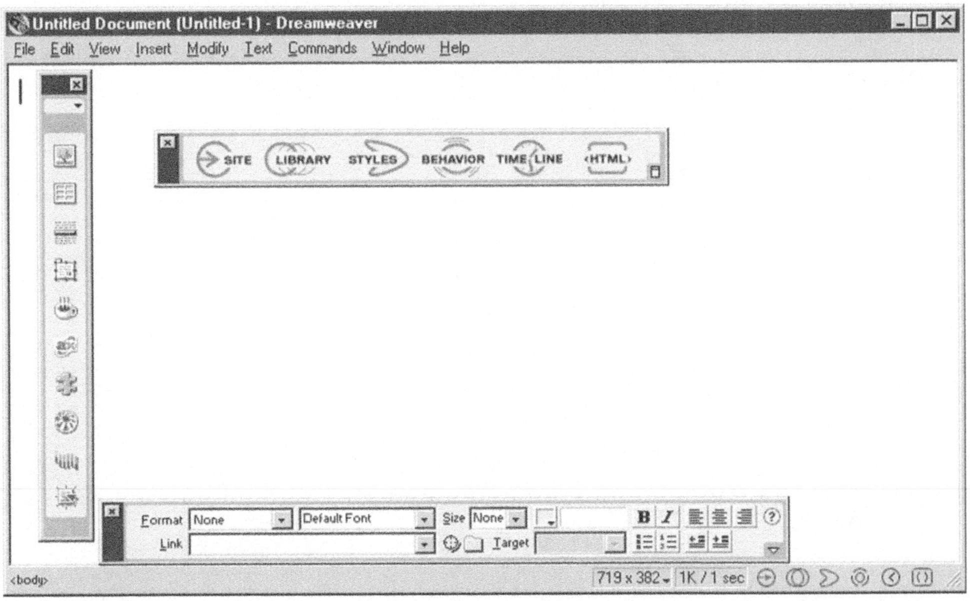

To define a time line for an event, which window in the Dreamweaver environment will you use?

A. Document window

B. Object Palette

C. Property Inspector

D. Launcher

E. No Answer is Correct

49. You are using Dreamweaver to develop your web site.

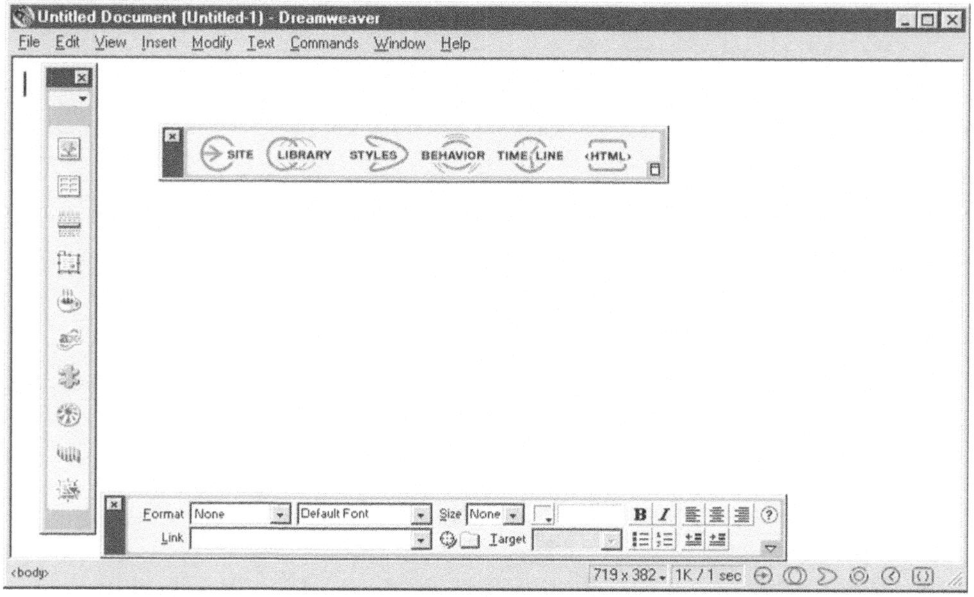

To define a time line for an event, which window in the Dreamweaver environment will you use?

A. Document window

B. Object Palette

C. Property Inspector

D. Launcher

***E. No Answer is Correct**

Explanation: Timeline is essential in designing behaviors and object movements. You are encouraged to actually gain hands on experience using Dreamweaver before taking the test. A copy of the Dreamweaver trial version can be downloaded at http://www.macromedia.com/software/dreamweaver/

50. How do you call up Netscape browser for preview from within Dreamweaver?

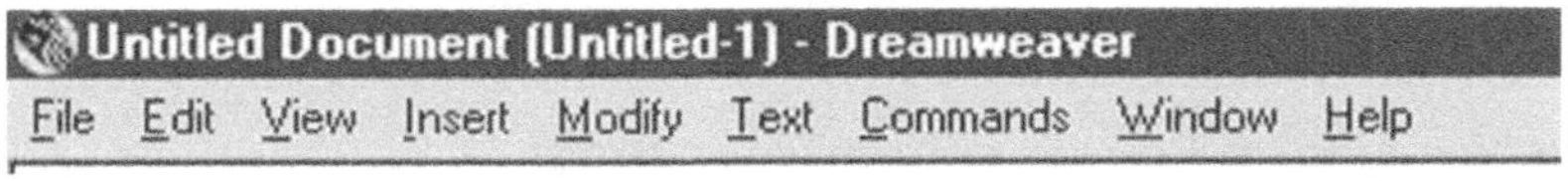

A. From the File Menu choose Preview in Browser - Netscape.

B. From the File Menu choose Preview - Netscape.

C. From the File Menu choose Browser Preview - Netscape.

D. From the File Menu choose Preview - Netscape - Onscreen.

E. No Answer is Correct

---

51. In Dreamweaver, how do you change the color of your text?

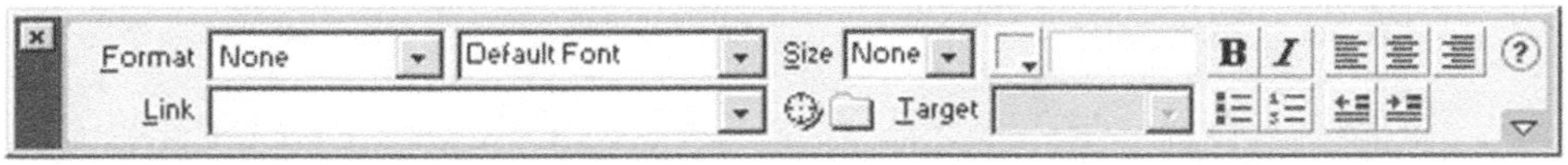

A. Select the text, then click the gray square to the right of the Size popup menu in the Property Inspector

B. Select the text, then click the gray square to the right of the Text popup menu in the Property Navigator

C. Select the text, then click the gray square to the right of the Text popup menu in the Object Inspector

D. Select the text, then click the gray square to the right of the Font popup menu in the Property Palette

E. No Answer is Correct

50. How do you call up Netscape browser for preview from within Dreamweaver?

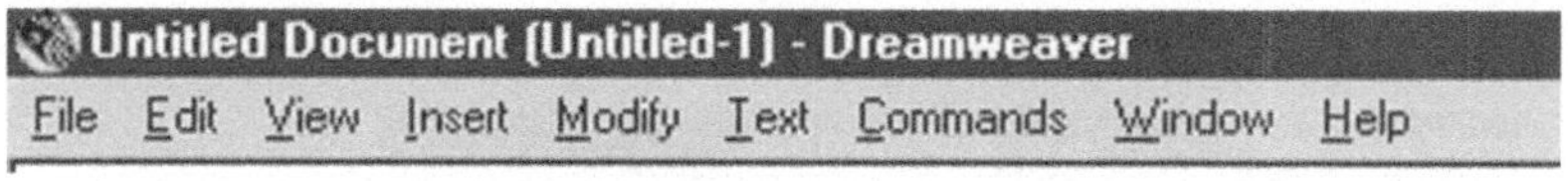

***A. From the File Menu choose Preview in Browser - Netscape.**

B. From the File Menu choose Preview - Netscape.

C. From the File Menu choose Browser Preview - Netscape.

D. From the File Menu choose Preview - Netscape - Onscreen.

E. No Answer is Correct

Explanation: You are encouraged to actually gain hands on experience using Dreamweaver before taking the test. A copy of the Dreamweaver trial version can be downloaded at http://www.macromedia.com/software/dreamweaver/

---

51. In Dreamweaver, how do you change the color of your text?

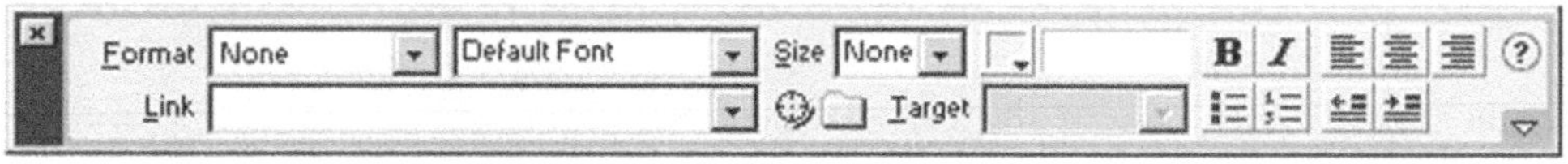

***A. Select the text, then click the gray square to the right of the Size popup menu in the Property Inspector**

B. Select the text, then click the gray square to the right of the Text popup menu in the Property Navigator

C. Select the text, then click the gray square to the right of the Text popup menu in the Object Inspector

D. Select the text, then click the gray square to the right of the Font popup menu in the Property Palette

E. No Answer is Correct

Explanation: Choice B, C and D do not exist. You are encouraged to actually gain hands on experience using Dreamweaver before taking the test. A copy of the Dreamweaver trial version can be downloaded at http://www.macromedia.com/software/dreamweaver/

52. In Dreamweaver, which window do you use to change the appearance of your text?

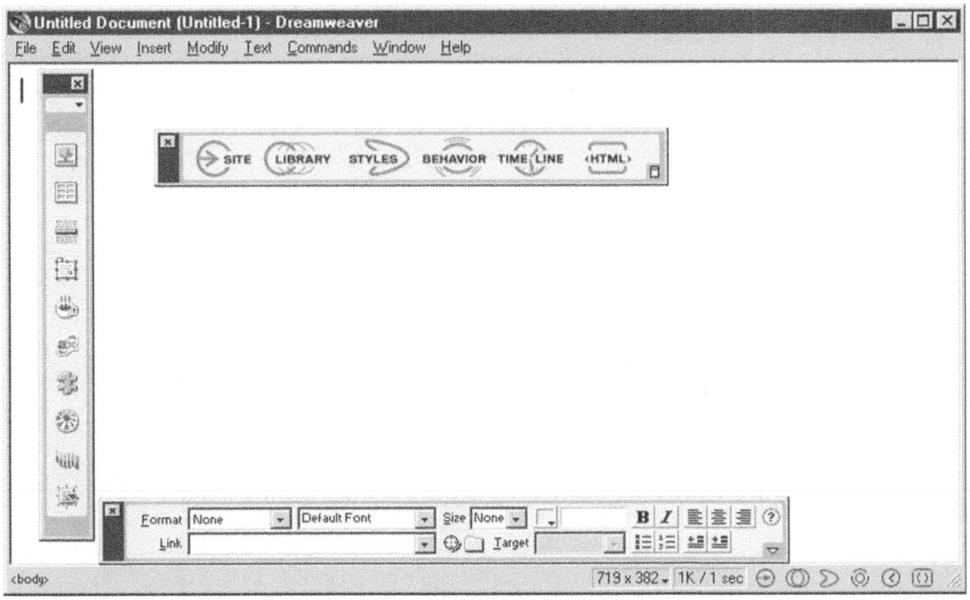

A. Document window

B. Object Palette

C. Property Inspector

D. App Launcher

E. No Answer is Correct

52. In Dreamweaver, which window do you use to change the appearance of your text?

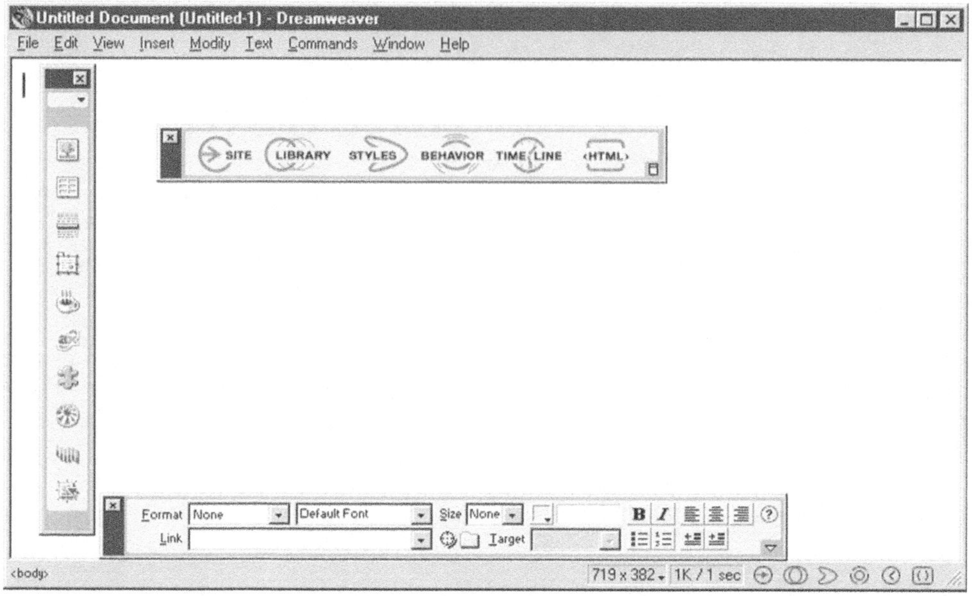

A. Document window

B. Object Palette

***C. Property Inspector**

D. App Launcher

E. No Answer is Correct

Explanation: You are encouraged to actually gain hands on experience using Dreamweaver before taking the test. A copy of the Dreamweaver trial version can be downloaded at http://www.macromedia.com/software/dreamweaver/

53. How do you request Dreamweaver to perform spell checking for your document?

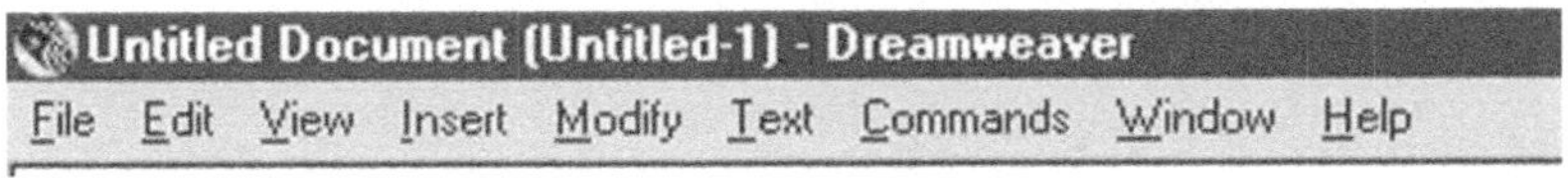

A. From the Text menu choose Check Spelling.

B. From the File menu choose Check Spelling.

C. From the Edit menu choose Check Spelling.

D. From the Commands menu choose Check Spelling.

E. No Answer is Correct

---

54. What menu command or equivalent short cut keys in Dreamweaver allows you to request Netscape to reload your page for preview?

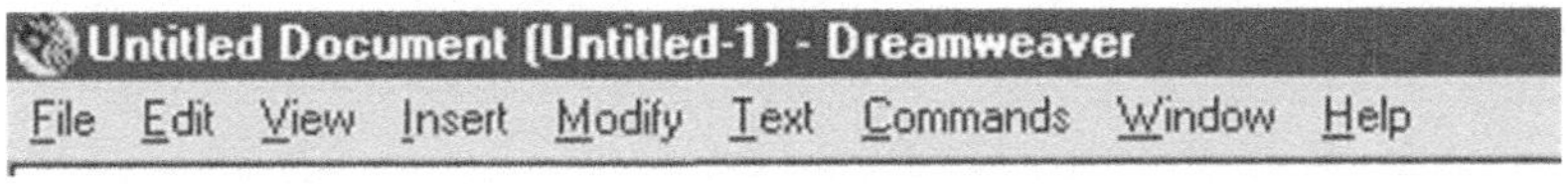

A. View - Browser - Reload

B. View - Browser - Refresh

C. F9

D. F12

E. Alt+P

53. How do you request Dreamweaver to perform spell checking for your document?

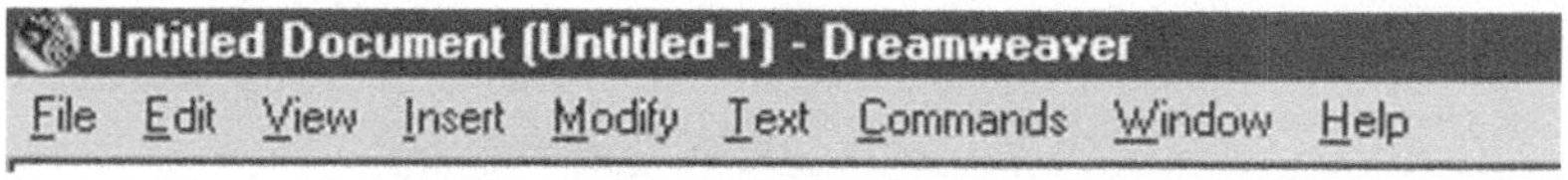

***A. From the Text menu choose Check Spelling.**

B. From the File menu choose Check Spelling.

C. From the Edit menu choose Check Spelling.

D. From the Commands menu choose Check Spelling.

E. No Answer is Correct

Explanation: You are encouraged to actually gain hands on experience using Dreamweaver before taking the test. A copy of the Dreamweaver trial version can be downloaded at http://www.macromedia.com/software/dreamweaver/

---

54. What menu command or equivalent short cut keys in Dreamweaver allows you to request Netscape to reload your page for preview?

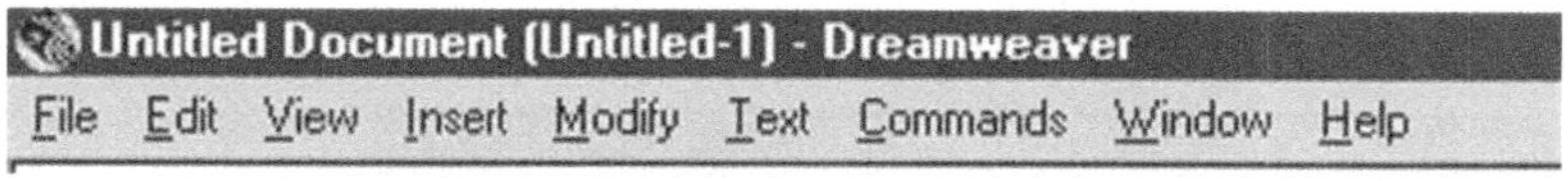

A. View - Browser - Reload

B. View - Browser - Refresh

C. F9

***D. F12**

E. Alt+P

Explanation: You are encouraged to actually gain hands on experience using Dreamweaver before taking the test. A copy of the Dreamweaver trial version can be downloaded at http://www.macromedia.com/software/dreamweaver/

55. How do you create an unordered list with Dreamweaver?

A. Click the Unordered List button in the Property Inspector window.

B. Click the Unordered List button in the Object Palette window.

C. Click the Unordered List button in the Property Palette window.

D. Click the Unordered List button in the Launcher window.

E. No Answer is Correct

---

56. You want to call your HTML window within Dreamweaver without the presence of the Launcher window. What alternative can you use?

A. File - Commands - View HTML

B. File - View HTML

C. Edit - View HTML

D. Mini Launcher

E. No Answer is Correct

55. How do you create an unordered list with Dreamweaver?

***A. Click the Unordered List button in the Property Inspector window.**

B. Click the Unordered List button in the Object Palette window.

C. Click the Unordered List button in the Property Palette window.

D. Click the Unordered List button in the Launcher window.

E. No Answer is Correct

Explanation: You are encouraged to actually gain hands on experience using Dreamweaver before taking the test. A copy of the Dreamweaver trial version can be downloaded at http://www.macromedia.com/software/dreamweaver/

---

56. You want to call your HTML window within Dreamweaver without the presence of the Launcher window. What alternative can you use?

A. File - Commands - View HTML

B. File - View HTML

C. Edit - View HTML

***D. Mini Launcher**

E. No Answer is Correct

Explanation: The mini launcher is in the lower right corner of your document window. You are encouraged to actually gain hands on experience using Dreamweaver before taking the test. A copy of the Dreamweaver trial version can be downloaded at http://www.macromedia.com/software/dreamweaver/

57. In Dreamweaver, how do you invoke the Insert Table dialog box?

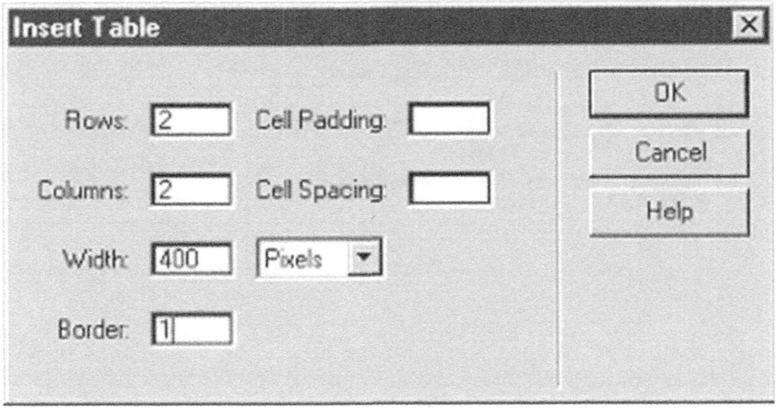

A. Choose Insert - Table

B. Choose Modify - Insert Table

C. Choose Edit - Insert Table

D. Choose Table - Insert

E. No Answer is Correct

57. In Dreamweaver, how do you invoke the Insert Table dialog box?

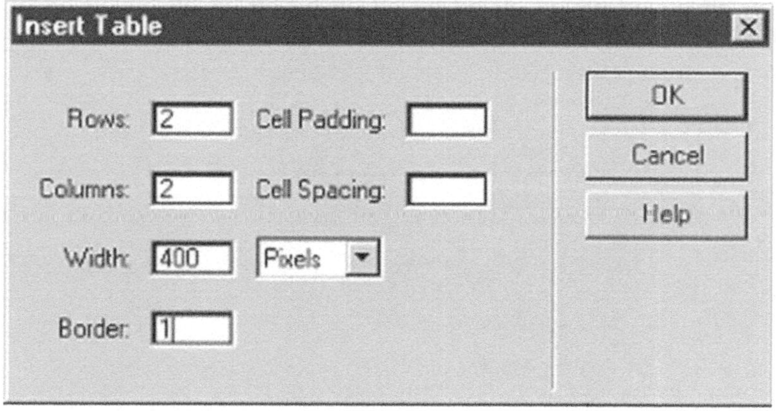

***A. Choose Insert - Table**

B. Choose Modify - Insert Table

C. Choose Edit - Insert Table

D. Choose Table - Insert

E. No Answer is Correct

Explanation: You are encouraged to actually gain hands on experience using Dreamweaver before taking the test. A copy of the Dreamweaver trial version can be downloaded at http://www.macromedia.com/software/dreamweaver/

58. In Dreamweaver, you found that the Object Palette is not visible. How do you enable it again?

A. Choose View - Objects

B. Choose Window - Objects

C. Choose View - Object Window

D. Press F12

E. No Answer is Correct

58. In Dreamweaver, you found that the Object Palette is not visible. How do you enable it again?

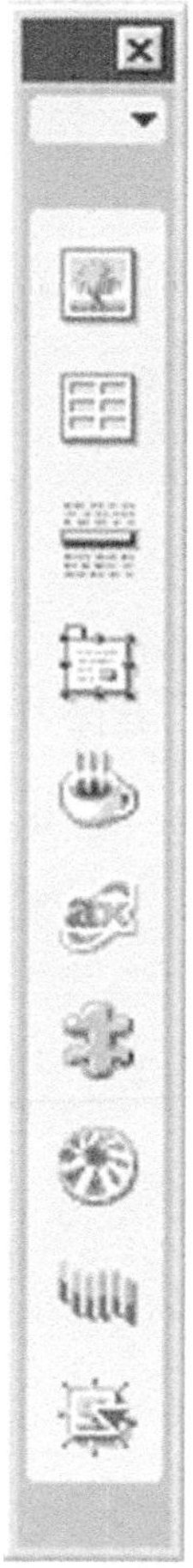

A. Choose View - Objects

***B. Choose Window - Objects**

C. Choose View - Object Window

D. Press F12

E. No Answer is Correct

Explanation: You are encouraged to actually gain hands on experience using Dreamweaver before taking the test. A copy of the Dreamweaver trial version can be downloaded at http://www.macromedia.com/software/dreamweaver/

59. You need to adjust the page color of your HTML document. In Dreamweaver, how do you call up the Page Properties window?

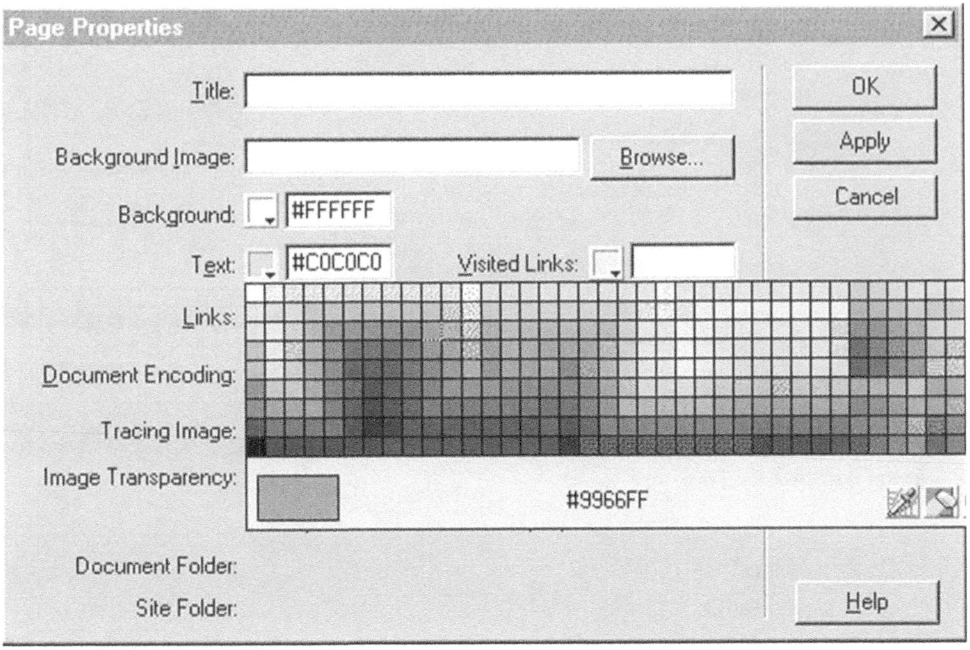

A. Choose Modify - Page Properties

B. Choose Format - Page Properties

C. Choose Edit - Page Properties

D. Choose Window - Page Properties

E. No Answer is Correct

59. You need to adjust the page color of your HTML document. In Dreamweaver, how do you call up the Page Properties window?

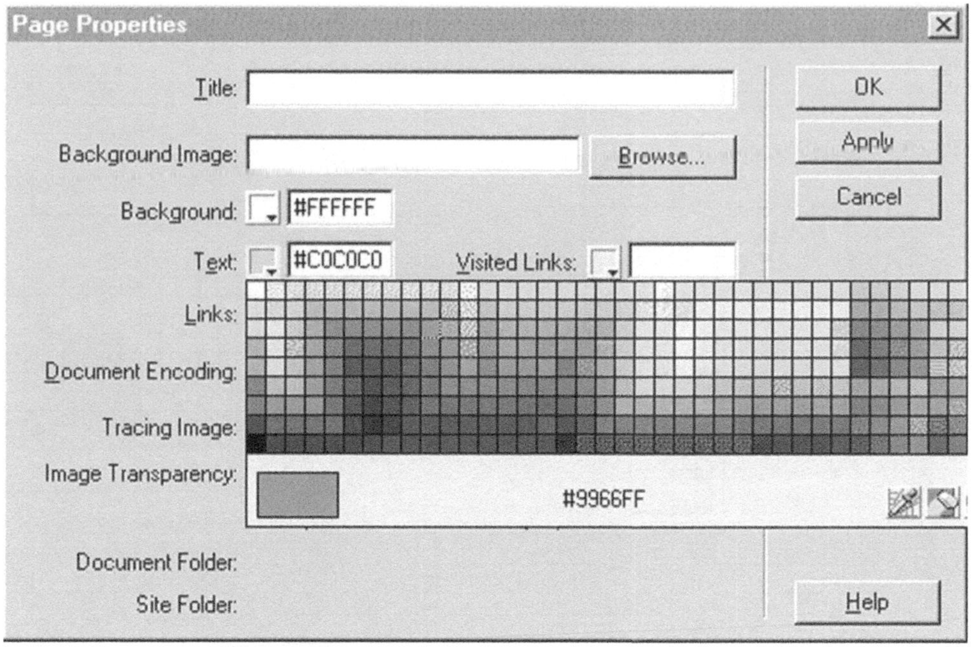

***A. Choose Modify - Page Properties**

B. Choose Format - Page Properties

C. Choose Edit - Page Properties

D. Choose Window - Page Properties

E. No Answer is Correct

Explanation: You are encouraged to actually gain hands on experience using Dreamweaver before taking the test. A copy of the Dreamweaver trial version can be downloaded at http://www.macromedia.com/software/dreamweaver/

60. In Dreamweaver, you want to create a file link. Which window will you refer to?

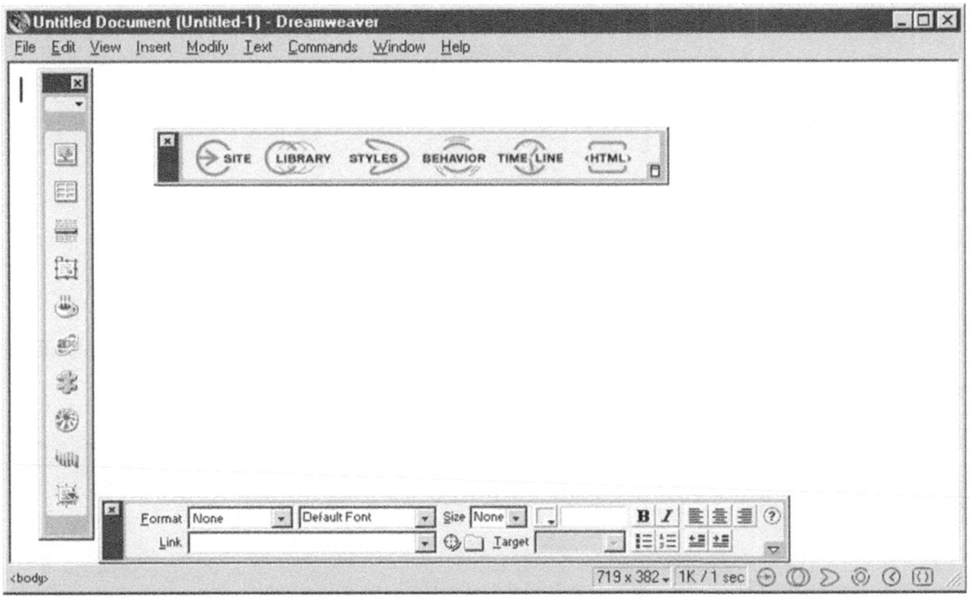

A. Document window

B. Object Palette

C. Property Inspector

D. App Launcher

E. No Answer is Correct

60. In Dreamweaver, you want to create a file link. Which window will you refer to?

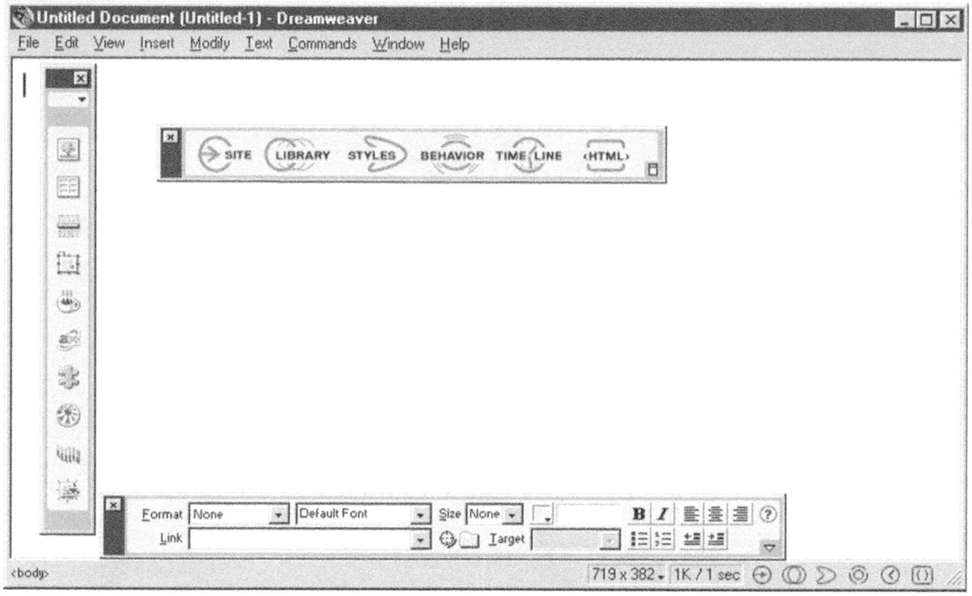

A. Document window

B. Object Palette

***C. Property Inspector**

D. App Launcher

E. No Answer is Correct

Explanation: You may go to the Property Inspector and click on the Browse for File icon. You are encouraged to actually gain hands on experience using Dreamweaver before taking the test. A copy of the Dreamweaver trial version can be downloaded at http://www.macromedia.com/software/dreamweaver/

61. You want to create an email link so that your visitors can click on it and send you mail instantly. From which window / dialog / field in Dreamweaver can you enable this?

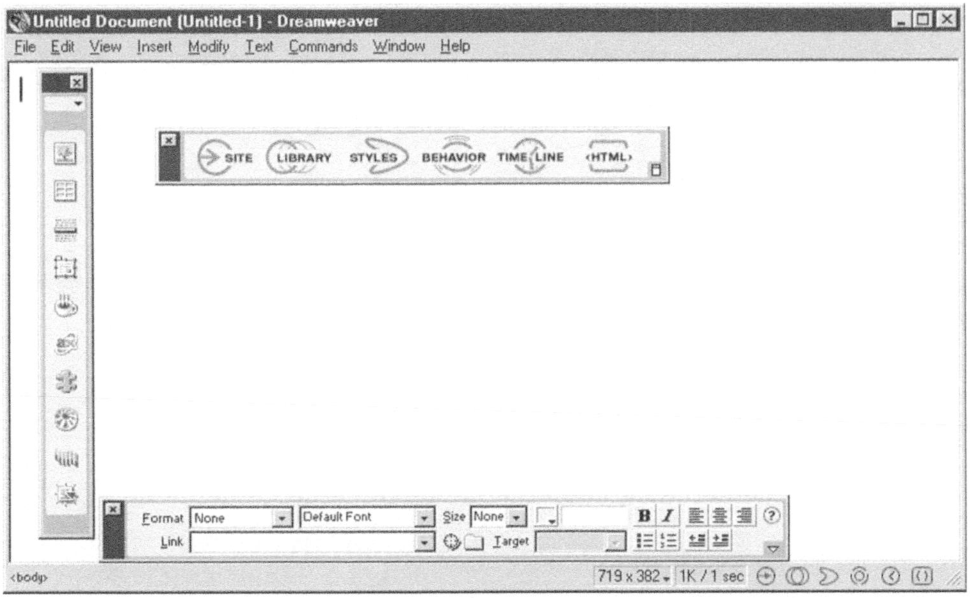

A. In the Property Inspector's Link field, type in the mailto:clause

B. In the Object Inspector's Link field, type in the mailto:clause

C. In the Object Palette's Email field, type in the mailto:clause

D. In the Property Inspector's SMTP field, type in the mailto:clause

E. No Answer is Correct

61. You want to create an email link so that your visitors can click on it and send you mail instantly. From which window / dialog / field in Dreamweaver can you enable this?

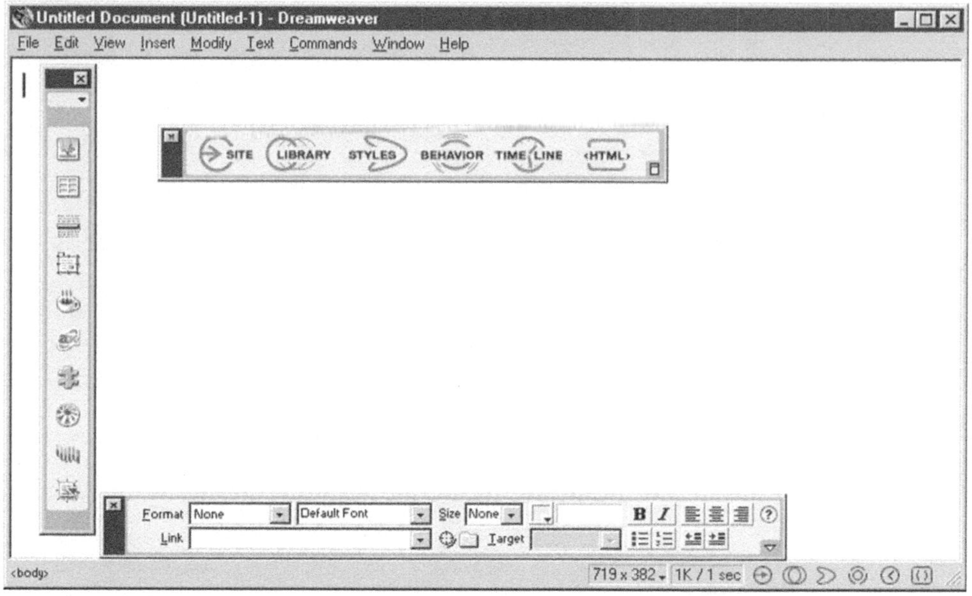

***A. In the Property Inspector's Link field, type in the mailto:clause**

B. In the Object Inspector's Link field, type in the mailto:clause

C. In the Object Palette's Email field, type in the mailto:clause

D. In the Property Inspector's SMTP field, type in the mailto:clause

E. No Answer is Correct

Explanation: An example of the mailto clause is "mailto:yourname@email.com" .You are encouraged to actually gain hands on experience using Dreamweaver before taking the test. A copy of the Dreamweaver trial version can be downloaded at http://www.macromedia.com/software/dreamweaver/

62. In HomeSite, how do you select a browser for viewing documents in HomeSite?

A. Open the Settings > Browse dialog

B. Open the Settings > Browser tag

C. Open the Settings > Browsing

D. Press F7

E. No Answer is Correct

---

63. HomeSite will look for a number of common browsers on your system and generates a list of the ones it finds. How do you review and edit this list?

A. Click Options > Configure External Browsers

B. Click Options > Configure Browsers

C. Click Options > Set Browsers

D. Click Options > Set External Browsers

E. No Answer is Correct

62. In HomeSite, how do you select a browser for viewing documents in HomeSite?

***A. Open the Settings > Browse dialog**

B. Open the Settings > Browser tag

C. Open the Settings > Browsing

D. Press F7

E. No Answer is Correct

Explanation: For detailed information please refer to the web link.

---

63. HomeSite will look for a number of common browsers on your system and generates a list of the ones it finds. How do you review and edit this list?

***A. Click Options > Configure External Browsers**

B. Click Options > Configure Browsers

C. Click Options > Set Browsers

D. Click Options > Set External Browsers

E. No Answer is Correct

Explanation: For detailed information please refer to the web link.

64. When configuring HomeSite, what is the option "Relative from server-assigned directory" for?

A. specify whether the initial directory should be set from the server-assigned user directory or from the removable drive

B. specify whether the initial directory should be set from the server-assigned user directory or from the client root

C. specify whether the initial directory should be set from the client-assigned user directory or from the server root

D. specify whether the initial directory should be set from the server-assigned user directory or from the server root

E. No Answer is Correct

64. When configuring HomeSite, what is the option "Relative from server-assigned directory" for?

A. specify whether the initial directory should be set from the server-assigned user directory or from the removable drive

B. specify whether the initial directory should be set from the server-assigned user directory or from the client root

C. specify whether the initial directory should be set from the client-assigned user directory or from the server root

***D. specify whether the initial directory should be set from the server-assigned user directory or from the server root**

E. No Answer is Correct

Explanation: HomeSite is cooperating closely with the web server. For detailed information please refer to the web link.

65. When configuring HomeSite, what is the option "Assume UTC file times" for?

A. adjust for servers that use the Universal Coordinated Time format

B. adjust for servers that use the Greenwich Time format

C. adjust for servers that use the System Time format

D. adjust for servers that use the Network Coordinated Time format.

E. No Answer is Correct

---

66. When configuring HomeSite, why would you use the option "Disable passive mode"?

A. when your server uses frequent flapping connections

B. when your server uses passive connections constantly

C. when your server does not use passive connections

D. when your server uses irregular and unstable connections

E. No Answer is Correct

65. When configuring HomeSite, what is the option "Assume UTC file times" for?

***A. adjust for servers that use the Universal Coordinated Time format**

B. adjust for servers that use the Greenwich Time format

C. adjust for servers that use the System Time format

D. adjust for servers that use the Network Coordinated Time format.

E. No Answer is Correct

Explanation: HomeSite is cooperating closely with the web server. For detailed information please refer to the web link.

---

66. When configuring HomeSite, why would you use the option "Disable passive mode"?

A. when your server uses frequent flapping connections

B. when your server uses passive connections constantly

***C. when your server does not use passive connections**

D. when your server uses irregular and unstable connections

E. No Answer is Correct

Explanation: HomeSite is cooperating closely with the web server. For detailed information please refer to the web link.

67. In HomeSite, how would you define server mapping for testing purpose?

A. Add mapping information in the Mapping dialog box

B. Select mapping from the internal browser

C. Go to File -> Mapping

D. Go to File -> Options -> Mapping

E. No Answer is Correct

---

68. In HomeSite, the Editor toolbar contains buttons for configuring the Editor pane display. Which option is for splitting the current editor document into two separate viewing panes?

A. Split document

B. Split into

C. Split current document

D. Split current view

E. No Answer is Correct

67. In HomeSite, how would you define server mapping for testing purpose?

***A. Add mapping information in the Mapping dialog box**

B. Select mapping from the internal browser

C. Go to File -> Mapping

D. Go to File -> Options -> Mapping

E. No Answer is Correct

Explanation: For developing a serious Web site you need to view the pages as visitors to the site and actually experience them. This can be done with server mapping - to route HTML documents through a Web server. For detailed information please refer to the web link.

---

68. In HomeSite, the Editor toolbar contains buttons for configuring the Editor pane display. Which option is for splitting the current editor document into two separate viewing panes?

A. Split document

B. Split into

***C. Split current document**

D. Split current view

E. No Answer is Correct

Explanation: For detailed information please refer to the web link.

69. In HomeSite, the Editor toolbar contains buttons for configuring the Editor pane display. Which option is for quickly setting the alignment of text and code blocks?

A. Indent/Unindent

B. Indent/Deindent

C. Tag/Untag

D. Indent/Reindent

E. No Answer is Correct

---

70. In HomeSite, we have the Auto Completion features. Which of the following are valid triggers built in of this feature
(Choose all that apply)?

A. Double quotes

B. Comments

C. Pound signs

D. ASP tags

E. No Answer is Correct

69. In HomeSite, the Editor toolbar contains buttons for configuring the Editor pane display. Which option is for quickly setting the alignment of text and code blocks?

***A. Indent/Unindent**

B. Indent/Deindent

C. Tag/Untag

D. Indent/Reindent

E. No Answer is Correct

Explanation: For detailed information please refer to the web link.

---

70. In HomeSite, we have the Auto Completion features. Which of the following are valid triggers built in of this feature
(Choose all that apply)?

***A. Double quotes**

***B. Comments**

***C. Pound signs**

***D. ASP tags**

E. No Answer is Correct

Explanation: Auto Completion provides automatic completion of user defined strings while editing. For detailed information please refer to the web link.

71. In HomeSite, we have the Auto Completion features. Which of the following are valid strings supported by default of this feature (Choose all that apply)?

A. (" ")

B. (<!-- -->)

C. (# *)

D. (<% %>)

E. No Answer is Correct

---

72. In HomeSite, functions available for use with Function Insight are controlled by:

A. Expression Builder function library

B. Procedure Builder function library

C. Function Builder library

D. Addin Builder function library

E. No Answer is Correct

71. In HomeSite, we have the Auto Completion features. Which of the following are valid strings supported by default of this feature (Choose all that apply)?

***A. (" ")**

***B. (<!-- -->)**

C. (# *)

***D. (<% %>)**

E. No Answer is Correct

Explanation: Auto Completion provides automatic completion of user defined strings while editing. For detailed information please refer to the web link.

---

72. In HomeSite, functions available for use with Function Insight are controlled by:

***A. Expression Builder function library**

B. Procedure Builder function library

C. Function Builder library

D. Addin Builder function library

E. No Answer is Correct

Explanation: Basically, Function Insight provides automatic function argument "insight" assistance for developers. For detailed information please refer to the web link.

73. In HomeSite, how do you enable quick access to all supported tags?

A. Use Tag Help

B. Use Tag Chooser

C. Use Tag List

D. Use Tag Generator

E. No Answer is Correct

---

74. While editing a page in HomeSite, you want to enable the Tag Chooser. How do you do that?

A. Ctrl + C

B. Ctrl + T

C. Ctrl + E

D. Ctrl + S

E. No Answer is Correct

73. In HomeSite, how do you enable quick access to all supported tags?

A. Use Tag Help

***B. Use Tag Chooser**

C. Use Tag List

D. Use Tag Generator

E. No Answer is Correct

Explanation: Tag Chooser allows you to choose from a list of all supported tags. For detailed information please refer to the web link.

---

74. While editing a page in HomeSite, you want to enable the Tag Chooser. How do you do that?

A. Ctrl + C

B. Ctrl + T

***C. Ctrl + E**

D. Ctrl + S

E. No Answer is Correct

Explanation: Tag Chooser allows you to choose from a list of all supported tags. For detailed information please refer to the web link.

75. When you click on a QuickBar icon in HomeSite, what will happen as a result of the click (choose 2)?

A. inserts the tag directly into the document

B. inserts pointer of the tag into the document

C. opens a dialog box for tags that require attributes

D. opens a dialog box for tags that do not require attributes

E. No Answer is Correct

---

76. In HomeSite, how do you set color values for different tag attributes (choose 3)?

A. Tag Inspector

B. Tag Insight

C. Individual tag editors

D. File - Options - Preference

E. No Answer is Correct

75. When you click on a QuickBar icon in HomeSite, what will happen as a result of the click (choose 2)?

***A. inserts the tag directly into the document**

B. inserts pointer of the tag into the document

***C. opens a dialog box for tags that require attributes**

D. opens a dialog box for tags that do not require attributes

E. No Answer is Correct

Explanation: Note that in HomeSite you may easily customize the QuickBar display and organize tool buttons. For detailed information please refer to the web link.

---

76. In HomeSite, how do you set color values for different tag attributes (choose 3)?

***A. Tag Inspector**

***B. Tag Insight**

***C. Individual tag editors**

D. File - Options - Preference

E. No Answer is Correct

Explanation: All these tools support the Windows 16 color palette with the Custom color option. For detailed information please refer to the web link.

77. Which view in FrontPage 2000 allows you to see the various statistics of the current web, including broken links and slow pages?

A. Navigation View

B. Page View

C. Folder View

D. Reports View

E. Site Summary View

---

78. What type of editors are FrontPage 2000, Allaire HomeSite, and Net Object's Fusion?

A. Line Editors

B. WSYIWYG Editors

C. Image Editors

D. Document Editors

77. Which view in FrontPage 2000 allows you to see the various statistics of the current web, including broken links and slow pages?

A. Navigation View

B. Page View

C. Folder View

***D. Reports View**

E. Site Summary View

Explanation: To get detailed statistics of the current web, you use the Report View. It provide information on the number of linked files, images used, broken links, slow pages, and other important data. Even though you can generate these statistics by creating a Site Summary, this takes you to the Reports view to see the information.

---

78. What type of editors are FrontPage 2000, Allaire HomeSite, and Net Object's Fusion?

A. Line Editors

***B. WSYIWYG Editors**

C. Image Editors

D. Document Editors

Explanation: Front Page 2000, Allaire HomeSite, and NetObjects Fusion are examples of WYSIWYG (What You See Is What You Get) editors. Notepad is a line editor. Photoshop and JASC Paint Shop are image editors. Word Perfect is a document editor.

Chapter 5: Scripting and Advanced HTML Features

1. You have the following code fragment:

```
<STYLE TYPE="text/css">
<!--
A: link        {color: #400080}
A: visited     {color: #C40000}
A: active      {background-color: #FFFFFF;
                text-decoration: underline}
A: hover       {background-color: #FFFFE8;
                text-decoration: underline}
-->
</STYLE>
```

Where would you place the code?

A. in within the <HEAD> section

B. in within the <TITLE> section

C. in within the <BODY> section

D. in within the <CODE> section

E. No Answer is Correct

---

2. What is selector in CSS?

A. patterns

B. conditions

C. rules

D. styles

E. No Answer is Correct

1. You have the following code fragment:

```
<STYLE TYPE="text/css">
<!--
A: link      {color: #400080}
A: visited   {color: #C40000}
A: active    {background-color: #FFFFFF;
              text-decoration: underline}
A: hover          {background-color: #FFFFE8;
              text-decoration: underline}
-->
</STYLE>
```

Where would you place the code?

***A. in within the <HEAD> section**

B. in within the <TITLE> section

C. in within the <BODY> section

D. in within the <CODE> section

E. No Answer is Correct

Explanation: This is an example of style sheet.

---

2. What is selector in CSS?

***A. patterns**

B. conditions

C. rules

D. styles

E. No Answer is Correct

Explanation: Selector is pattern that may range from simple element names to rich contextual patterns.

3. In CSS, media types are for:

A. specifying how a document is to be presented on different browsers

B. specifying how a document is to be presented on different media

C. specifying how a document is to be presented on different computers

D. specifying how a document is to be presented on different locale

E. No Answer is Correct

---

4. In CSS, what construct allows style sheet rules for various media in the same style sheet?

A. @medias

B. @media

C. @rule

D. @rules

E. No Answer is Correct

3. In CSS, media types are for:

A. specifying how a document is to be presented on different browsers

***B. specifying how a document is to be presented on different media**

C. specifying how a document is to be presented on different computers

D. specifying how a document is to be presented on different locale

E. No Answer is Correct

Explanation: A document can be presented on different media, such as on the screen, on paper, with a speech synthesizer, with a Braille device, etc.

---

4. In CSS, what construct allows style sheet rules for various media in the same style sheet?

A. @medias

***B. @media**

C. @rule

D. @rules

E. No Answer is Correct

Explanation: An @media rule specifies the target media types of a set of rules.

5. You want to deploy CSS for documents viewed on screen in print preview mode. What media type would you use?

A. embossed

B. handheld

C. print

D. projection

E. No Answer is Correct

---

6. You want to use CSS for terminals with limited display capabilities. What media type can you use?

A. embossed

B. handheld

C. print

D. projection

E. tty

5. You want to deploy CSS for documents viewed on screen in print preview mode. What media type would you use?

A. embossed

B. handheld

***C. print**

D. projection

E. No Answer is Correct

Explanation: CSS media types reflect chosen target devices.

---

6. You want to use CSS for terminals with limited display capabilities. What media type can you use?

A. embossed

B. handheld

C. print

D. projection

***E. tty**

Explanation: CSS media types reflect chosen target devices.

7. What correctly describe WebFonts
   (Choose all that apply)?

   A. client-side font matching

   B. font synthesis

   C. progressive rendering,

   D. fonts downloadable over the Web

   E. No Answer is Correct

---

8. In order to be able to change the appearance of multiple Web pages by tweaking a single file, how would you implement your CSS?

   A. linking to a style sheet from your HTML file.

   B. embedding a style sheet

   C. using inline style

   D. using CSS control software

   E. No Answer is Correct

7. What correctly describe WebFonts (Choose all that apply)?

***A. client-side font matching**

***B. font synthesis**

***C. progressive rendering,**

***D. fonts downloadable over the Web**

E. No Answer is Correct

Explanation: These are possible with CSS2.

---

8. In order to be able to change the appearance of multiple Web pages by tweaking a single file, how would you implement your CSS?

***A. linking to a style sheet from your HTML file.**

B. embedding a style sheet

C. using inline style

D. using CSS control software

E. No Answer is Correct

Explanation: The same style file can be used by multiple pages.

9. What is the structure of a style definition?

A. an HTML tag followed by a listing of properties for that tag within double quotes

B. an HTML tag followed by a listing of properties for that tag within single quote

C. an HTML tag followed by a listing of properties for that tag within curly braces.

D. a listing of properties for that tag within curly braces followed by an HTML tag

E. No Answer is Correct

---

10. You want to link to an external style file. What file extension would that file use?

A. a .CS file extension

B. a .CSS file extension

C. a .CSA file extension

D. a .CSSS file extension

E. No Answer is Correct

9. What is the structure of a style definition?

A. an HTML tag followed by a listing of properties for that tag within double quotes

B. an HTML tag followed by a listing of properties for that tag within single quote

***C. an HTML tag followed by a listing of properties for that tag within curly braces.**

D. a listing of properties for that tag within curly braces followed by an HTML tag

E. No Answer is Correct

Explanation: You should remember this "syntax" for the exam.

---

10. You want to link to an external style file. What file extension would that file use?

A. a .CS file extension

***B. a .CSS file extension**

C. a .CSA file extension

D. a .CSSS file extension

E. No Answer is Correct

Explanation: External style file uses .CSS as the extension.

11. You have the following code fragment:

```
<HEAD>
<TITLE>Title of article</TITLE>
<LINK REL=STYLESHEET
HREF="}{WebURL1=http://internet-name/mystyles.css"
TYPE="text/css">
</HEAD>
```

Which method of style sheet deployment are you using?

A. linking to a style sheet from your HTML file.

B. embedding a style sheet

C. using inline style

D. using CSS control software

E. No Answer is Correct

---

12. To embed a style sheet, what tag will you use?

A. <STYLE>

B. <STY>

C. <EMBED>

D. <STYLE EMBED>

E. No Answer is Correct

11. You have the following code fragment:

```
<HEAD>
<TITLE>Title of article</TITLE>
<LINK REL=STYLESHEET
HREF="}{WebURL1=http://internet-name/mystyles.css"
TYPE="text/css">
</HEAD>
```

Which method of style sheet deployment are you using?

***A. linking to a style sheet from your HTML file.**

B. embedding a style sheet

C. using inline style

D. using CSS control software

E. No Answer is Correct

Explanation: The same style file can be used by multiple pages.

---

12. To embed a style sheet, what tag will you use?

***A. <STYLE>**

B. <STY>

C. <EMBED>

D. <STYLE EMBED>

E. No Answer is Correct

Explanation: You place this code between <HEAD> and <BODY>

13. To embed a style sheet, where will you place the code containing the styles?

A. between <BODY>

B. between <HEAD> and <TITLE>

C. between <CODE>

D. between <EMBED>

E. between <HEAD> and <BODY>

---

14. In order to create variations for a single HTML tag, what feature of CSS can you use?

A. Class

B. Unit

C. Code

D. Script

E. No Answer is Correct

13. To embed a style sheet, where will you place the code containing the styles?

A. between <BODY>

B. between <HEAD> and <TITLE>

C. between <CODE>

D. between <EMBED>

***E. between <HEAD> and <BODY>**

Explanation: You place the style sheet code between <HEAD> and <BODY>.

---

14. In order to create variations for a single HTML tag, what feature of CSS can you use?

***A. Class**

B. Unit

C. Code

D. Script

E. No Answer is Correct

Explanation: You may use classes to create variations for a single HTML tag.

15. In CSS, the position property can be set to (Choose all that apply)?

A. absolute

B. relative

C. static

D. linked

E. double

---

16. You are coding your JavaScript program. You have the keyboard's caps lock on all the time. What will happen?

A. nothing wrong

B. all display appears in capital letters

C. program execute hangs

D. may not execute at all

E. No Answer is Correct

15. In CSS, the position property can be set to (Choose all that apply)?

***A. absolute**

***B. relative**

***C. static**

D. linked

E. double

Explanation: Among the three values, the default is static.

---

16. You are coding your JavaScript program. You have the keyboard's caps lock on all the time. What will happen?

A. nothing wrong

B. all display appears in capital letters

C. program execute hangs

***D. may not execute at all**

E. No Answer is Correct

Explanation: JavaScript is case sensitive.

17. What are the decision making statements in JavaScript (Choose all that apply)?

A. if

B. switch

C. for

D. while

E. No Answer is Correct

---

18. You are using JavaScript variables. Tom told you that JavaScript variables are loosely typed. What does that mean?

A. you must declare the variable first

B. the variable case must match

C. the variable case does not need to match

D. you must garbage collect the variables

E. No Answer is Correct

17. What are the decision making statements in JavaScript (Choose all that apply)?

***A. if**

***B. switch**

C. for

D. while

E. No Answer is Correct

Explanation: C and D are conditional looping statements.

---

18. You are using JavaScript variables. Tom told you that JavaScript variables are loosely typed. What does that mean?

A. you must declare the variable first

B. the variable case must match

C. the variable case does not need to match

D. you must garbage collect the variables

***E. No Answer is Correct**

Explanation: JavaScript variables do not need to be pre-declared, and can be used for different data types.

19. You want to use JavaScript within your web page. In what tags will you place the code?

A. <script>

B. <jscript>

C. <body>

D. <declare>

E. No Answer is Correct

---

20. In JavaScript, what is a sequence of commands that are executed when the function is called?

A. procedure

B. group

C. function

D. parameter

E. No Answer is Correct

19. You want to use JavaScript within your web page. In what tags will you place the code?

***A. <script>**

B. <jscript>

C. <body>

D. <declare>

E. No Answer is Correct

Explanation: To use JavaScript in HTML, you enclose JavaScript commands inside the <script> .... </script> tags.

---

20. In JavaScript, what is a sequence of commands that are executed when the function is called?

A. procedure

B. group

***C. function**

D. parameter

E. No Answer is Correct

Explanation: There is no procedure in JavaScript.

21. What will you use to end every line of your JavaScript code and to tell the browser that it has reached the end of your JavaScript statement?

A. ;

B. ,

C. .

D. :

E. ""

---

22. You want to make sure that people who browse the Internet without the capability to view documents that contain JavaScript can still read your page. How could you do this?

A. place JavaScript commands in <code> tags

B. place JavaScript commands in <head> tags

C. place JavaScript commands in comment tags

D. place JavaScript commands in <hide> tags

E. No Answer is Correct

21. What will you use to end every line of your JavaScript code and to tell the browser that it has reached the end of your JavaScript statement?

***A. ;**

B. ,

C. .

D. :

E. ""

Explanation: You use ; to end the statement.

---

22. You want to make sure that people who browse the Internet without the capability to view documents that contain JavaScript can still read your page. How could you do this?

A. place JavaScript commands in <code> tags

B. place JavaScript commands in <head> tags

***C. place JavaScript commands in comment tags**

D. place JavaScript commands in <hide> tags

E. No Answer is Correct

Explanation: This are the comment tags: <!-- -->

23. How do you provide additional information for non-JavaScript compatible client?

A. you cannot

B. add extra HTML code using the <stealthscript> tag

C. add extra HTML code using the <hidescript> tag

D. add extra HTML code using the <noscript> .... </noscript> tags

E. No Answer is Correct

24. In JavaScript, you use ______________ to call a JavaScript function in response to a mouse movement.

A. event handlers

B. event schedulers

C. event dispatchers

D. object sensor

E. No Answer is Correct

23. How do you provide additional information for non-JavaScript compatible client?

A. you cannot

B. add extra HTML code using the <stealthscript> tag

C. add extra HTML code using the <hidescript> tag

***D. add extra HTML code using the <noscript> .... </noscript> tags**

E. No Answer is Correct

Explanation: You normally put these tags within the HTML body.

---

24. In JavaScript, you use ______________ to call a JavaScript function in response to a mouse movement.

***A. event handlers**

B. event schedulers

C. event dispatchers

D. object sensor

E. No Answer is Correct

Explanation: JavaScript is an event driven language.

25. Which of the following corresponds to user changing the value of a form field?

A. onChange

B. onClick

C. onCheck

D. onClear

E. No Answer is Correct

26. In JavaScript how do you detect when user clicks a specified button?

A. onChange

B. onClick

C. onCheck

D. onClear

E. No Answer is Correct

25. Which of the following corresponds to user changing the value of a form field?

***A. onChange**

B. onClick

C. onCheck

D. onClear

E. No Answer is Correct

Explanation: Please refer to the web link for detailed coverage of the various events available in JavaScript.

---

26. In JavaScript how do you detect when user clicks a specified button?

A. onChange

***B. onClick**

C. onCheck

D. onClear

E. No Answer is Correct

Explanation: Please refer to the web link for detailed coverage of the various events available in JavaScript.

27. How do you detect if a user moves the mouse off of a specified link in JavaScript?

A. onChange

B. onClick

C. onCheck

D. onMouseOut

E. onMouseOff

28. Why would you prefer to place your Javascripts within the <HEAD></HEAD> section
(Choose all that apply)?

A. information in the header is not usually displayed by the browser

B. statements in the header are processed before the document is displayed

C. support non JavaScript capable browser

D. support MAC clients

E. No Answer is Correct

27. How do you detect if a user moves the mouse off of a specified link in JavaScript?

A. onChange

B. onClick

C. onCheck

***D. onMouseOut**

E. onMouseOff

Explanation: Please refer to the web link for detailed coverage of the various events available in JavaScript.

---

28. Why would you prefer to place your Javascripts within the <HEAD></HEAD> section
(Choose all that apply)?

***A. information in the header is not usually displayed by the browser**

***B. statements in the header are processed before the document is displayed**

C. support non JavaScript capable browser

D. support MAC clients

E. No Answer is Correct

Explanation: Please refer to the web link for detailed coverage of the JavaScript techniques.

29. Instead of having all JavaScript codes in the same HTML file, how do you include separate JavaScript files?

A. use the <SCRIPT> attribute DST.

B. use the <SCRIPT> attribute SRC.

C. use the <SCRIPT> attribute UBC.

D. use the <SCRIPT> attribute URL.

E. No Answer is Correct

---

30. What is the syntax of incorporating external JavaScript file?

A. <SCRIPT LANGUAGE="JavaScript" SRC="script.js">

B. <SCRIPT LANG="JavaScript" SOURCE="\script.js">

C. <SCRIPT LANG="JavaScript" URL="script.js">

D. <SCRIPT LANGUAGE="JavaScript" URL="\\script.js">

E. No Answer is Correct

29. Instead of having all JavaScript codes in the same HTML file, how do you include separate JavaScript files?

A. use the <SCRIPT> attribute DST.

***B. use the <SCRIPT> attribute SRC.**

C. use the <SCRIPT> attribute UBC.

D. use the <SCRIPT> attribute URL.

E. No Answer is Correct

Explanation: External JavaScript file usually has a .js extension.

---

30. What is the syntax of incorporating external JavaScript file?

***A. <SCRIPT LANGUAGE="JavaScript" SRC="script.js">**

B. <SCRIPT LANG="JavaScript" SOURCE="\script.js">

C. <SCRIPT LANG="JavaScript" URL="script.js">

D. <SCRIPT LANGUAGE="JavaScript" URL="\\script.js">

E. No Answer is Correct

Explanation: External JavaScript file usually has a .js extension.

31. Dynamic HTML allows you to change the look and content of their pages by:

A. connecting to a server

B. connecting to a dynamic server

C. without connecting to a server

D. connecting to the local COM object

E. No Answer is Correct

---

32. DHTML is a language that relies heavily on (Choose all that apply)?

A. JavaScript

B. Style Sheet

C. Visual Basic

D. C++

E. No Answer is Correct

31. Dynamic HTML allows you to change the look and content of their pages by:

A. connecting to a server

B. connecting to a dynamic server

***C. without connecting to a server**

D. connecting to the local COM object

E. No Answer is Correct

Explanation: You do not need to connect to the server when using DHTML.

---

32. DHTML is a language that relies heavily on
(Choose all that apply)?

***A. JavaScript**

***B. Style Sheet**

C. Visual Basic

D. C++

E. No Answer is Correct

Explanation: Basically you write DHTML with JavaScript.

33. You have the following code fragment in your web page that deploys DHTML:

```
<STYLE TYPE="text/css">
<!--
A: link        {color: #400080}
A: visited     {color: #C40000}
A: active      {background-color: #FFFFFF;
                text-decoration: underline}
A: hover            {background-color: #FFFE8;
                text-decoration: underline}
-->
</STYLE>
```

What type of code is it?

A. JavaScript

B. VBScript

C. DHTML

D. Style Sheets

E. No Answer is Correct

---

34. You want to create the effect whereby a link image changes when you move the mouse cursor over it. How would you do this (Choose all that apply)?

A. create two images to be your links

B. use JavaScript

C. load the mouse driver on startup

D. use animated GIF

E. No Answer is Correct

33. You have the following code fragment in your web page that deploys DHTML:

```
<STYLE TYPE="text/css">
<!--
A: link         {color: #400080}
A: visited      {color: #C40000}
A: active       {background-color: #FFFFFF;
                 text-decoration: underline}
A: hover              {background-color: #FFFFE8;
                 text-decoration: underline}
-->
</STYLE>
```

What type of code is it?

A. JavaScript

B. VBScript

C. DHTML

***D. Style Sheets**

E. No Answer is Correct

Explanation: This is an example of style sheet.

---

34. You want to create the effect whereby a link image changes when you move the mouse cursor over it. How would you do this (Choose all that apply)?

***A. create two images to be your links**

***B. use JavaScript**

C. load the mouse driver on startup

D. use animated GIF

E. No Answer is Correct

Explanation: You need to create a mouse over event for this.

35. Typically where would you place your JavaScript code at?

A. an external file

B. text/JavaScript

C. the <HEAD> of your document

D. .ext file

E. No Answer is Correct

---

36. To inform your JavaScript code that the mouse cursor is currently on top of the image, what event can you use?

A. onMouseOver

B. onMouseOut

C. onMouseIn

D. onMouseOn

E. No Answer is Correct

35. Typically where would you place your JavaScript code at?

A. an external file

B. text/JavaScript

***C. the <HEAD> of your document**

D. .ext file

E. No Answer is Correct

Explanation: Generally you want to place the code in the <head> section so the code will be loaded for sure.

---

36. To inform your JavaScript code that the mouse cursor is currently on top of the image, what event can you use?

***A. onMouseOver**

B. onMouseOut

C. onMouseIn

D. onMouseOn

E. No Answer is Correct

Explanation: You want to place onMouseOver in the anchor.

37. To inform your JavaScript code that the mouse cursor is currently on top of the image, where will you place the corresponding event code?

A. in within <body>

B. in within <title>

C. in within <head>

D. in within <href>

E. in within <a>

---

38. You want to be able to fully support the many different versions of browsers while maximizing the benefits of DHTML. What should you do?

A. sniff the browser type and version and then serve up appropriate content for the browser concerned

B. create different static pages for different browser

C. ask the user to select a browser version

D. write dummy code for all versions

E. No Answer is Correct

37. To inform your JavaScript code that the mouse cursor is currently on top of the image, where will you place the corresponding event code?

A. in within <body>

B. in within <title>

C. in within <head>

D. in within <href>

***E. in within <a>**

Explanation: You want to place onMouseOver in the anchor.

---

38. You want to be able to fully support the many different versions of browsers while maximizing the benefits of DHTML. What should you do?

***A. sniff the browser type and version and then serve up appropriate content for the browser concerned**

B. create different static pages for different browser

C. ask the user to select a browser version

D. write dummy code for all versions

E. No Answer is Correct

Explanation: This is the suggested way of handling the compatibility issue.

39. What method will open a new instance of the browser and load the document a particular URL specifies?

A. window.open

B. windows.open

C. window.opens

D. window=open

E. No Answer is Correct

---

40. Which type of dialog box allows a user to interact with the original window while the dialog box is open?

A. modal

B. modeless

C. mode=no

D. open

E. No Answer is Correct

39. What method will open a new instance of the browser and load the document a particular URL specifies?

***A. window.open**

B. windows.open

C. window.opens

D. window=open

E. No Answer is Correct

Explanation: You use this to open a separate instance of the browser.

---

40. Which type of dialog box allows a user to interact with the original window while the dialog box is open?

A. modal

***B. modeless**

C. mode=no

D. open

E. No Answer is Correct

Explanation: Modal window is the exact opposite.

41. What is true of the Document Object Model in DHTML
(Choose all that apply)?

A. it is the foundation for Dynamic HTML

B. supported by Microsoft across all platform releases of Internet Explorer 4.0

C. does not work with JavaScript

D. does not support Macintosh client

E. No Answer is Correct

---

42. What is a scriptlet?

A. a Web page authored with Dynamic HTML that content providers can use as a component

B. a Web page authored with Dynamic HTML that content providers can use as a server side engine

C. an ActiveX control

D. part of a Java component

E. No Answer is Correct

41. What is true of the Document Object Model in DHTML (Choose all that apply)?

***A. it is the foundation for Dynamic HTML**

***B. supported by Microsoft across all platform releases of Internet Explorer 4.0**

C. does not work with JavaScript

D. does not support Macintosh client

E. No Answer Is Correct

Explanation: MS supports DOM in all versions of IE4 and above.

---

42. What is a scriptlet?

***A. a Web page authored with Dynamic HTML that content providers can use as a component**

B. a Web page authored with Dynamic HTML that content providers can use as a server side engine

C. an ActiveX control

D. part of a Java component

E. No Answer is Correct

Explanation: With scriptlets, content providers can author content once and easily reuse them in other Web pages.

43. Using a table as an example, how would you describe the relationship between HTML, CSS and DHTML
(Choose all that apply)?

A. you use HTML to specify that there is a table

B. you use CSS to control the style of the table

C. you use DHTML to update the table contents

D. you use CSS to control the table 's behavior

E. No Answer is Correct

---

44. How would you describe DHTML behavior?

A. heavyweight components that encapsulate specific functionality on a page

B. lightweight components that encapsulate specific style on a page

C. lightweight components that encapsulate specific functionality on a page

D. ActiveX Control

E. No Answer is Correct

43. Using a table as an example, how would you describe the relationship between HTML, CSS and DHTML
(Choose all that apply)?

***A. you use HTML to specify that there is a table**

***B. you use CSS to control the style of the table**

***C. you use DHTML to update the table contents**

D. you use CSS to control the table 's behavior

E. No Answer is Correct

Explanation: DHTML provides an object model (DOM) and API to allow interaction with HTML and CSS.

---

44. How would you describe DHTML behavior?

A. heavyweight components that encapsulate specific functionality on a page

B. lightweight components that encapsulate specific style on a page

***C. lightweight components that encapsulate specific functionality on a page**

D. ActiveX Control

E. No Answer is Correct

Explanation: DHTML Behavior is introduced in IE 5.5.

45. You want to create simple flying text on your page. How would you do this with the least amount of coding?

A. use Java applet

B. use DHTML to manipulate the position of elements on the page over time

C. use ActiveX control

D. use animated GIF

E. No Answer is Correct

---

46. Which of the following is true concerning XML (Choose all that apply)?

A. simplified version of SGML

B. designed for use on the web

C. simplified version of HTML

D. simplified version of EML

E. No Answer is Correct

45. You want to create simple flying text on your page. How would you do this with the least amount of coding?

A. use Java applet

***B. use DHTML to manipulate the position of elements on the page over time**

C. use ActiveX control

D. use animated GIF

E. No Answer is Correct

Explanation: DHTML supports dynamic positioning of elements.

---

46. Which of the following is true concerning XML (Choose all that apply)?

***A. simplified version of SGML**

***B. designed for use on the web**

C. simplified version of HTML

D. simplified version of EML

E. No Answer is Correct

Explanation: Please refer to the web link for detailed explanation of this topic.

47. With XML we can markup our document. What are the types of markup we can perform
(Choose all that apply)?

A. Stylistic

B. Structural

C. Semantic

D. Logical

E. No Answer is Correct

---

48. With XML we can markup our document. What are the types of markup we can perform to tell how the document is to be styled?

A. Stylistic

B. Structural

C. Semantic

D. Logical

E. No Answer is Correct

47. With XML we can markup our document. What are the types of markup we can perform
(Choose all that apply)?

***A. Stylistic**

***B. Structural**

***C. Semantic**

D. Logical

E. No Answer is Correct

Explanation: Please refer to the web link for detailed explanation of this topic.

---

48. With XML we can markup our document. What are the types of markup we can perform to tell how the document is to be styled?

***A. Stylistic**

B. Structural

C. Semantic

D. Logical

E. No Answer is Correct

Explanation: Please refer to the web link for detailed explanation of this topic.

49. With XML we can markup our document. What are the types of markup we can perform to tell how the document is to be structured?

A. Stylistic

B. Structural

C. Semantic

D. Logical

E. No Answer is Correct

---

50. In XML, empty tags must be in a special format. This format is denoted by:

A. <emptytag>

B. <empty>

C. <emptag>

D. <emptytags>

E. No Answer is Correct

49. With XML we can markup our document. What are the types of markup we can perform to tell how the document is to be structured?

A. Stylistic

***B. Structural**

C. Semantic

D. Logical

E. No Answer is Correct

Explanation: Please refer to the web link for detailed explanation of this topic.

---

50. In XML, empty tags must be in a special format. This format is denoted by:

***A. <emptytag>**

B. <empty>

C. <emptag>

D. <emptytags>

E. No Answer is Correct

Explanation: Please refer to the web link for detailed explanation of this topic.

51. In XML, codes are case sensitive.

A. True

B. False

---

52. When writing an XML tag, you need to keep in mind that tags are (Choose all that apply)?

A. can start with a letter

B. can start with a colon

C. can start with an underscore

D. can start with a dash

E. No Answer is Correct

51. In XML, codes are case sensitive.

***A. True**

B. False

Explanation: Please refer to the web link for detailed explanation of this topic.

---

52. When writing an XML tag, you need to keep in mind that tags are (Choose all that apply)?

***A. can start with a letter**

B. can start with a colon

***C. can start with an underscore**

D. can start with a dash

E. No Answer is Correct

Explanation: Please refer to the web link for detailed explanation of this topic.

53. XML tag allows what characters in the name
(Choose all that apply)?

A. letters

B. digits

C. period

D. underscore

E. hyphen

---

54. In XML, for a document to be considered as well formed, it must obey the following simple rules
(Choose all that apply)?

A. It must contain at least one element

B. It must contain a unique opening and closing tag to contain the whole document

C. All other tags must be nested

D. All other tags cannot overlap

E. No Answer is Correct

53. XML tag allows what characters in the name
    (Choose all that apply)?

***A. letters**

***B. digits**

***C. period**

***D. underscore**

***E. hyphen**

Explanation: Please refer to the web link for detailed explanation of this topic.

---

54. In XML, for a document to be considered as well formed, it must obey the following simple rules
    (Choose all that apply)?

***A. It must contain at least one element**

***B. It must contain a unique opening and closing tag to contain the whole document**

***C. All other tags must be nested**

***D. All other tags cannot overlap**

E. No Answer is Correct

Explanation: Keep in mind that a well formed document is not the same as a valid document. Please refer to the web link for detailed explanation of this topic.

55. Where can we place the XML DTD
(Choose all that apply)?

A. in the prolog of the document

B. in a separate file

C. in the body tag

D. in the heading section

E. No Answer is Correct

---

56. In XML, document type declaration can be done with which tag?

A. <!DOCTYPES.....>

B. <!DTYPE.....>

C. <!DOC.....>

D. <!DOCTYPE.....>

E. No Answer is Correct

55. Where can we place the XML DTD
(Choose all that apply)?

***A. in the prolog of the document**

***B. in a separate file**

C. in the body tag

D. in the heading section

E. No Answer is Correct

Explanation: DTD is not a REQUIRED option for XML. Please refer to the web link for detailed explanation of this topic.

---

56. In XML, document type declaration can be done with which tag?

A. <!DOCTYPES.....>

B. <!DTYPE.....>

C. <!DOC.....>

***D. <!DOCTYPE.....>**

E. No Answer is Correct

Explanation: Please refer to the web link for detailed explanation of this topic.

57. You have the following code fragment:

```
<!ATTLIST element_name
attribute_name attribute_type defaultvalue>
```

What type of tag is this?

A. attribute formation

B. attribute declaration

C. attribute removal

D. attribute modification

E. No Answer is Correct

---

58. What is the nature of the CDATA type of attribute in XML?

A. any text

B. common text

C. data record text

D. database markup tag

E. No Answer is Correct

57. You have the following code fragment:

```
<!ATTLIST element_name
attribute_name attribute_type defaultvalue>
```

What type of tag is this?

A. attribute formation

***B. attribute declaration**

C. attribute removal

D. attribute modification

E. No Answer is Correct

Explanation: Please refer to the web link for detailed explanation of this topic.

---

58. What is the nature of the CDATA type of attribute in XML?

***A. any text**

B. common text

C. data record text

D. database markup tag

E. No Answer is Correct

Explanation: Keep in mind that CDATA as comment is a totally different thing in XML. Please refer to the web link for detailed explanation of this topic.

59. Which of the following is true concerning an entity in XML (Choose all that apply)?

A. a storage unit for data

B. can be character data

C. can be binary data

D. can be graphical data

E. No Answer is Correct

---

60. What is true about a binary entity in XML?

A. anything that is not an XML document

B. anything that is an XML document

C. anything that is a compiled XML document

D. anything that is not a compiled XML document

E. No Answer is Correct

59. Which of the following is true concerning an entity in XML (Choose all that apply)?

***A. a storage unit for data**

***B. can be character data**

***C. can be binary data**

D. can be graphical data

E. No Answer is Correct

Explanation: Please refer to the web link for detailed explanation of this topic.

---

60. What is true about a binary entity in XML?

***A. anything that is not an XML document**

B. anything that is an XML document

C. anything that is a compiled XML document

D. anything that is not a compiled XML document

E. No Answer is Correct

Explanation: Please refer to the web link for detailed explanation of this topic.

61. Cookie is a type of ________ object that resides on the client computer.

A. State

B. Time

C. Data

D. Source

E. No Answer is Correct

62. In general Cookie is in __________ format when stored in the client's PC.

A. binary

B. text

C. compiled

D. raw

E. No Answer is Correct

61. Cookie is a type of ________ object that resides on the client computer.

***A. State**

B. Time

C. Data

D. Source

E. No Answer is Correct

Explanation: Please refer to the web link for detailed specification of cookies.

---

62. In general Cookie is in __________ format when stored in the client's PC.

A. binary

***B. text**

C. compiled

D. raw

E. No Answer is Correct

Explanation: Please refer to the web link for detailed specification of cookies.

63. You have the following code fragment:

Set-Cookie: NAME=VALUE; expires=DATE; path=PATH; domain=DOMAIN_NAME; secure

What is this code about?

A. syntax used by the Set-Cookie HTTP Response Header

B. syntax used by the Get-Cookie HTTP Response Header

C. syntax used by the Retrieve-Cookie HTTP Script

D. syntax used by the Configure-Cookie Response Header

E. No Answer is Correct

---

64. In general, a single server response can issue how many Set-Cookie headers?

A. 1 only

B. more than 1

C. maximum 2

D. maximum 5

E. No Answer is Correct

63. You have the following code fragment:

Set-Cookie: NAME=VALUE; expires=DATE;
path=PATH; domain=DOMAIN_NAME; secure

What is this code about?

***A. syntax used by the Set-Cookie HTTP Response Header**

B. syntax used by the Get-Cookie HTTP Response Header

C. syntax used by the Retrieve-Cookie HTTP Script

D. syntax used by the Configure-Cookie Response Header

E. No Answer is Correct

Explanation: Please refer to the web link for detailed specification of cookies.

---

64. In general, a single server response can issue how many Set-Cookie headers?

A. 1 only

***B. more than 1**

C. maximum 2

D. maximum 5

E. No Answer is Correct

Explanation: Please refer to the web link for detailed specification of cookies.

65. Which of the following is true concerning the expires header for cookies (Choose all that apply)?

A. it lets the client know when it is safe to save the mapping

B. it forces the client to purge the mapping

C. it help the client to purge the mapping automatically

D. it lets the client know when it is safe to purge the mapping

E. No Answer is Correct

---

66. What is limitation on the number of cookies that a client can store at any one time?

A. 100

B. 200

C. 300

D. 400

E. unlimited

65. Which of the following is true concerning the expires header for cookies (Choose all that apply)?

A. it lets the client know when it is safe to save the mapping

B. it forces the client to purge the mapping

C. it help the client to purge the mapping automatically

***D. it lets the client know when it is safe to purge the mapping**

E. No Answer is Correct

Explanation: Please refer to the web link for detailed specification of cookies.

---

66. What is limitation on the number of cookies that a client can store at any one time?

A. 100

B. 200

***C. 300**

D. 400

E. unlimited

Explanation: Please refer to the web link for detailed specification of cookies.

67. What is the limitation on the size of a cookie that a client can accept?

A. 1KB

B. 2KB

C. 4KB

D. 8KB

E. No Answer is Correct

---

68. What is limitation on the number of cookies that a client can store at any one time on a PER DOMAIN BASIS?

A. 20 cookies per domain

B. 30 cookies per domain

C. 40 cookies per domain

D. 50 cookies per domain

E. No Answer is Correct

67. What is the limitation on the size of a cookie that a client can accept?

A. 1KB

B. 2KB

***C. 4KB**

D. 8KB

E. No Answer is Correct

Explanation: Please refer to the web link for detailed specification of cookies.

---

68. What is limitation on the number of cookies that a client can store at any one time on a PER DOMAIN BASIS?

***A. 20 cookies per domain**

B. 30 cookies per domain

C. 40 cookies per domain

D. 50 cookies per domain

E. No Answer is Correct

Explanation: Please refer to the web link for detailed specification of cookies.

69. How can you delete a cookie via a CGI script?

A. return a cookie with the same name and with an expires time which is in the future

B. return a cookie with another name and with an expires time which is in the past

C. return a cookie with no name and with an expires time which is in the past

D. return a cookie with the same name and with an expires time which is in the past

E. No Answer is Correct

---

70. On the Set-Cookie header, how many attribute is REQUIRED?

A. 1

B. 2

C. 3

D. 4

E. No Answer is Correct

69. How can you delete a cookie via a CGI script?

A. return a cookie with the same name and with an expires time which is in the future

B. return a cookie with another name and with an expires time which is in the past

C. return a cookie with no name and with an expires time which is in the past

***D. return a cookie with the same name and with an expires time which is in the past**

E. No Answer is Correct

Explanation: Please refer to the web link for detailed specification of cookies.

---

70. On the Set-Cookie header, how many attribute is REQUIRED?

***A. 1**

B. 2

C. 3

D. 4

E. No Answer is Correct

Explanation: Please refer to the web link for detailed specification of cookies.

71. On the Set-Cookie header, which attributes are NOT REQUIRED (Choose all that apply)?

A. name

B. expires

C. path

D. domain

E. secure

---

72. What would happen when the path attribute of a cookie is not set?

A. cookie error

B. server set-cookie error

C. server send cookie error

D. server get cookie error

E. no error

71. On the Set-Cookie header, which attributes are NOT REQUIRED (Choose all that apply)?

A. name

***B. expires**

***C. path**

***D. domain**

***E. secure**

Explanation: Only the name attribute is required. Please refer to the web link for detailed specification of cookies.

---

72. What would happen when the path attribute of a cookie is not set?

A. cookie error

B. server set-cookie error

C. server send cookie error

D. server get cookie error

***E. no error**

Explanation: If the path is not specified, it will be assumed as the same path of the document being described by the header containing the cookie. Please refer to the web link for detailed specification of cookies.

73. How can we force the user to receive the cookie?

A. by setting the force option to true

B. by setting the force option to 1

C. by code signing the cookie

D. by renaming the extension of the cookie to .MAN

E. you cannot do this

---

74. An hacker attempts to use a cookie to include macro virus for attacking client's computers. What can the client do to avoid this situation?

A. turn on anti-virus functions

B. instruct the browser to reject cookies

C. install a firewall

D. change the IP address

E. do nothing

73. How can we force the user to receive the cookie?

A. by setting the force option to true

B. by setting the force option to 1

C. by code signing the cookie

D. by renaming the extension of the cookie to .MAN

***E. you cannot do this**

Explanation: The user can always instruct the browser to reject cookies. Please refer to the web link for detailed specification of cookies.

---

74. An hacker attempts to use a cookie to include macro virus for attacking client's computers. What can the client do to avoid this situation?

A. turn on anti-virus functions

B. instruct the browser to reject cookies

C. install a firewall

D. change the IP address

***E. do nothing**

Explanation: A cookie is a simple text file that cannot hold any macro virus. The user does not need to take any action against this attempt. Please refer to the web link for detailed specification of cookies.

75. Your company is designing multimedia content for clients. Client A asks you to deliver Authorware content over the web site. What plug in would their visitors need in order to play the file?

A. Nothing

B. Just Netscape Browser will do

C. Just IE will do

D. All versions 3 and above browsers will do

E. Shockwave

---

76. Your company is designing multimedia content for clients. Client B asks you to deliver Director version 5 content over the web site. What plug in would their visitors need in order to play the file?

A. Nothing

B. Just Netscape Browser will do

C. Just IE will do

D. All versions 3 and above browsers will do

E. Shockwave

75. Your company is designing multimedia content for clients. Client A asks you to deliver Authorware content over the web site. What plug in would their visitors need in order to play the file?

A. Nothing

B. Just Netscape Browser will do

C. Just IE will do

D. All versions 3 and above browsers will do

***E. Shockwave**

Explanation: This is a technology from Macromedia. Please refer to the web link for further explanation.

---

76. Your company is designing multimedia content for clients. Client B asks you to deliver Director version 5 content over the web site. What plug in would their visitors need in order to play the file?

A. Nothing

B. Just Netscape Browser will do

C. Just IE will do

D. All versions 3 and above browsers will do

***E. Shockwave**

Explanation: This is a technology from Macromedia. Please refer to the web link for further explanation.

77. Your company is designing multimedia content for clients. Client C asks you to deliver Java content over the web site. What plug in would their visitors need in order to play the file?

A. Nothing

B. Just Netscape Browser will do

C. Just IE will do

D. Flash

E. Shockwave

---

78. Your company is designing multimedia content for clients. Client D asks you to deliver ActiveX content over the web site. What plug in would their visitors need in order to play the file?

A. Flash

B. Javaplay

C. IE 5 will do. No need for special plug in.

D. VRML

E. Shockwave

77. Your company is designing multimedia content for clients. Client C asks you to deliver Java content over the web site. What plug in would their visitors need in order to play the file?

***A. Nothing**

B. Just Netscape Browser will do

C. Just IE will do

D. Flash

E. Shockwave

Explanation: All major browsers in the market support Java. Please refer to the web link for further explanation.

---

78. Your company is designing multimedia content for clients. Client D asks you to deliver ActiveX content over the web site. What plug in would their visitors need in order to play the file?

A. Flash

B. Javaplay

***C. IE 5 will do. No need for special plug in.**

D. VRML

E. Shockwave

Explanation: ActiveX controls work for browser running on Windows platform. Please refer to the web link for further explanation.

79. Your company is designing multimedia content for clients. Client E asks you to deliver 3D world content over the web site. What plug in would their visitors need in order to play the file?

A. Nothing

B. Just Netscape Browser will do

C. Just IE will do

D. WAD

E. VRML

---

80. Your company is designing multimedia content for clients. Client F asks you to deliver .RA music over the web site. What plug in would their visitors need in order to play the file?

A. Nothing

B. Just Netscape Browser will do

C. Just IE will do

D. RealAudio

E. WinAudio

79. Your company is designing multimedia content for clients. Client E asks you to deliver 3D world content over the web site. What plug in would their visitors need in order to play the file?

A. Nothing

B. Just Netscape Browser will do

C. Just IE will do

D. WAD

***E. VRML**

Explanation: VRML plug in is for playing back 3D virtual world. Please refer to the web link for further explanation.

---

80. Your company is designing multimedia content for clients. Client F asks you to deliver .RA music over the web site. What plug in would their visitors need in order to play the file?

A. Nothing

B. Just Netscape Browser will do

C. Just IE will do

***D. RealAudio**

E. WinAudio

Explanation: .RA is the file type for Real Audio. Please refer to the web link for further explanation.

81. Your company is designing multimedia content for clients. Client G asks you to deliver MPG content over the web site. What plug in would their visitors need in order to play the file?

A. Shockwave

B. Just Netscape Browser will do

C. Just IE will do

D. Flash

E. No Answer is Correct

---

82. Your company is designing multimedia content for clients. Client H asks you to construct the web site with ASP technology. What plug in would their visitors need in order to play the file?

A. Shockwave

B. VRML

C. RealPlayer

D. Flash

E. No Answer is Correct

81. Your company is designing multimedia content for clients. Client G asks you to deliver MPG content over the web site. What plug in would their visitors need in order to play the file?

A. Shockwave

B. Just Netscape Browser will do

C. Just IE will do

D. Flash

***E. No Answer is Correct**

Explanation: You need a separate MPEG player to play back MPEG files. Please refer to the web link for further explanation.

---

82. Your company is designing multimedia content for clients. Client H asks you to construct the web site with ASP technology. What plug in would their visitors need in order to play the file?

A. Shockwave

B. VRML

C. RealPlayer

D. Flash

***E. No Answer is Correct**

Explanation: You do not need any plug in to view ASP pages. Please refer to the web link for further explanation.

83. Your company is designing multimedia content for clients. Client I asks you to deliver AVI content over the web site. What plug in would their visitors need in order to play the file?

A. Shockwave

B. Just Netscape Browser will do

C. Just IE will do

D. Flash

E. Windows Media Player

---

84. Your company is designing multimedia content for clients. Client J asks you to deliver Animated GIF content over the web site. What plug in would their visitors need in order to play the file?

A. Shockwave

B. RealPlayer

C. MPG Player

D. Flash

E. No Answer is Correct

83. Your company is designing multimedia content for clients. Client I asks you to deliver AVI content over the web site. What plug in would their visitors need in order to play the file?

A. Shockwave

B. Just Netscape Browser will do

C. Just IE will do

D. Flash

***E. Windows Media Player**

Explanation: AVI is not a good choice for web due to its large size. Please refer to the web link for further explanation.

---

84. Your company is designing multimedia content for clients. Client J asks you to deliver Animated GIF content over the web site. What plug in would their visitors need in order to play the file?

A. Shockwave

B. RealPlayer

C. MPG Player

D. Flash

***E. No Answer is Correct**

Explanation: You do not need a separate player to play back Animated GIF. Please refer to the web link for further explanation.

85. Your company is designing multimedia content for clients. Client K asks you to deliver QuickTime content over the web site. What special requirement would their visitors need to fulfill in order to play the file, if these visitors are using the Windows platform?

A. Shockwave

B. QuickTime driver

C. Real Media Player

D. Flash

E. No Answer is Correct

---

86. Your company is designing multimedia content for clients. Client K asks you to deliver ActiveX content over the web site. What may prevent visitors from playing the file?

A. Firewall

B. Antivirus

C. Version 4 browsers

D. Flash

E. No Answer is Correct

85. Your company is designing multimedia content for clients. Client K asks you to deliver QuickTime content over the web site. What special requirement would their visitors need to fulfill in order to play the file, if these visitors are using the Windows platform?

A. Shockwave

***B. QuickTime driver**

C. Real Media Player

D. Flash

E. No Answer is Correct

Explanation: QuickTime is the native format for MAC clients. Please refer to the web link for further explanation.

---

86. Your company is designing multimedia content for clients. Client K asks you to deliver ActiveX content over the web site. What may prevent visitors from playing the file?

***A. Firewall**

B. Antivirus

C. Version 4 browsers

D. Flash

E. No Answer is Correct

Explanation: Some firewalls may be configured to filter ActiveX. Please refer to the web link for further explanation.

87. Your company is designing multimedia content for clients. Client K asks you to deliver ActiveX content over the web site. What technology may increase users' confidence towards the identity of the code you develop?

A. Firewall

B. Antivirus

C. Version 4 browsers

D. Flash

E. Code Signing

---

88. Your company is designing multimedia content for clients. Client L asks you to deliver multimedia content over the web site. What technology may be appropriate for real time video delivery?

A. MPEG

B. AVI

C. Streaming

D. Flash

E. Shockwave

87. Your company is designing multimedia content for clients. Client K asks you to deliver ActiveX content over the web site. What technology may increase users' confidence towards the identity of the code you develop?

A. Firewall

B. Antivirus

C. Version 4 browsers

D. Flash

***E. Code Signing**

Explanation: Please refer to the web link for further explanation.

---

88. Your company is designing multimedia content for clients. Client L asks you to deliver multimedia content over the web site. What technology may be appropriate for real time video delivery?

A. MPEG

B. AVI

***C. Streaming**

D. Flash

E. Shockwave

Explanation: Streaming media is the ideal choice for real time video delivery. Please refer to the web link for further explanation.

89. Your company is designing multimedia content for clients. Client L asks you to deliver multimedia content over the web site. What technology may be appropriate for electronic piano style music delivery?

A. MPEG

B. AVI

C. Streaming

D. Flash

E. MIDI

---

90. What are single line comments in Java applet codes?

A. /*

B. /

C. //

D. "

E. No Answer is Correct

89. Your company is designing multimedia content for clients. Client L asks you to deliver multimedia content over the web site. What technology may be appropriate for electronic piano style music delivery?

A. MPEG

B. AVI

C. Streaming

D. Flash

***E. MIDI**

Explanation: The good thing about MIDI is its extremely small size and fast download time. Please refer to the web link for further explanation.

---

90. What are single line comments in Java applet codes?

A. /*

B. /

***C.** //

D. "

E. No Answer is Correct

Explanation: Please refer to the web link for detailed coverage on Java Applet.

91. What does this line of Java code mean?

```
import java.applet.Applet;
```

A. inherits all of class Applets methods and data

B. inherits all of class Applets data only

C. inherits all of class Applets methods only

D. inherits all of class Applets' pointers

E. No Answer is Correct

---

92. GUI objects for Java applet are defined in?

A. OBT

B. OBJ

C. AWT

D. ICD

E. AWD

91. What does this line of Java code mean?

```
import java.applet.Applet;
```

***A. inherits all of class Applets methods and data**

B. inherits all of class Applets data only

C. inherits all of class Applets methods only

D. inherits all of class Applets' pointers

E. No Answer is Correct

Explanation: Please refer to the web link for detailed coverage on Java Applet.

---

92. GUI objects for Java applet are defined in?

A. OBT

B. OBJ

***C. AWT**

D. ICD

E. AWD

Explanation: Please refer to the web link for detailed coverage on Java Applet.

93. Which of the following are valid Java events (Choose all that apply)?

A. ComponentEvent

B. ContainerEvent

C. FocusEvent

D. ItemEvent

E. KeyEvent

---

94. What are valid GUI components in Java applet (Choose all that apply)?

A. Canvas

B. Label

C. Component

D. Spinner

E. No Answer is Correct

93. Which of the following are valid Java events
(Choose all that apply)?

***A. ComponentEvent**

***B. ContainerEvent**

***C. FocusEvent**

***D. ItemEvent**

***E. KeyEvent**

Explanation: Please refer to the web link for detailed coverage on Java Applet.

---

94. What are valid GUI components in Java applet
(Choose all that apply)?

***A. Canvas**

***B. Label**

***C. Component**

D. Spinner

E. No Answer is Correct

Explanation: Please refer to the web link for detailed coverage on Java Applet.

95. In your Java applet, what event will a scrollbar generate?

A. ItemEvent

B. AdjustmentEvent

C. ActionEvent

D. MessageEvent

E. No Answer is Correct

---

96. In your Java applet, what event will a button generate?

A. ItemEvent

B. AdjustmentEvent

C. ActionEvent

D. MessageEvent

E. No Answer is Correct

95. In your Java applet, what event will a scrollbar generate?

A. ItemEvent

***B. AdjustmentEvent**

C. ActionEvent

D. MessageEvent

E. No Answer is Correct

Explanation: Please refer to the web link for detailed coverage on Java Applet.

---

96. In your Java applet, what event will a button generate?

A. ItemEvent

B. AdjustmentEvent

***C. ActionEvent**

D. MessageEvent

E. No Answer is Correct

Explanation: Please refer to the web link for detailed coverage on Java Applet.

97. In your Java applet, what event will a choice generate?

A. ItemEvent

B. AdjustmentEvent

C. ActionEvent

D. MessageEvent

E. No Answer is Correct

---

98. In your Java applet, what event will a check box generate?

A. ItemEvent

B. AdjustmentEvent

C. ActionEvent

D. MessageEvent

E. No Answer is Correct

97. In your Java applet, what event will a choice generate?

***A. ItemEvent**

B. AdjustmentEvent

C. ActionEvent

D. MessageEvent

E. No Answer is Correct

Explanation: Please refer to the web link for detailed coverage on Java Applet.

---

98. In your Java applet, what event will a check box generate?

***A. ItemEvent**

B. AdjustmentEvent

C. ActionEvent

D. MessageEvent

E. No Answer is Correct

Explanation: Please refer to the web link for detailed coverage on Java Applet.

99. In a Java applet, what will you use to hold GUI objects for graphical display?

A. container

B. object

C. object lib

D. AWT

E. No Answer is Correct

---

100. In Java, which class provides all of the necessary mouse related functions?

A. GUILib

B. MouseAdapter

C. MouseLib

D. KBandMouse

E. No Answer is Correct

99. In a Java applet, what will you use to hold GUI objects for graphical display?

***A. container**

B. object

C. object lib

D. AWT

E. No Answer is Correct

Explanation: Please refer to the web link for detailed coverage on Java Applet.

---

100. In Java, which class provides all of the necessary mouse related functions?

A. GUILib

***B. MouseAdapter**

C. MouseLib

D. KBandMouse

E. No Answer is Correct

Explanation: Please refer to the web link for detailed coverage on Java Applet.

101. When designing your Java applet, why would you want to use thread?

A. to have several tasks share the use of the CPU

B. to have several tasks share the use of the source code

C. to have several tasks share the use of the memory

D. to have several tasks share the use of the pointers

E. No Answer is Correct

---

102. How do you implement threads in Java
(Choose all that apply)?

A. using the Thread class

B. using the Runnable interface

C. using the thread model

D. using SMP

E. No Answer is Correct

101. When designing your Java applet, why would you want to use thread?

***A. to have several tasks share the use of the CPU**

B. to have several tasks share the use of the source code

C. to have several tasks share the use of the memory

D. to have several tasks share the use of the pointers

E. No Answer is Correct

Explanation: Please refer to the web link for detailed coverage on Java Applet.

---

102. How do you implement threads in Java (Choose all that apply)?

***A. using the Thread class**

***B. using the Runnable interface**

C. using the thread model

D. using SMP

E. No Answer is Correct

Explanation: Please refer to the web link for detailed coverage on Java Applet.

103. In Java, a thread may stop and die if?

A. the GUI is reloaded

B. the display is refreshed

C. the button is pressed

D. the run function terminates

E. No Answer is Correct

---

104. What are valid standard data structures in Java?

A. Vector

B. Stack

C. Hashtable

D. BLOB

E. No Answer is Correct

103. In Java, a thread may stop and die if?

A. the GUI is reloaded

B. the display is refreshed

C. the button is pressed

***D. the run function terminates**

E. No Answer is Correct

Explanation: Please refer to the web link for detailed coverage on Java Applet.

---

104. What are valid standard data structures in Java?

***A. Vector**

***B. Stack**

***C. Hashtable**

D. BLOB

E. No Answer is Correct

Explanation: Please refer to the web link for detailed coverage on Java Applet.

105. What 3 technologies are used in creating DHTML web pages? Choose 3.

A. HTML

B. Java applets

C. Cascading Style Sheets

D. Document Object Model

E. JavaScript

---

106. Which of the following are examples of object oriented programming languages?

A. C++

B. JAVA

C. Pascal

D. JavaScript

E. Visual Basic

105. What 3 technologies are used in creating DHTML web pages? Choose 3.

***A. HTML**

B. Java applets

***C. Cascading Style Sheets**

***D. Document Object Model**

E. JavaScript

Explanation: To make Dynamic HTML pages, you incorporate HTML tags, Cascading Style Sheets, and the Document Object Model. This is a trick question in that many developers may say that JavaScript is a key component. However, it is possible to use other scripting languages to access the DOM (such as VBScript or ECMAScript). Java applets can be used in DHTML, but are not a required component.

---

106. Which of the following are examples of object oriented programming languages?

***A. C++**

***B. JAVA**

C. Pascal

D. JavaScript

***E. Visual Basic**

Explanation: C++, JAVA, and Visual Basic are object-oriented programming languages. They have the characteristic of using objects with defined properties, methods, and events. JavaScript is considered a object-based language in that it does not require compiling to execute, but is executed line by line. Pascal is considered a procedural language

107. Your company has decided to start using XML for all of its internal documentation. Why should you be excited about this use of technology?

A. Because XML is easier to use that HTML

B. Because XML will allow authors to create custom tags that will enhance results that the search engines on your intranet return.

C. Because XML is able to be viewed in all current browsers

D. Because all new applications read and write their data in XML formats, which will allow you to post all of this data seamlessly to your intranet site

107. Your company has decided to start using XML for all of its internal documentation. Why should you be excited about this use of technology?

A. Because XML is easier to use that HTML

***B. Because XML will allow authors to create custom tags that will enhance results that the search engines on your intranet return.**

C. Because XML is able to be viewed in all current browsers

D. Because all new applications read and write their data in XML formats, which will allow you to post all of this data seamlessly to your intranet site

Explanation: XML will enhance the searching features of your intranet because it allow authors to create custom tags in their documents. However, XML is much more strict than HTML, and therefore is considered more difficult to use than HTML. Also, XML is currently only supported in Internet Explorer 4.01+ and some third party browsers. It is true that many new applications are using XML as their default language, but porting this data to a web format involves style sheets and other filters, making it not very seamless.

Chapter 6: Working with Graphics and Multimedia

1. When designing web graphics, what is a valid concern?

A. Most Web audiences are accessing the Internet via modems

B. Most Web audiences are accessing the Internet via T1

C. Most ISP are accessing the Internet via T3

D. Most Web audiences are accessing the Internet via ISDN

E. No Answer is Correct

---

2. Why would you choose not to use Full-screen graphic menu?

A. not beautiful enough

B. not enough color depth

C. take much longer to download

D. take much longer to decode

E. No Answer is Correct

1. When designing web graphics, what is a valid concern?

***A. Most Web audiences are accessing the Internet via modems**

B. Most Web audiences are accessing the Internet via T1

C. Most ISP are accessing the Internet via T3

D. Most Web audiences are accessing the Internet via ISDN

E. No Answer is Correct

Explanation: This means the connections can be very slow. This situation will not change until broadband access become a common property.

---

2. Why would you choose not to use Full-screen graphic menu?

A. not beautiful enough

B. not enough color depth

***C. take much longer to download**

D. take much longer to decode

E. No Answer is Correct

Explanation: It would take a long time to download big graphics.

3. What is a "palette" or "index" when referring to web graphics?

A. never contain more than 256 colors

B. never contain more than 16 colors

C. never contain more than 16 bits colors

D. never contain more than 24 bits colors

E. No Answer is Correct

---

4. For MAC users, what is the ideal dpi setting for graphics?

A. 16

B. 64

C. 72

D. 128

E. 256

3. What is a "palette" or "index" when referring to web graphics?

***A. never contain more than 256 colors**

B. never contain more than 16 colors

C. never contain more than 16 bits colors

D. never contain more than 24 bits colors

E. No Answer is Correct

Explanation: An example is GIF.

---

4. For MAC users, what is the ideal dpi setting for graphics?

A. 16

B. 64

***C. 72**

D. 128

E. 256

Explanation: 72 dpi is the most common setting for MAC clients.

5. For Windows users, what is the ideal dpi setting for graphics?

A. 16

B. 64

C. 75

D. 128

E. 256

---

6. PNG graphic format has enhanced support on:

A. graphic image compatibility

B. browser support

C. image contrast

D. image brightness

E. No Answer is Correct

5. For Windows users, what is the ideal dpi setting for graphics?

A. 16

B. 64

***C. 75**

D. 128

E. 256

Explanation: 75 - 100 dpi is the most common setting for Windows clients.

---

6. PNG graphic format has enhanced support on:

A. graphic image compatibility

B. browser support

C. image contrast

***D. image brightness**

E. No Answer is Correct

7. To assist visually impaired visitors who depend on speech synthesizers to read things out, what technique can you use?

A. Use the ALT attribute

B. Use the ALTS attribute

C. Use the ALTERNATE attribute

D. Use the IMAGE attribute

E. No Answer is Correct

---

8. What type of graphical background is smaller and downloads faster?

A. Tiling

B. Full Screen

C. Half Screen

D. Split

E. No Answer is Correct

7. To assist visually impaired visitors who depend on speech synthesizers to read things out, what technique can you use?

***A. Use the ALT attribute**

B. Use the ALTS attribute

C. Use the ALTERNATE attribute

D. Use the IMAGE attribute

E. No Answer is Correct

Explanation: ALT allows you to define the description of the image with text.

---

8. What type of graphical background is smaller and downloads faster?

***A. Tiling**

B. Full Screen

C. Half Screen

D. Split

E. No Answer is Correct

Explanation: This type of background has background image repeated on the page.

9. GIF incorporates a compression scheme to keep files sizes at a minimum. What scheme is this?

A. PKI

B. ZIP

C. LSH

D. LZW

E. LEI

---

10. For site with many photo quality pictures, what is the reason that discourage the use of GIF?

A. When converting a full-color image to a 256-color GIF , image detail will be lost

B. When converting a full-color image to a 256-color GIF , image contrast will change

C. When converting a full-color image to a 256-color GIF , image brightness will change

D. When converting a full-color image to a 256-color GIF , animation will be disabled

E. No Answer is Correct

9. GIF incorporates a compression scheme to keep files sizes at a minimum. What scheme is this?

A. PKI

B. ZIP

C. LSH

***D. LZW**

E. LEI

Explanation: LZW squeezes out inefficiencies in the data storage.

---

10. For site with many photo quality pictures, what is the reason that discourage the use of GIF?

***A. When converting a full-color image to a 256-color GIF , image detail will be lost**

B. When converting a full-color image to a 256-color GIF , image contrast will change

C. When converting a full-color image to a 256-color GIF , image brightness will change

D. When converting a full-color image to a 256-color GIF , animation will be disabled

E. No Answer is Correct

Explanation:

11. What is so special about the Non-interlaced GIF?

A. smaller size

B. higher color depth

C. more colorful

D. higher compression

E. downloads proceed one line of pixels at a time

---

12. How many colors are identical in the system palettes of Windows and Mac?

A. 16

B. 216

C. 256

D. 16bit

E. 24bit

11. What is so special about the Non-interlaced GIF?

A. smaller size

B. higher color depth

C. more colorful

D. higher compression

***E. downloads proceed one line of pixels at a time**

Explanation: This way users can see the graphics appearing gradually

---

12. How many colors are identical in the system palettes of Windows and Mac?

A. 16

***B. 216**

C. 256

D. 16bit

E. 24bit

Explanation: System palettes for the Mac and Windows are not entirely the same.

13. Which graphic format uses discrete cosine transformation to produce a sliding scale of compression?

A. GIF

B. JPG

C. PNG

D. BMP

E. PCX

---

14. What is the term Halo in web graphic?

A. additional color dots appear between foreground object and background image

B. additional color lines appear between foreground object and background image

C. additional transparent dots appear between foreground object and background image

D. additional blocks of pixels appear between foreground object and background image

E. No Answer is Correct

13. Which graphic format uses discrete cosine transformation to produce a sliding scale of compression?

A. GIF

***B. JPG**

C. PNG

D. BMP

E. PCX

Explanation: JPG supports full-color images at 24 bit.

---

14. What is the term Halo in web graphic?

A. additional color dots appear between foreground object and background image

***B. additional color lines appear between foreground object and background image**

C. additional transparent dots appear between foreground object and background image

D. additional blocks of pixels appear between foreground object and background image

E. No Answer is Correct

Explanation: This is usually caused by anti-aliasing together with transparent color.

15. What would be your solution to the Halo problem (Choose all that apply)?

A. turn on Anti-aliasing

B. use multiple 24 bit color

C. turn off Anti-aliasing

D. use multiple transparent color

E. No Answer is Correct

---

16. What does the browser client need in order to play most of the multimedia files?

A. plug in

B. add in

C. extension

D. connector

E. No Answer is Correct

15. What would be your solution to the Halo problem (Choose all that apply)?

A. turn on Anti-aliasing

B. use multiple 24 bit color

***C. turn off Anti-aliasing**

***D. use multiple transparent color**

E. No Answer is Correct

Explanation: Horizontal or vertical object edges do not need anti aliasing in general.

---

16. What does the browser client need in order to play most of the multimedia files?

***A. plug in**

B. add in

C. extension

D. connector

E. No Answer is Correct

Explanation: Client needs plug-ins to extend the browser's capability.

17. To enable a user to download plug-ins for use, what should you do?

A. use the "Plugin" attribute

B. use the "Plugins" attribute

C. use the "Pluginspace" attribute

D. use the "Plug = true" attribute

E. No Answer is Correct

---

18. To set up your web server to accommodate new file formats, what should you do?

A. set up the MIME types

B. set up the plug in

C. set up the add in types

D. set up the encoding types

E. No Answer is Correct

17. To enable a user to download plug-ins for use, what should you do?

A. use the "Plugin" attribute

B. use the "Plugins" attribute

***C. use the "Pluginspace" attribute**

D. use the "Plug = true" attribute

E. No Answer is Correct

Explanation: Client needs plug-ins to extend the browser's capability.

---

18. To set up your web server to accommodate new file formats, what should you do?

***A. set up the MIME types**

B. set up the plug in

C. set up the add in types

D. set up the encoding types

E. No Answer is Correct

Explanation: On the server side you need to set up the MIME type for the different file formats.

19. What is a characteristic of inline media?

A. plays when the page is uploaded

B. plays when the page is downloaded

C. plays when the page is clicked

D. plays when the mouse is over the page

E. No Answer is Correct

---

20. You like to create inline media for your web page. How do you do this?

A. use the <EMBEDD> tag

B. use the <EMBEDS> tag

C. use the <EMBED> tag

D. use the <EMBEDDING> tag

E. No Answer is Correct

19. What is a characteristic of inline media?

A. plays when the page is uploaded

***B. plays when the page is downloaded**

C. plays when the page is clicked

D. plays when the mouse is over the page

E. No Answer is Correct

Explanation:

---

20. You like to create inline media for your web page. How do you do this?

A. use the <EMBEDD> tag

B. use the <EMBEDS> tag

***C. use the <EMBED> tag**

D. use the <EMBEDDING> tag

E. No Answer is Correct

Explanation: You use this tag to embed the media into the page.

21. You are asked to play background music in IE. How would you do this?

A. use the <BSOUND> tag

B. use the <BSOUNDS> tag

C. use the <BGSOUNDS> tag

D. use the <BGSOUND> tag

E. No Answer is Correct

---

22. Which of the following object types do not require the use of plug-in when being played back
(Choose all that apply)?

A. Animated GIF

B. Java

C. JavaScript

D. Shockwave

E. No Answer is Correct

21. You are asked to play background music in IE. How would you do this?

A. use the <BSOUND> tag

B. use the <BSOUNDS> tag

C. use the <BGSOUNDS> tag

***D. use the <BGSOUND> tag**

E. No Answer is Correct

Explanation: This enable background music while the page is downloaded

---

22. Which of the following object types do not require the use of plug-in when being played back
(Choose all that apply)?

***A. Animated GIF**

***B. Java**

***C. JavaScript**

D. Shockwave

E. No Answer is Correct

Explanation: All version 3 browsers can support these objects without the need of any plug in.

23. What media type does Shockwave plug-in play (Choose all that apply)?

A. Authorware

B. Director

C. Flash

D. VRML

E. No Answer is Correct

---

24. What are the file extensions of 3D world on the web (Choose all that apply)?

A. .VRML

B. .WRL

C. .WRZ

D. .VML

E. No Answer is Correct

23. What media type does Shockwave plug-in play
(Choose all that apply)?

***A. Authorware**

***B. Director**

***C. Flash**

D. VRML

E. No Answer is Correct

Explanation: All these are the creations of Macromedia.

---

24. What are the file extensions of 3D world on the web
(Choose all that apply)?

***A. .VRML**

***B. .WRL**

***C. .WRZ**

D. .VML

E. No Answer is Correct

Explanation: You need specific viewer to play back these files.

25. What can you do to reduce the size of sound files (Choose all that apply)?

A. Reduce sound bit depth

B. Reduce sampling rate

C. Use mono sound

D. Use stereo sound

E. No Answer is Correct

---

26. How do you reduce size of an animation file (Choose all that apply)?

A. reduce the number of frames

B. reduce the Image size

C. reduce the number of colors

D. reduce the play back speed

E. increase the bit depth

25. What can you do to reduce the size of sound files (Choose all that apply)?

***A. Reduce sound bit depth**

***B. Reduce sampling rate**

***C. Use mono sound**

D, Use stereo sound

E. No Answer is Correct

Explanation:

---

26. How do you reduce size of an animation file (Choose all that apply)?

***A. reduce the number of frames**

***B. reduce the Image size**

***C. reduce the number of colors**

D. reduce the play back speed

E. increase the bit depth

Explanation: You do these at the expense of animation quality.

27. How do you minimize the download time for your background music?

A. place the sound tag at the page heading

B. place the sound tag at the page body

C. place the sound tag at the page end

D. place the sound tag at an external location

E. No Answer is Correct

---

28. What is the standard audio format for Macintosh computers ?

A. AIF

B. AIG

C. AIFF

D. AIV

E. No Answer is Correct

27. How do you minimize the download time for your background music?

A. place the sound tag at the page heading

B. place the sound tag at the page body

***C. place the sound tag at the page end**

D. place the sound tag at an external location

E. No Answer is Correct

Explanation: By placing the sound tag at the end it will be downloaded later, and will not delay the page download.

---

28. What is the standard audio format for Macintosh computers ?

A. AIF

B. AIG

***C. AIFF**

D. AIV

E. No Answer is Correct

Explanation: This format uses 8-bit mono or stereo waveforms.

29. Which standard provide a video resolution of 352-by-240 at 30 frames per second?

A. MPEG-1

B. MPEG-2

C. MPEG-3

D. MPEG-4

E. No Answer is Correct

---

30. Which of the following standard supports streaming?

A. AVI

B. MPG

C. JPG

D. QuickTime

E. RealVideo

29. Which standard provide a video resolution of 352-by-240 at 30 frames per second?

***A. MPEG-1**

B. MPEG-2

C. MPEG-3

D. MPEG-4

E. No Answer is Correct

Explanation: MPEG achieves high compression rate purely by storing the changes rather than complete data from one frame to another.

---

30. Which of the following standard supports streaming?

A. AVI

B. MPG

C. JPG

***D. QuickTime**

***E. RealVideo**

Explanation: This is a streaming technology developed by Real Networks for transmitting live video over WWW.

31. PSP's filters, layers, masks and antialiasing features do not work in which color mode (Choose all that apply)?

A. 16 color

B. 256 color

C. 16bit

D. 24bit

E. No Answer is Correct

---

32. You have an image that you need to crop. What command will you use?

A. Image - Crop to Selection

B. Picture - Crop to Selection

C. Image - Cut to Selection

D. Image - Resize to Selection

E. Image - Cropping

31. PSP's filters, layers, masks and antialiasing features do not work in which color mode (Choose all that apply)?

***A. 16 color**

***B. 256 color**

C. 16bit

D. 24bit

E. No Answer is Correct

Explanation: Features not supported in these color mode will be "grayed out".

---

32. You have an image that you need to crop. What command will you use?

***A. Image - Crop to Selection**

B. Picture - Crop to Selection

C. Image - Cut to Selection

D. Image - Resize to Selection

E. Image - Cropping

Explanation: This cropping function is similar to those available in Photo Editor and Photoshop.

33. In Paintshop Pro, what is the equivalent to hitting the DEL key?

A. select Edit - Delete

B. select File - Clear

C. select Edit - Clear

D. select Edit - Clean

E. No Answer is Correct

---

34. In Paintshop Pro, if you choose Edit - Clear on the base layer, what will happen (Choose all that apply)?

A. it clears the layer

B. it fills the cleared part with the background color

C. it fills the cleared part with the foreground color

D. it fills the cleared part with white

E. No Answer is Correct

33. In Paintshop Pro, what is the equivalent to hitting the DEL key?

A. select Edit - Delete

B. select File - Clear

***C. select Edit - Clear**

D. select Edit - Clean

E. No Answer is Correct

Explanation: You should be familiar with the different options available in the toolbar and the menus.

---

34. In Paintshop Pro, if you choose Edit - Clear on the base layer, what will happen (Choose all that apply)?

***A. it clears the layer**

***B. it fills the cleared part with the background color**

C. it fills the cleared part with the foreground color

D. it fills the cleared part with white

E. No Answer is Correct

Explanation: If you are working on a No Answer is Correct base layer, it will just clear the layer without filling in color.

35. What is the following tool for in Paintshop Pro?

A. flood fill a selection with a solid color

B. used with premade tubes

C. erases all color down to the base image

D. apply photo retouching effects to an image

E. No Answer is Correct

---

36. What is the following tool for in Paintshop Pro?

A. flood fill a selection with a solid color

B. used with premade tubes

C. erases all color down to the base image

D. apply photo retouching effects to an image

E. No Answer is Correct

35. What is the following tool for in Paintshop Pro?

A. flood fill a selection with a solid color

B. used with premade tubes

C. erases all color down to the base image

***D. apply photo retouching effects to an image**

E. No Answer is Correct

Explanation: You need to be familiar with the different tools available in Paintshop Pro.

---

36. What is the following tool for in Paintshop Pro?

A. flood fill a selection with a solid color

***B. used with premade tubes**

C. erases all color down to the base image

D. apply photo retouching effects to an image

E. No Answer is Correct

Explanation: You need to be familiar with the different tools available in Paintshop Pro.

37. You are creating some artistic text for your web site. You need to ensure smooth edge. How can you do this?

A. flood fill a selection with a solid color

B. used with premade tubes

C. erases all color down to the base image

D. apply photo retouching effects to an image

E. turn on anti aliasing

---

38. You have the following toolbar in Paintshop Pro:

You need to further customize it. Which menu command will you choose?

A. File|Preferences|Customize

B. File|Options|Customize

C. File|Edit|Customize

D. File| Customize

E. No Answer is Correct

37. You are creating some artistic text for your web site. You need to ensure smooth edge. How can you do this?

A. flood fill a selection with a solid color

B. used with premade tubes

C. erases all color down to the base image

D. apply photo retouching effects to an image

***E. turn on anti aliasing**

Explanation: Anti aliasing avoid jagged edges.

---

38. You have the following toolbar in Paintshop Pro:

You need to further customize it. Which menu command will you choose?

***A. File|Preferences|Customize**

B. File|Options|Customize

C. File|Edit|Customize

D. File| Customize

E. No Answer is Correct

Explanation: You need to be familiar with the different tools available in Paintshop Pro.

39. You finish working on your web graphics with Paintshop Pro. You click save to save it. What file format will the graphic be in?

A. gif

B. psp

C. pst

D. ppt

E. jpg

40. You finish working on your web graphics with Paintshop Pro. You want to save it. You also want the program to remember the last settings you used to save a graphic. What command will you use?

A. Save

B. Save as

C. Save copy as

D. Export

E. No Answer is Correct

39. You finish working on your web graphics with Paintshop Pro. You click save to save it. What file format will the graphic be in?

A. gif

***B. psp**

C. pst

D. ppt

E. jpg

Explanation: When you save a new graphic, it defaults to the "psp" format.

---

40. You finish working on your web graphics with Paintshop Pro. You want to save it. You also want the program to remember the last settings you used to save a graphic. What command will you use?

A. Save

B. Save as

***C. Save copy as**

D. Export

E. No Answer is Correct

Explanation: Paintshop Pro can remember the last setting and the last folder you saved to.

41. In Paintshop Pro, what tool is this?

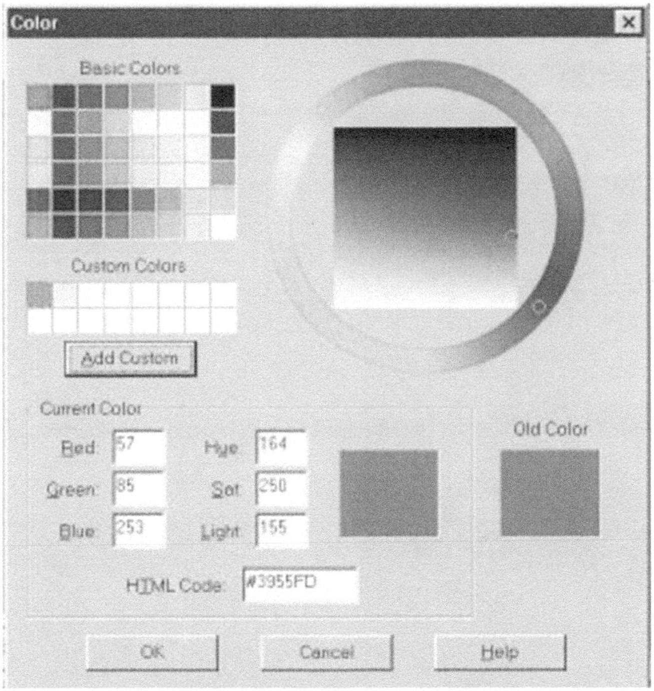

A. color picker

B. format picker

C. style picker

D. font picker

E. No Answer is Correct

41. In Paintshop Pro, what tool is this?

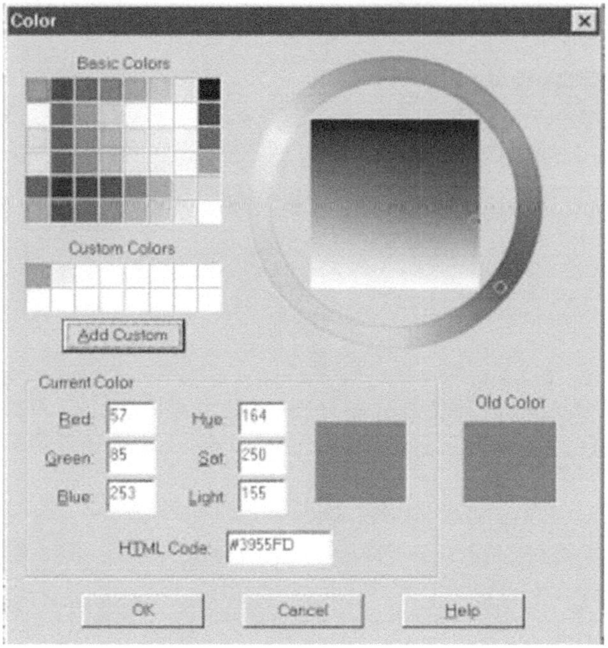

***A. color picker**

B. format picker

C. style picker

D. font picker

E. No Answer is Correct

Explanation: You need to be familiar with the different tools available in Paintshop Pro.

42. In Paintshop Pro, how do you reach the following screen:

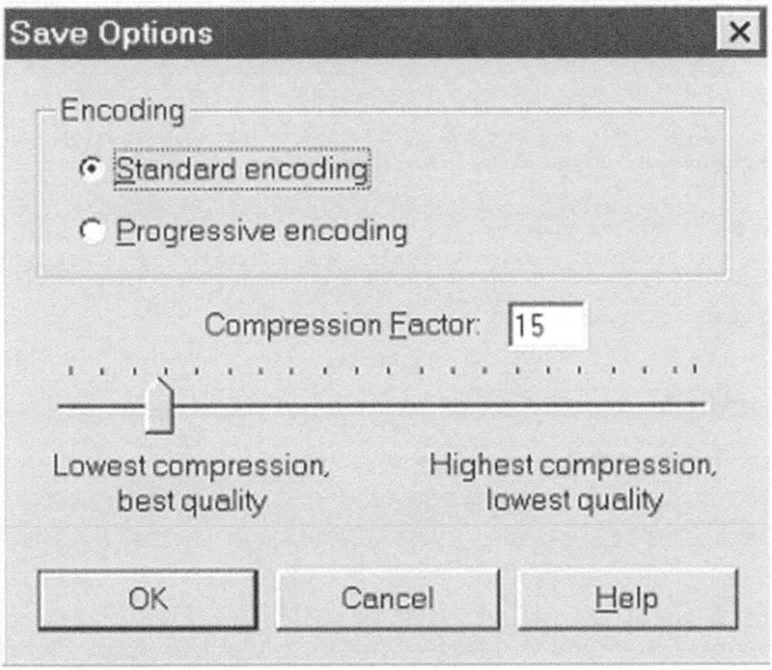

A. save the file as jpg and click Options

B. save the file as gif and click Options

C. save the file as pgp and click Options

D. save the file as bmp and click Options

E. No Answer is Correct

42. In Paintshop Pro, how do you reach the following screen:

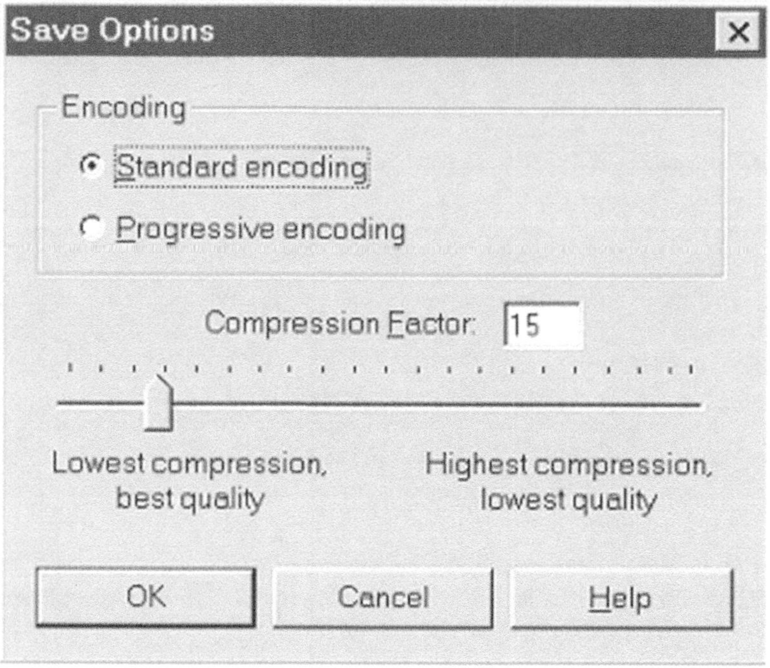

***A. save the file as jpg and click Options**

B. save the file as gif and click Options

C. save the file as pgp and click Options

D. save the file as bmp and click Options

E. No Answer is Correct

Explanation: For web graphics, only JPG allows progressive rendering.

43. In Paintshop Pro, what is the shortcut key to paste a selection as a new Image?

A. ctrl o

B. ctrl n

C. ctrl p

D. ctrl v

E. ctrl h

---

44. You want to be able to easily line things up on your web graphic in Paintshop Pro. What feature will you need?

A. Grid

B. Rulers

C. Toolbars

D. Units

E. No Answer is Correct

43. In Paintshop Pro, what is the shortcut key to paste a selection as a new Image?

A. ctrl o

B. ctrl n

C. ctrl p

***D. ctrl v**

E. ctrl h

Explanation: Refer to the web link for a list of shortcut keys in Paintshop Pro.

---

44. You want to be able to easily line things up on your web graphic in Paintshop Pro. What feature will you need?

***A. Grid**

B. Rulers

C. Toolbars

D. Units

E. No Answer is Correct

Explanation: Grid is for lining things up, while ruler is for precise measurement.

45. You want to save your own personal information together with the image you created. How would you do that?

A. go to File - Image Information

B. go to View - Creator Information

C. go to View - Author Information

D. go to View - Image Information

E. No Answer is Correct

---

46. You want to create straight line in Flash. What tool will you use?

A. Art tool

B. Draw tool

C. Line tool

D. Pencil tool

E. No Answer is Correct

45. You want to save your own personal information together with the image you created. How would you do that?

A. go to File - Image Information

B. go to View - Creator Information

C. go to View - Author Information

***D. go to View - Image Information**

E. No Answer is Correct

Explanation: There is a tab in here called Creator Information.

---

46. You want to create straight line in Flash. What tool will you use?

A. Art tool

B. Draw tool

***C. Line tool**

D. Pencil tool

E. No Answer is Correct

Explanation: This is the line tool icon:

47. You want to tweak the level of assistance you receive from Flash. Where will you go to for modifying this setting?

A. File - Help

B. File - Assist

C. File - Assistant

D. Edit -Help

E. No Answer is Correct

---

48. You have the following screen with you:

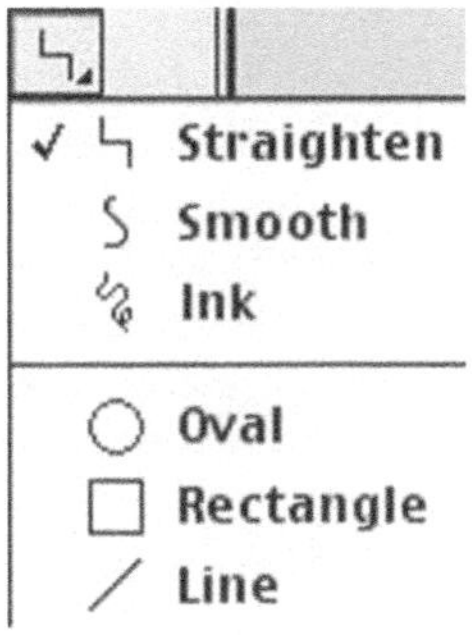

What does Straighten do?

A. automatically shape your drawing

B. automatically clean your drawing

C. automatically resize your drawing

D. automatically optimize your drawing

E. No Answer is Correct

47. You want to tweak the level of assistance you receive from Flash. Where will you go to for modifying this setting?

A. File - Help

B. File - Assist

***C. File - Assistant**

D. Edit -Help

E. No Answer is Correct

Explanation: You should be familiar with the different menus and options available in Flash.

---

48. You have the following screen with you:

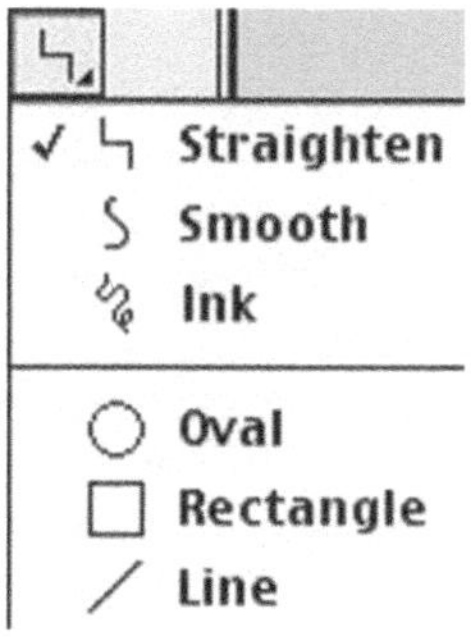

What does Straighten do?

***A. automatically shape your drawing**

B. automatically clean your drawing

C. automatically resize your drawing

D. automatically optimize your drawing

E. No Answer is Correct

Explanation: You should be familiar with the different menus and options available in Flash.

49. You have the following screen with you:

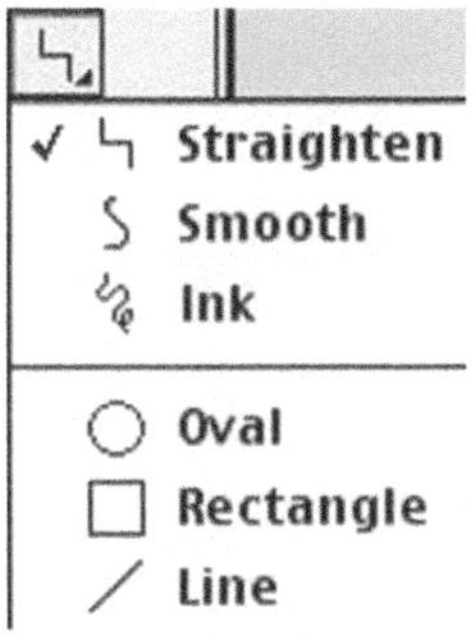

Of the above choices, which items are for reducing imperfections in shapes (Choose all that apply)?

A. Straighten

B. Smooth

C. Oval

D. Line

E. Rectangle

49. You have the following screen with you:

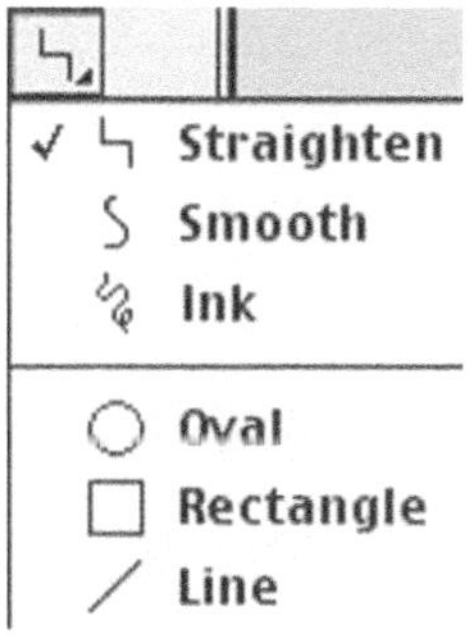

Of the above choices, which items are for reducing imperfections in shapes (Choose all that apply)?

***A. Straighten**

***B. Smooth**

C. Oval

D. Line

E. Rectangle

Explanation: These options can automatically shape your drawing to some degree.

50. You have the following screen:

Which of the above allows you to select the line type to create?

A. first one

B. second one

C. third one

D. fourth one

E. No Answer is Correct

50. You have the following screen:

Which of the above allows you to select the line type to create?

***A. first one**

B. second one

C. third one

D. fourth one

E. No Answer is Correct

Explanation: You should be familiar with the different menus and options available in Flash.

51. You want to expert your flash movie as SWF format. How could you do this?

A. File > Export Movie

B. File > Export > SWF Movie

C. File > Export SWF Movie

D. File > Export > Movies

E. File > Save as > Movie

---

52. What component is essential in the process of creating SWF file from Flash?

A. Macromedia Shock

B. Macromedia Aftershock

C. Macromedia ShockAfter

D. Macromedia ShockEngine

E. No Answer is Correct

51. You want to expert your flash movie as SWF format. How could you do this?

***A. File > Export Movie**

B. File > Export > SWF Movie

C. File > Export SWF Movie

D. File > Export > Movies

E. File > Save as > Movie

Explanation: You should be familiar with the different menus and options available in Flash.

---

52. What component is essential in the process of creating SWF file from Flash?

A. Macromedia Shock

***B. Macromedia Aftershock**

C. Macromedia ShockAfter

D. Macromedia ShockEngine

E. No Answer is Correct

Explanation: This is a program that comes installed with Flash.

53. In Flash, when you upload your animation to your site, what components must be included
(Choose all that apply)?

A. alternate image

B. SWF

C. HTML

D. MIDI

E. No Answer is Correct

---

54. You have the following screen:

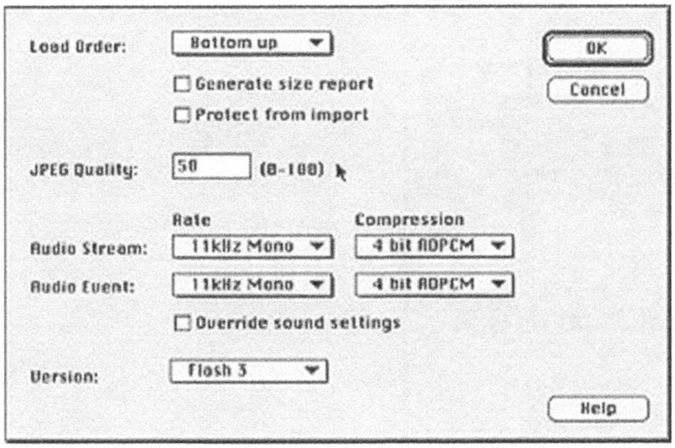

What action are you trying to perform in Flash?

A. Screen setup

B. Page setup

C. Preview setup

D. Export Options

E. No Answer is Correct

53. In Flash, when you upload your animation to your site, what components must be included
(Choose all that apply)?

***A. alternate image**

***B. SWF**

***C. HTML**

D. MIDI

E. No Answer is Correct

Explanation: You need the HTML code to call the SWF file.

---

54. You have the following screen:

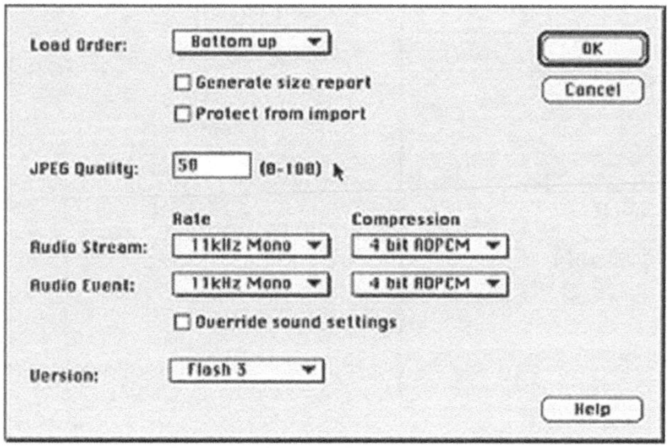

What action are you trying to perform in Flash?

A. Screen setup

B. Page setup

C. Preview setup

***D. Export Options**

E. No Answer is Correct

Explanation: This is the screen you will encounter when exporting to SWF.

55. In a Flash action script, what is used to tell the play head to jump to a specific frame?

A. go to

B. jump to

C. skip to

D. play to

E. No Answer is Correct

---

56. How do you increase or decrease the playback quality in Flash Action Script?

A. Toggle Play Back

B. Toggle Play Quality

C. Toggle Quality

D. Toggle High Quality

E. No Answer is Correct

55. In a Flash action script, what is used to tell the play head to jump to a specific frame?

***A. go to**

B. jump to

C. skip to

D. play to

E. No Answer is Correct

Explanation: Refer to the web link for detailed information on Action Script.

---

56. How do you increase or decrease the playback quality in Flash Action Script?

A. Toggle Play Back

B. Toggle Play Quality

C. Toggle Quality

***D. Toggle High Quality**

E. No Answer is Correct

Explanation: Refer to the web link for detailed information on Action Script.

57. How do you link a Flash movie to an external HTML in Flash Action Script?

A. Get Link

B. Get URL

C. Set Link

D. Set URL

E. No Answer is Correct

---

58. How do you allow a Flash movie to load another movie into itself in Flash Action Script?

A. not possible

B. Load/Unload Movie

C. Load/Reload Movie

D. Load/Offload Movie

E. Load/Deload SWF

57. How do you link a Flash movie to an external HTML in Flash Action Script?

A. Get Link

***B. Get URL**

C. Set Link

D. Set URL

E. No Answer is Correct

Explanation: Refer to the web link for detailed information on Action Script.

---

58. How do you allow a Flash movie to load another movie into itself in Flash Action Script?

A. not possible

***B. Load/Unload Movie**

C. Load/Reload Movie

D. Load/Offload Movie

E. Load/Deload SWF

Explanation: Refer to the web link for detailed information on Action Script.

59. How do you manipulate the value of variables in Flash Action Script?

A. Not possible

B. Tune Variable

C. Alter Variable

D. Set Variable

E. Change Variable

---

60. In conjunction with the OnMouseEvent script, what can you use in the Flash Action Script to make a main stage moveable?

A. Drag Movie Clip

B. Move Movie Clip

C. Drag Movie Stage

D. Move Movie Stage

E. No Answer is Correct

59. How do you manipulate the value of variables in Flash Action Script?

A. Not possible

B. Tune Variable

C. Alter Variable

***D. Set Variable**

E. Change Variable

Explanation: Refer to the web link for detailed information on Action Script.

---

60. In conjunction with the OnMouseEvent script, what can you use in the Flash Action Script to make a main stage moveable?

***A. Drag Movie Clip**

B. Move Movie Clip

C. Drag Movie Stage

D. Move Movie Stage

E. No Answer is Correct

Explanation: Refer to the web link for detailed information on Action Script.

61. You wish to create a website that will showcase the artwork of upcoming artists. The images that you use may have transparency and will need to be capable of displaying, as close as possible, the true color nature of the photos.

Required Results:

Display the photos in "true color"

Optional Results:

The images should be capable of using transparency

Don't require users to download any plug-ins or upgrades to view the photos

Proposed Solution:

Use the PNG format for the images

A. The solution does not meet the required result

B. The solution meets the required result and none of the optional results

C. The solution meets the required result and one of the optional results

D. The solution meets the required result and all of the optional results

61. You wish to create a website that will showcase the artwork of upcoming artists. The images that you use may have transparency and will need to be capable of displaying, as close as possible, the true color nature of the photos.

Required Results:

Display the photos in "true color"

Optional Results:

The images should be capable of using transparency

Don't require users to download any plug-ins or upgrades to view the photos

Proposed Solution:

Use the PNG format for the images

A. The solution does not meet the required result

B. The solution meets the required result and none of the optional results

***C. The solution meets the required result and one of the optional results**

D. The solution meets the required result and all of the optional results

Explanation: The PNG format allows for a wider range of colors than 256, unlike GIFs. PNG also allows for transparency in images like GIFs. However, many older browsers do not support PNG or require a plug-in. Therefore, the proposed solution meets the required result, and only one of the optional results.

62. Two guns in a monitor are firing, they are blue and red. What color do they produce?

A. Black

B. White

C. Magenta

D. Yellow

E. Purple

62. Two guns in a monitor are firing, they are blue and red. What color do they produce?

A. Black

B. White

***C. Magenta**

D. Yellow

E. Purple

Explanation: The RGB color method used by monitors is known as a Additive Color method. This means that unlike your standard color wheel, blue and red do not make purple, but instead make Magenta. By varying the intensity of the three guns, various hues and tones are created. When all three guns are fired at full intensity, white is created. When all three guns are left unfired, the result is black.

63. What is the proper breakdown of the six digit hexadecimal RGB code used in HTML?

A. #RRGGBB

B. #GGRRBB

C. #BGRBGR

D. #RGBRGB

---

64. Your boss just returned from a Flash demonstration and is set on creating the next version of your website in Flash. What can you do to ensure that users without Flash enabled browsers can still use your site. Choose two

A. Create a JavaScript detection script that will redirect users without the Flash plug-in to the Flash site so that they can download the plug-in

B. Create a JavaScript detection script that will redirect users without the Flash plug-in to an HTML version of your site

C. Add a hyperlink to your pages to the Flash site so users can download the plug-in

D. Add a popup message that informs users that they cannot use your site without the Flash plug-in and that they should get the plug-in and return later

63. What is the proper breakdown of the six digit hexadecimal RGB code used in HTML?

***A. #RRGGBB**

B. #GGRRBB

C. #BGRBGR

D. #RGBRGB

Explanation: The 6 digit hexadecimal code used in HTML represents #RRGGBB. Because each color has two digits with 16 possible values (0-F), there are a possible 16,777,215 colors that can be created with this code. Remember that only 216 of the colors are guaranteed to work properly on all systems.

---

64. Your boss just returned from a Flash demonstration and is set on creating the next version of your website in Flash. What can you do to ensure that users without Flash enabled browsers can still use your site. Choose two

A. Create a JavaScript detection script that will redirect users without the Flash plug-in to the Flash site so that they can download the plug-in

***B. Create a JavaScript detection script that will redirect users without the Flash plug-in to an HTML version of your site**

***C. Add a hyperlink to your pages to the Flash site so users can download the plug-in**

D. Add a popup message that informs users that they cannot use your site without the Flash plug-in and that they should get the plug-in and return later

Explanation: One mistake that many web designers make is trying to force users to upgrade their software in order to use their site. The best way to handle this situation is to create a JavaScript detection script that will redirect users without Flash to an HTML version of your site. On this page, you should add a short message that tells users that a more interactive version of your site exists with a link to the Flash site where they can download the plug-in.

Notes:

Money Back Book Guarantee

This guarantee applies only to books published by TotalRecallPress.com! We are so confident in our products, we are prepared to offer the following guarantee to YOU our valued customer: If you do not pass your certification exam after two attempts, we will give money back!

Visit www.TotalRecallPress.com

Select "Money Back Book Guarantee" for details.

Registered book purchasers will receive

1. Receive a 50% cash refund of purchase price

OR

2. Receive a free TotalRecallPress.com book of less or equal value.

To qualify for this www.TotalRecallPress.com Guarantee you must meet these requirements and perform the following tasks:

1. Register your purchase at **www.TotalRecallPress.com** web site before taking the Real Exam.
2. Fail the corresponding exam twice (No time Limit)
3. Contact TotalRecall for the RMA # and to claim this guarantee
4. Send a notification email to **Guarantee@TotalRecallPress.com**
5. Subject must contain your Membership # or Registration #

Ship the following to claim your refund.

1. RMA # from returned email
2. Documents of exam scores (Copy) for both failed attempts
3. Return the Book to the following address

TotalRecall Publications
Attn: Corby Tate
1103 Middlecreek
Friendswood, TX 77546

888-992-3131	**bfquiz@swbell.net**
281-992-3131	**http://www.BFQOnline.com**
281-482-5390 Fax	**http://www.BFQ.com**

It's a Passing day here at the BeachFront.

Thank you for using the TotalRecallPress.com Success Program.

Bruce Moran President

Registration Instructions

BeachFront Quizzer Inc. (BFQ) version 4.0

With the purchase of this book you qualify for a Free
30 DAY BeachFront Quizzer, Inc. Online Practice exam

Visit www.TotalRecallPress.com for details.

Register your book purchase at www.totalrecallpress.com
Your Registration Code is: = EW-43420-3000

System Requirements: Internet connection:

BeachFront Quizzer

888-992-3131

www.bfq.com

Call: 281-992-3131

Good Luck with your certification!

Your Book Registration Number is EW-43420-3000

You cannot go wrong with this book because it is GUARANTEED:

See details at www.TotalRecallPress.com

Made in United States
Cleveland, OH
05 November 2026

47670549R00308